Praise for *U.S. Strategy in the Asian Century*

"As disruptive tailwinds propel Asia and the Indo-Pacific to the center of global politics, Abraham M. Denmark's meticulous research provides a pragmatic rationale and a lucid strategy to recalibrate American engagements in the region with old and new partners. A must-read."

> —SAMIR SARAN, PRESIDENT OF OBSERVER RESEARCH
> FOUNDATION, INDIA

"This excellent book shows with terrifying plausibility how quickly American power can become hollow leadership unless we return to reliable and creative emboldenment of our allies. Competing successfully with China will require it."

> —KORI SCHAKE, DIRECTOR OF FOREIGN AND DEFENSE POLICY
> STUDIES, AMERICAN ENTERPRISE INSTITUTE

"At a time when the speed of change in the Asia-Pacific seems to only be accelerating, Denmark's calls for an evolved set of American alliances and partnerships resonate deeply with all who seek a stronger liberal order in the region and beyond."

> —YOICHI FUNABASHI, CO-FOUNDER AND CHAIRMAN
> OF THE ASIA PACIFIC INITIATIVE

"Wealth and power are moving eastward, toward Asia. One of Washington's advantages at this historic moment is its powerful and cost-effective network of regional allies and partners. Denmark's timely book contains useful recommendations for both the United States and its friends as they navigate the Asian century."

> —MICHAEL FULLILOVE, EXECUTIVE DIRECTOR
> OF THE LOWY INSTITUTE, AUSTRALIA

U.S. STRATEGY IN THE ASIAN CENTURY

WOODROW WILSON CENTER SERIES

W|Wilson Center
WOODROW WILSON CENTER SERIES

The Woodrow Wilson International Center for Scholars was chartered by the US Congress in 1968 as the living memorial to the nation's twenty-eighth president. It serves as the country's key nonpartisan policy forum, tackling global challenges through independent research and open dialogue. Bridging the worlds of academia and public policy, the Center's diverse programmatic activity informs actionable ideas for Congress, the administration, and the broader policy community.

The Woodrow Wilson Center Series shares in the Center's mission by publishing outstanding scholarly and public policy-related books for a global readership. Written by the Center's expert staff and international network of scholars, our books shed light on a wide range of topics, including US foreign and domestic policy, security, the environment, energy, and area studies.

Conclusions or opinions expressed in Center publications and programs are those of the authors and speakers and do not necessarily reflect the views of the Center staff, fellows, trustees, advisory groups, or any individuals or organizations that provide financial support for the Center.

Please visit us online at www.wilsoncenter.org.

William H. Hill, *No Place for Russia: European Security Institutions Since 1989*

Donald R. Wolfensberger, *Changing Cultures in Congress: From Fair Play to Power Plays*

Samuel F. Wells Jr., *Fearing the Worst: How Korea Transformed the Cold War*

U.S. STRATEGY IN THE ASIAN CENTURY

EMPOWERING ALLIES AND PARTNERS

ABRAHAM M. DENMARK

Columbia University Press
New York

Columbia University Press
Publishers Since 1893
New York   Chichester, West Sussex
cup.columbia.edu

Library of Congress Cataloging-in-Publication Data

Names: Denmark, Abraham, author.
Title: U.S. strategy in the Asian century : empowering allies
    and partners / Abraham M. Denmark.
Other titles: United States strategy in the Asian century
Description: New York : Columbia University Press, 2020. |
    Series: Woodrow Wilson Center series | Includes bibliographical
    references and index.
Identifiers: LCCN 2020009103 (print) | LCCN 2020009104 (ebook) |
    ISBN 9780231197649 (cloth) | ISBN 9780231197656 (paperback) |
    ISBN 9780231552271 (ebook)
Subjects: LCSH: Indo-Pacific Region—Foreign relations—United
    States. | United States—Foreign relations—Indo-Pacific Region. |
    Geopolitics—Indo-Pacific Region. | United States—Foreign
    relations—China. | China—Foreign relations—United States.
Classification: LCC JZ1480.A55 D46 2020 (print) | LCC JZ1480.A55
    (ebook) | DDC 327.7305—dc23
LC record available at https://lccn.loc.gov/2020009103
LC ebook record available at https://lccn.loc.gov/2020009104

Columbia University Press books are printed on permanent and
durable acid-free paper.
Printed in the United States of America

Cover design: Noah Arlow
Cover image: Alamy

CONTENTS

PREFACE

When Japanese prime minister Shinzo Abe visited President Obama in April 2015, I was an analyst several years removed from my previous government service and a few months away from joining the Obama administration as deputy assistant secretary of defense for East Asia. I was invited to the White House. for the ceremony welcoming the prime minister on the South Lawn. It was a beautiful spring day in Washington, and I enjoyed the sun next to the South Portico while Abe and Obama reviewed the troops and gave brief remarks to the assembled crowd.

It was a day when the United States and Japan would begin a new chapter in their decades-old alliance and dramatically shape the tour in government upon which I was about to embark. It was also a day of remarkable, if largely unnoticed, historical significance. In 1960, Prime Minister Abe's grandfather—Prime Minister Nobusuke Kishi—had likewise agreed with President Dwight D. Eisenhower to amend and update the US–Japan alliance. Standing in the sun at the White House fifty-five years later, I thought about the history of those two men and marveled at their ability to overcome wartime enmity and adjust their nation's policies to the geopolitical realities of the day.

There was a sense that Abe and Obama were building on the accomplishments of their predecessors by updating the defense guidelines that defined the scope of defense cooperation between the two sides. It heralded the beginning of a new era for the alliance, in which Japan would finally begin to contribute more to its own defense and in which US and Japanese forces would be more flexible and better prepared to cooperate on a range of challenges, from maritime security to disaster response, by planning, training, and operating together.

This was especially important for me at the time, because I was in the midst of researching strategies to encourage allies and partners in Asia to do more—a project that resulted in this book. Through this research, and then through my experiences in the Pentagon, I became increasingly convinced that the United States faces profound challenges in the Indo-Pacific, and became committed to the idea that we should again adjust our policies for these new geopolitical realities.

I began to write this book during the middle of the Obama administration, when I was working at the National Bureau of Asian Research (NBR). The project was shelved when I was appointed deputy assistant secretary of defense for East Asia in 2015, and I was delighted to be able to return to the project after the end of the Obama administration. Yet I found myself needing to revise my thinking substantially—both because of what I had learned during my time in the Pentagon, but also because of President Donald Trump.

President Trump has been clear in his desire to see our allies and partners to "do more," even while questioning the utility and fairness of those alliances themselves. This had several implications for the book I was writing, and I realized that it should go beyond describing *how* the United States should do more with its allies and partners, to also describe *why*. More fundamentally, this book seeks to describe the utility of alliances and partnerships themselves and why they are critical for American power in the world's most geopolitically important and dynamic region.

This book is also, though implicitly, an argument for the critical role that allies and partners should play in American foreign policy and national security strategy in the Indo-Pacific. Within this context looms President Trump, who has regularly expressed deep skepticism about the utility of allies and partners while—often in the same breath—praising America's enemies.[1] Because this book was written during the Trump administration and was completed in the midst of its third year, it does not attempt to catalogue the administration's approach to alliances and partnerships in Asia; nor does it attempt to grapple with the inheritance of its policies. This is an ongoing story, and one beyond the scope of this book. Yet the Trump administration also provides a context that cannot be ignored.

I would like to express my deep appreciation to the Smith-Richardson Foundation, the NBR, and the Wilson Center for supporting this project, and for their patience as I navigated its rapidly changing subject matter. I am especially thankful to Al Song for his thoughtfulness, support, and partnership. I am also deeply thankful to Lindsey Ford, Prashanth Parameswaran, Eric Sayers, Ashley Townsend, Van Jackson, and Thomas Wright for their thoughtful reviews of drafts. I would also like to thank Allison Szalwinski at NBR for her exceptional project management, and to Melanie Berry, Brian O'Keefe, Mary Ratliff, Nicole Smolinske, Taylor Washburn, and Zane Zovak for their research and editing support. I am also deeply grateful for my editors—Alfred Imhoff and Stephen Wesley—as well as my colleagues at the Woodrow Wilson International Center for Scholars—especially Robert Litwak and former US representative Jane Harman.

Finally, I am thankful to my wife, Laura, for her support in the late nights and during weekend writing sessions. Taking care of two small children is difficult under any circumstance; doing it with a husband first working at the Pentagon and then glued to a laptop has been above and beyond the call of duty.

The views expressed here are mine alone, and not of the U.S. government or any of its departments or agencies.

U.S. STRATEGY IN THE ASIAN CENTURY

INTRODUCTION

Challenged Friendships in Challenging Times

We cannot always assure the future of our friends; we have a better chance of assuring our future if we remember who our friends are.

—HENRY KISSINGER

Allies and partners have played a highly consequential role in America's foreign and national security policy since before its founding. France was a key supporter of the colonists during the American Revolution, providing George Washington and the Continental Army with supplies, weapons, financing, and the much-needed diversion of an English focus outside North America in their global competition for power. Despite President Washington's admonitions to future generations that "the great rule of conduct for us, in regard to foreign nations, is in extending our commercial relations, to have with them as little political connection as possible," the United States has long understood that its power was augmented with strong foreign relationships.[1]

Historically, allies and partners have functioned both as a complement to American power and a conduit for it. Though not formal allies at the time, the United States came to the aid of France and Great Britain for World War I and World War II, laying the foundation for a collective defense arrangement that has lasted for decades. It was during the postwar era when the United States established the structure of its East Asian alliances and partnerships, which during the Cold War served to deter large-scale Soviet aggression and contain the spread of communism while also enabling the United States to exert its influence around the world.

As the geopolitical environment has evolved and American interests have changed, Washington's approach to alliances and partnerships have evolved as well. Since the collapse of the Soviet Union and the Eastern Bloc, NATO has acted to stop genocide in the former Yugoslavia and later augmented the United States' liberation of Afghanistan after the terrorist attacks of September 11, 2001. In Southeast Asia, the spread of terrorist organizations spurred the United States to revitalize its alliances and partnerships in the region to fight their spread and counter their attacks.

Today, the Indo-Pacific looms as a vital region for American economic, political, and security interests. The region includes the world's largest economies, representing two-thirds of global growth; it accounts for 60 percent of global gross domestic product; and it is home to some of the world's largest and most advanced militaries and several of nuclear powers.[2] The Indo-Pacific's tremendous strategic importance to the United States, and to the fate of global geopolitics, was the motivating factor behind the Obama administration's rebalance to the Asia-Pacific and the Trump administration's strategy to build a free and open Indo-Pacific.

Yet just as this region continues to grow in significance for the United States, the essential dynamics of its geopolitics are in the midst of a fundamental change. China is steadily growing more powerful, and it is becoming increasingly assertive in the pursuit of its objectives. Concurrently, American engagement in the region is seen across the region as both insufficient and unreliable.

This book argues that these changes in the regional balance of power threaten the existing liberal regional order, which has been fundamental to regional stability and prosperity for decades. It also argues that the regional balance of power is no longer only about military capacity, but instead involves multiple measures of national power—including trade and investment flows, economic throw-weight, soft power, and military potential. This book explores how US allies and partners are increasingly adopting hedging strategies to account for these changes, and proposes a strategy for the United States to empower its regional allies and partners to help strengthen these critical relationships and defend the key principles that are the foundation of the liberal regional order.

This strategy will require the United States to adjust the original conceit of its approach to alliances and partnerships, which were as much about restraining allies as about confronting threats. Indeed, as persuasively argued by Georgetown University professor Victor Cha, the United States established its alliances with Korea (in 1953) and the Republic of China (1954) in order to both contain communism and to stop Syngman Rhee's and Chiang Kai-shek's governments from, respectively, provoking conflicts with North Korea and mainland China.[3] For the US alliance with Japan (1951), Washington was less concerned about Tokyo entrapping it in an unwanted conflict, but more that Japan's postwar recovery would occur without US involvement. Although the rationales for these alliances have evolved significantly over time, the military-centric, hub-and-spokes system that grew out of the US approach to Asian alliances in the early 1950s remains the foundation of its strategy today.

Yet a military-centric approach is insufficient in a region where the balance of power in the Indo-Pacific is increasingly measured via a continually evolving assessment of hierarchies of relative levels of existing and potential national power. Further states will perceive a series of power hierarchies among various measures of national power, be it overall economic strength, the resilience of domestic politics and economics, per capita income and innovation, defense budgets, qualitative assessments of military capabilities, geography, and soft power. These multiple, interrelated hierarchies—referred to here as a "heterarchy" (see chapter 2)—will inform great power competition in the Indo-Pacific and likewise drive the development of strategies by the region's middle powers to hedge against tremendous strategic uncertainty.[4] This means that the United States cannot focus solely on military power, but must also become involved in all aspects of national power in its strategy toward the Indo-Pacific. From trade and investment to development and security assistance, this book argues that the United States needs to tailor its regional strategy to fit the demands of the emerging era of complex regional competition.

This book primarily focuses on the need for the United States to empower its key allies and partners in the Indo-Pacific, many of which are focusing more on the role they will play in the emerging regional heterarchy. The scope of this book encompasses the American allies (Australia, Japan, the Philippines, and South Korea) and partners (India, Indonesia, New Zealand, Singapore, Taiwan, and Vietnam) that are most critical for a US strategy in Asia. This is certainly not an exhaustive list, but instead an examination of some of the most critical alliance and partner relationships in the Indo-Pacific. Discussions of Thailand, for instance, are not a major feature of this book—largely because there is little potential for the US–Thai Alliance to substantially change as long as the military government remains in power.

At times, the book also discusses the role that allies and partners outside Asia—and especially in Europe—can play in US strategy in the region. Although other observers may group American allies and partners differently—potentially focusing on treaty allies only, or solely grouping nations based on allies and partners that are democratically governed—this book focuses on allies and partners whose interests in strengthening aspects of a liberal order in Asia align with those of the United States and that are generally comfortable with the United States playing a significant role in the region's geopolitics.

As their power rises, America's allies and partners in Asia have an opportunity to contribute more to the health and success of a rules-based liberal order that has been critical to the region's stability and prosperity for generations. Successfully empowering allies and partners in this way, however, will require the United States to broaden the aperture of these relationships and place a greater emphasis on political coordination and economic integration in addition to military cooperation. It will also require an intensified effort to build allied capabilities in a way that enables them to play a larger role in contributing to the liberal order and providing public goods while also mitigating the potential for arms races or the fueling of lingering intraregional rivalries.

This book describes a broad strategy that involves a diverse set of initiatives designed to empower US allies and partners in the Indo-Pacific:

Developing a shared vision for the regional order
- Sustaining critical principles
- Competing with a rising China
- Navigating a multipolar Asia
- Providing public goods
- Confronting a belligerent North Korea

Bolstering American power and leadership in the Indo-Pacific
- Domestic investments as foundations of national power
- Investing in tools of American foreign policy
- Protecting against disengagement

Maximizing US engagement and influence
- Alliances as a comprehensive platform for cooperation
- Robust economic engagement
- Building governance and fighting corruption

Developing military capabilities and presence
- Strengthening and reforming security assistance
- Buttressing regional maritime security capabilities, including building regional coast guards and developing a regional maritime domain awareness network
- Expanding missile defense
- Enhancing island and shore defense
- Coordinating with allies and partners
- Managing unintended consequences

Expanding economic interconnectivity
- Strengthening economic integration under US leadership
- Building physical and digital infrastructure

Deepening diplomatic coordination
- Maritime security
- Space
- The digital domain

Networking alliances and partnerships

By implementing a strategy to empower its allies and partners in the Indo-Pacific and more effectively drive them to contribute to the health and success of the regional liberal order, the United States has an opportunity to proactively address emerging regional challenges and sustain American regional power and leadership. Such a strategy will not only enhance regional stability and prosperity—it will also enhance the ability of the United States to compete with China. Although this is not an anti-China strategy, it does recognize the extent of the challenge posed by China and proposes a positive approach to advance the interests of the United States and its allies and partners.

In pursuing this strategy, the United States will face two significant dilemmas in the Indo-Pacific. First, if the United States continues to shoulder the vast majority of costs for the defense of its allies and the preservation of the liberal order, this will simply reinforce allied tendencies toward free riding and will not help address the changing balance of power in the region. Conversely, an unconsidered reduction in US capabilities and engagement in the region (or threats to do so) may backfire and diminish US influence while undermining the perceived reliability of American commitments. The possible results—a rising China that threatens to undermine liberal internationalism across the region, and a retrenching United States—would threaten the overall stability of the region and set conditions for Beijing to establish dominance in the world's most geopolitically critical region.

Second, building up the power and capabilities of US allies and partners in the Indo-Pacific—if done capriciously or without a robust understanding of the region's underlying geopolitical dynamics—could unintentionally fuel lingering intraregional rivalries and incite regional instability. In the case of US allies, greater capabilities could increase concerns about entrapment in the United States. Moreover, allied overinvestment in some types of capabilities (e.g., antiaccess / area denial capabilities) could diminish their investments in other areas (e.g., power projection). The potential for arms racing, entrapment, and misaligned investments are certainly challenges that would need to be addressed, but can be mitigated by the adroit selection of capabilities to be built and the policies to be pursued.

Navigating these dilemmas will pose significant challenges for the United States. Specifically, Washington must update its approach to its allies and partners in the Indo-Pacific to encourage more active and independent allies and partners in ways that support the critical features of the liberal order without inflaming fears of abandonment or entrapment, sparking a regional arms race, or jeopardizing American influence in the region. It can do this by emphasizing integration and interoperability, and by tailoring empowerment efforts to best match the interests and capabilities of the specific ally or partner.

This book is fundamentally about power, order, and developing a new regional strategy in an era of profound change. It describes the Indo-Pacific's rapidly changing power dynamics, explains how change has affected the regional order in the past, and proposes an approach to empower US allies and partners in the Indo-Pacific in order to successfully adjust to these new realities.

The core argument of this book is that as the geopolitics of the Indo-Pacific evolve and the United States seeks to adapt, our allies and partners need us now more than ever. And we need them. Here is why.

1

ORDER AND POWER
IN THE INDO-PACIFIC

International politics, like all politics, is a struggle for power.

—HANS MORGENTHAU, *POLITICS AMONG NATIONS*

The character of the Indo-Pacific's strategic environment is very different from that of Europe or the Middle East. Indeed, the region's order flows from the ability of its constituent states to build, marshal, and utilize their national power in the pursuit of their interests. This is far different from Europe's neoliberal institutionalism or the Middle East's mix of strongmen, weak states, and nonstate actors scheming in the pursuit of their own ambitions. Rather, Asia's geopolitical dynamics more closely represent classic power competition between states—similar to Europe in the eighteenth and nineteenth centuries (but with a few billion more people and nuclear weapons).

The international environment of Asia is fundamentally anarchic, in that states are generally able to act according to how they perceive their interests and their threat environment without the significant constraints of strong multinational institutions. Asia is not Europe—history and geopolitics remain forces of discord and tension, and Asia's institutions are not even close to capable of providing the relative cohesion and stability that NATO has had for Europe since the early years of the Cold War. Indeed, Henry Kissinger notes that "the global order during the nineteenth century and the first half of the twentieth century was predominantly European, designed to maintain a rough balance of power between the major European countries."[1]

In Asia, the United States is the dominant power and the center of a hub-and-spokes alliance model that is fundamentally different from NATO's networked approach to collective self-defense. Nonetheless, the Indo-Pacific exists within an order that, to a degree, constrains the freedom of action of its composite nations. After a brief examination of the liberal order as a concept and as the foundation for tremendous international benefits, this chapter surveys the tectonic changes that have transformed Asia's international political environment during the last two centuries.[2] It concludes with a description of the postwar order established and sustained by the United States, and argues that it is an order that has been tremendously beneficial for global peace, stability, and prosperity.

ON ORDER

The concept of an established "order" within an anarchic system may seem oxymoronic. Indeed, one of the defining features of the international system is the absence of any sovereign power with the authority or capability to unilaterally enforce a legal regime that uniformly and effectively binds all members of the international community in the way that domestic laws bind the citizens or subjects of an individual state.[3] It is precisely this absence of a central authority that has led some to describe the international system as anarchic, and others to question the very existence of a rules-based liberal order.[4]

Yet, though the absence of an order-giving leviathan is one salient characteristic of the international environment, it is also possible to identify other features that help define how the system functions and how entities within it interact. Although war has been a persistent feature of human life, it is rare for the international realm to descend into pure Hobbesian struggle of *bellum omnium contra omnes*.[5] It is far more common for leading international actors to create arrangements and rules to shape and constrain their actions and those of others, despite the anarchic system in which they live and the competition and struggle that may exist between them.[6] In other words, there can still be an order, even if it is not entirely "orderly."

Considering the importance of the concept of "order" to this book, it is necessary to delve a bit more deeply into what it is and what it is not. It may be surprising, therefore, that there is no settled singular definition for "order" within the academic community. Although several definitions have been proposed in various books and articles,[7] for the purpose of clarity and simplicity, this book uses the definition of order from the remarkable series of studies by Michael Mazarr and his colleagues at the RAND Corporation on the future of the liberal order, which defines order as "the body of rules, norms, and institutions that govern relations among the key players in the international environment."[8]

Mazarr and his colleagues make an important contribution to the field by offering conceptions of order in both conservative and liberal terms.[9] A conservative understanding of order starts with the idea that order is based on power and the need for states to manage competing or contradictory interests, and with the understanding that such arrangements—both the balance of power and how a nation defines its interests—are temporary. Historical examples of this more conservative approach to order include the Westphalian system and its norm of territorial integrity, as well as (as is demonstrated just below) past Asian orders based on the primacy of one country over all others. Yet a liberal approach to order seeks to go beyond conceptions of the balance of power and, instead, establish norms, laws, and institutions that shape the behavior of states and seeks to channel disputes over competitive and contradictory interests into more diplomatic, and less conflict-prone, modes of dispute resolution.

Academics have likewise also long debated sources of liberal order. Although realists have argued that order is the result of the balance of power or hegemony and that a decline of the hegemon's geopolitical power will likewise lead to the unraveling of the established order, others point out that order is the reflection of more than power.[10] For instance, Princeton University's G. John Ikenberry argues that order can persist in the face of changes to the balance of power because of the role of strong institutions and if other actors see the order as favorable to their interests. For Ikenberry, the international order sustains autonomy, growth, and international participation for every state beyond the American hegemon; as such, developing states have incentives to maintain the structure while pursuing changes in their favors.[11] This is especially true when the alternative is an order led by China, as Ikenberry argues: "If these potential partner states did not experience substantial material benefits from participating in the Chinese-led order, China would need to spend resources to entice and bully these states into cooperation."[12]

Both arguments have merit, and an accurate understanding of order in the Indo-Pacific would be incomplete without elements from both schools of thought. For example, although Ikenberry is correct to highlight the attractiveness of a liberal order to several developing states in Asia, the region's geopolitics cannot be understood without recognizing both the weakness of regional institutions as compared with those of Europe along with the importance of raw calculations of power in determining the region's alignments and behaviors.

For much of the twentieth and twenty-first centuries, American foreign policy has employed strategies that feature elements of both realism and liberalism. From the exercise of hard power and the use of military force to prevent other major powers from dominating broad swaths of territory to creating and strengthening institutions and international laws that seek to constrain the actions of nations, the United States has employed a hybrid strategy that reflects the fundamental link between power and order.

Though strongly linked, it is important to note that the concepts of power and of order are fundamentally distinct. The power of a nation or group of nations is rooted in their national characteristics (e.g., wealth, political stability, and military might), as well as the ability of their national leaders to translate these characteristics into power and influence on the world stage.[13] Power subsequently imbues the nation or group of nations to create, sustain, shape, or undermine a given liberal order.

Considering such factors, it may be possible to identify paradigmatic adjustments to the balance of geopolitical power that coincide with tectonic shifts in the liberal order of either the globe or a particular region. One particular order could reign in part of the world for centuries, only to crumble when its defining features are altered by changes in the balance of power.

However, measures of power alone are insufficient to understand the nature of a given order. Indeed, the character of any given order is defined by norms, laws, customs, relationships, and transnational or multilateral institutions that influence a nation-state's conduct. It is the relative balance of power among the nation-states within this order that enable them to set the terms of the order's norms, laws, and institutions and the ability of these features to inform and shape behavior within the order. Powerful nation-states with little interest in a liberal order will tend to prefer a rather self-supporting system whose benefits for other actors are primarily coincidental or would serve the dominant powers. Conversely, powerful nation-states that believe in the importance of a robust and influential liberal order will tend to create an order that constrains the behavior of all nation-states, even their own, in the pursuit of general stability and prosperity.

This is a critical distinction, because discussions about China will often conflate China's rising power—an undeniable change in the regional distribution of power—as an automatic threat to the established regional order. As we will see in subsequent chapters, China's approach to the existing liberal order is far more complex than one may assume.

THE TRANSFORMATIONS OF ASIAN ORDERS

This book does not seek to solve these persistent questions in the context of academia, but rather to explore how these issues are evolving across the Indo-Pacific. Historically, changes in the Asian balance of power have correlated with changes in the regional order. One should therefore expect recent and ongoing shifts in the regional balance of power to have profound implications for today's regional order. To understand the Indo-Pacific order and the implications of changing power dynamics, one must understand how it has evolved before. The following brief historical review is not simply an academic exercise, but is essential for understanding the relationship between power and order in the Indo-Pacific. This context fundamentally informs how regional actors view themselves and their place in the world.

Speaking generally, the Asian regional order has undergone several tectonic transformations in its fundamental shape and character.[14] And as the balance of power in Asia has evolved, its regional order has generally evolved as well.

THE MIDDLE KINGDOM

For centuries, until the mid-nineteenth century, the Asian balance of power was broadly predicated on Chinese geopolitical supremacy. As the so-called Middle Kingdom, China's leaders saw themselves as ruling under the "Mandate of Heaven," and they established a tributary system that emphasized a formal hierarchy (with China as the hegemon) while allowing smaller nations a significant amount of autonomy under the suzerainty of the Chinese emperor.[15] The Sinocentric order of this period continues to echo throughout the region. Countries around the region remain greatly influenced by Chinese culture—its writing system, religions and philosophies, art, and literature—yet nostalgia for Sinocentrism is virtually nonexistent outside China itself.

For China's leaders during this period, foreign relations were little more than an afterthought. China's place atop the global hierarchy was thought of as a law of nature that only required ritualized attention. John K. Fairbank, the founding father of modern Chinese studies in the United States, described China's approach to foreign affairs at this time thusly: "The Chinese tended to think of their foreign relations as giving expression externally to the same principles of social and political order that were manifested internally within the Chinese state and society. China's foreign relations were accordingly hierarchic and nonegalitarian, like Chinese society itself."[16]

Indeed, from the seventh to the mid-nineteenth centuries, China's foreign relations were managed by the Ministry of Rites (礼部), which also supervised the imperial court's ceremonies, oversaw registers for Buddhist and Taoist priests, and managed imperial examinations. Foreign relations, therefore, were seen as another ritualized aspect of the emperor's duties. Interactions with foreign nations, especially on an equal basis as sovereign states, was an incomprehensible idea for China's leaders. Responsibility for foreign relations was finally made its own office—the Zongli Yamen—in 1861, which gives a sense of how slow China's leaders were to recognize how wrong they were about the importance of foreign relations.

Although some scholars have argued that premodern Asia was peaceful, in contrast to contemporaneous Europe,[17] the Sinocentric order was nonetheless created and maintained through an implicit threat of subjugation—and at times via the actual use of force. China and Vietnam clashed as early as the second century BCE, and were often at war throughout the millennia that followed. As for Korea, its status as a Chinese tributary was established and enforced by the Mongols and the Manchus, whose successful invasions of China, in, respectively, the thirteenth and seventeenth centuries CE, were accompanied by bloody attacks on the Korean Peninsula. For centuries, primarily because of its geographic separation, Japan largely existed on the periphery of the Sinocentric order. Kublai Khan launched the only attempted invasions of Japan from China, in 1274 and 1281, both of which failed.

The Sinocentric order frayed in the mid-nineteenth century as a result of the Qing Dynasty's failure to govern and its inability to reform, and because of pressure from Western colonial forces.[18] Western colonialism in China presented a fundamental challenge to each major power in Asia, and their ability (or inability) to adjust accordingly directly shaped the subsequent regional balance of power. Indeed, it is this period—when China was subject to a series of military defeats, colonial exploitation, and unequal treaties that undermined Chinese territorial integrity—that China's leaders refer to as the "Century of Humiliation" and a driving factor in its current approach to foreign affairs.[19]

THE RISING SUN

The order established in the wake of the collapsing Qing Dynasty was similarly driven by Tokyo's rapidly expanding geopolitical power. In fact, the rapid expansion of Japanese economic and military power had profound implications for the East Asian order. Using ships acquired from Europe and having studied Western military theorists, Japan instituted a period of rapid military expansion. In 1876, Meiji Japan opened Choseon Korea, obtaining lopsided treaty rights of its own, and it then won wars against China (1895) and Russia (1905), to become Northeast Asia's unrivaled hegemon.

Initially, Japan seemed content to join the club of major powers. Yet the Japanese were stung by the reversal of their capture of China's Liaodong Peninsula through the "Triple Intervention" of Germany, Russia, and France; by the rejection of their Racial Equality Proposal at the Paris Peace Conference in 1919; by the Immigration Act of 1924, which was designed to curtail Japanese immigration to the United States; and by London's and Washington's assiduous efforts to limit the size of the Japanese navy. As Japan's foreign policy came to be increasingly dominated by the military in the wake of the Great Depression, Tokyo embarked on an aggressive course of action that would bring it into conflict with a diminished China, the European countries still entrenched in Southeast Asia, and, eventually, the United States.

The order that Japan sought to establish in Asia was fundamentally coercive, yet was conceived of in terms that sought to justify Japanese aggression. Although Japanese troops invaded countries across East Asia, these efforts were painted as intended to end Western colonialization and to integrate Asia into a regional economy that would benefit all—the so-called Greater East Asian Co-Prosperity Sphere. And though such justifications were certainly propaganda, some Japanese strategists believed their cause was one of liberation, while others saw it as a path to Japanese hegemony over the region. Indeed, some Japanese military planners thought the invasion and occupation of the Philippines would be aided by local Filipinos, whom they thought would rise up and fight their nominal American colonial oppressors. Japanese military planners were therefore surprised when the people of the Philippines fought side by side with the Americans.

For a relatively brief moment, it may have appeared that the next Asian order would be orchestrated from an Asian capital. But Japan's disastrous attack on the United States in 1941, and its devastating defeat in 1945, put Washington and Moscow in the cockpit—a pairing that immediately broke apart on ideological grounds. As for Japan, the ravaged Asian power was remade to serve as a fortress of American liberalism—a vital component of the new order that would emerge—but not as its architect.

THE POSTWAR PACIFIC, 1946 TO THE PRESENT

Although Japanese expansion failed to produce Tokyo's desired Greater East Asian Co-Prosperity Sphere, dominated by Imperial Japan, it did succeed in dealing a mortal blow to the European colonial project. In the years after 1945, old names like "British India," "British Malaya," "the Dutch East Indies," and "French Indochina" would be gradually (and often violently) replaced by those of India, Pakistan, Malaysia, Singapore, Indonesia, Vietnam, Cambodia, and Laos. The Philippines, site of some of the bloodiest battles in the Pacific War, was granted the independence long promised by the United States, and Korea and Taiwan were freed from Japanese control. The peoples of Australia and New Zealand, meanwhile, would attenuate their old ties to London and further develop national identities distinct from their colonial roots.

As the strongest Allied power in the Pacific and the only major nation not ravaged by the fighting, the United States was primed to become Asia's predominant power. Yet establishing this dominance was not automatic, immediate, or peaceful. Indeed, the United States was engaged in an active conflict in Asia for twenty-three of the Cold War's forty-four years, leading to the death of over 95,000 Americans and millions of people in Asia.[20] Moreover, a poor and militarily obsolescent China fought the United States to a stalemate in Korea and deterred Washington from escalating in Vietnam—demonstrating that even economic and political predominance does not always translate into assured military victory, especially in continental Asia.

As the United States fought these wars in Asia, it also laid the groundwork for an international order that was neither hierarchical nor colonial; it was liberal. ("Liberalism" has a different meaning in international politics than it does in domestic politics. This book refers to "liberalism" as a concept in international politics that emphasizes international laws, norms, and institutions as a means to overcome the instability caused by pure power politics in international relations.)[21]

The American Cold War strategy of containment was first detailed in a 1950 memo written by Secretary of State Paul Nitze. Titled "United States Objectives and Programs for National Security," and generally referred to as "NSC-68," the memo argues that "even if there were no Soviet Union," the United States must "face the fact that in a shrinking world the absence of order among nations is becoming less and less tolerable."[22]

Throughout the Cold War, the United States—often in concert with its allies—built a liberal order that sought to restrain the actions of states and to channel geopolitical competition into forums of diplomacy and negotiation rather than coercion and war. The result has been what Ikenberry describes as an order composed of open markets, economic security and the social bargain, multilateral institutional cooperation, human rights and progressive change, security binding, Western democratic solidarity, and American hegemonic leadership.[23] Add to these the preservation of the open and secure global commons that has facilitated closer economic integration and greater political interaction, and one can see how this order has encouraged regional stability (through American military dominance and extended deterrence commitments), economic integration (through the Bretton Woods institutions), the peaceful resolution of disputes through international laws and institutions (e.g., the United Nations), and the promotion of democratic governance. The result has been a remarkable period of economic growth, regional stability, and rapid democratization.

US alliances and partnerships served as the backbone of Asia's postwar liberal order. These alliances and partnerships included some that predated the fall of Japan (e.g., Thailand, the Philippines, and Australia), but it was from the Cold War that two of the key US alliances in Asia emerged: with South Korea, after American forces helped save the new government from destruction at the hands of the North; and with Japan, which became one of the world's premier trading nations and economic powers while the United States guaranteed its security.

For much of the Cold War, several key American allies and partners in Asia (and elsewhere) were not governed democratically. Both South Korea and Taiwan were led by military dictatorships, as were the South Vietnamese. Indeed, despite all the Cold War rhetoric of defending the Free World from the spread of communism, the United States was still willing to work with—and defend—undemocratic governments that aligned against communism. Yet this order also provided the necessary international context that enabled South Korea and Taiwan to eventually transition to the robust, flourishing democracies they are today. This is important for two reasons: First, it demonstrates that, historically, the United States has worked with undemocratic governments if their national interests aligned. Second, these undemocratic states were nonetheless generally supportive of some aspects of a liberal order that were conducive for regional stability and supportive of international trade.[24]

These alliances and partnerships—in conjunction with the laws, norms, and institutions that composed the postwar liberal order—allowed states to compete peaceably with one another and avoid military conquest as the preferred means for resolving differences. It also established mechanisms and institutions that enabled greater political and economic integration around the world, which in turn raised living standards and promoted liberal principles.

On the Asian mainland, meanwhile, the victory of Mao Zedong's People's Liberation Army in 1949 began the process of redefining regional strategic dynamics. For the first decades of the Cold War, before the Cultural Revolution, China was actively hostile to American power in Asia and to a liberal order internationally. China intervened heavily in Korea and, to check perceived American imperialism, supported revolutionary groups around the world in support of Mao's dream of "perpetual revolution," and sought to establish itself as a leader in the Non-Aligned Movement.[25] Yet during the Cultural Revolution, Beijing largely looked inward because it was consumed by a struggle to solidify and expand its authority over the troubled nation and convulsed by a series of horrific political experiments that rendered its intellectual life as barren as its fields.

When Washington became aware of Beijing's rivalry with its ostensible ideological allies in Moscow, President Richard Nixon's argument that "to leave the present and future leaders of China isolated, nurturing their resentments and even hatred of the United States . . . is senseless and counterproductive" drove Washington to precipitate a process that reintroduced the world to China and China to the world.[26]

With the end of the Cold War and in the subsequent years, the liberal order both deepened and expanded in parallel with unparalleled American geopolitical dominance. By the time the Soviet Union dissolved in 1991, South Korea had become a democracy and Taiwan was well on its way to doing the same. Germany reunified, and NATO expanded to include several former Soviet satellites, and in 1995 the General Agreement on Tariffs and Trade was replaced with the World Trade Organization. Deng Xiaoping's economic reforms were only a decade old, and the Chinese economy was but a fraction of the size of those in Western Europe, let alone those of the United States and Japan. The world Washington inherited in 1991 was unipolar, structured on venerable Cold War and pre–Cold War security partnerships—in Europe, NATO; in Asia, the hub-and-spokes system of close bilateral alliances—but cemented by unchallenged US economic and military might.

Some prominent scholars have argued that the post–World War II order is distinct from the order that emerged after the Cold War. John Mearsheimer, for example, argues that the postwar order was fundamentally realist, and that this order became more liberal with the end of the Cold War and the emergence of an American unipolarity.[27] Conversely, other scholars note that the order that emerged from World War II was created during a vast asymmetry of power, yet reflected a broad embrace of institutionalism. G. John Ikenberry, for example, argues that the post–Cold War era demonstrated the durability of institutions and of relations among advanced industrial countries.[28]

For the purposes of this book, the key variable to understand is that the order that was largely created by the United States after the end of World War II was fundamentally liberal and was buttressed by a realist approach to power. Although the breadth and depth of this order certainly changed over time, and American ambitions for an international liberal order expanded, the fundamental character of the order—its embrace of liberalism as a bulwark against instability—remained fundamentally unchanged.

Ultimately, the post–World War II liberal order has been tremendously beneficial to the United States and a major boon to global stability and prosperity. Built from the ashes of World War II, the liberal order made the world far more peaceful, stable, and prosperous than it has ever been before.[29] The post–World War II era saw the disappearance of wars between major developed powers, the end of great power wars (since 1953), and the absence of interstate wars in Western Europe.[30] It has also seen a dramatic reduction in the number and deadliness of other international conflicts, the construction of institutions and mechanisms that have promoted and facilitated trade and investment, and the strengthening (although far from perfecting) of norms that have proscribed the use of force, except in self-defense or with the approval of the United Nations Security Council.

The end of the Cold War, and its attendant expansion of the liberal order, have seen a further reduction of conflict within states and a renewed level of activism for conflict prevention and dispute management by the international community. If current trends continue, researchers at the Peace Research Institute in Oslo argue that the proportion of the world's countries afflicted by civil wars will be halved by 2050.[31] Joshua Goldstein writes of the post–Cold War era thusly:

> In the first half of the twentieth century, world wars killed tens of millions and left whole continents in ruins. In the second half of that century, during the Cold War, proxy wars killed millions, and the world feared a nuclear war that could have wiped out our species. Now, in the early twenty-first century, the worst wars, such as Iraq, kill hundreds of thousands. We fear terrorist attacks that could destroy a city, but not life on the planet. The fatalities still represent a large number and the impacts of wars are still catastrophic for those caught in them, but overall, war has diminished dramatically.[32]

The benefits of this historically unprecedented era of peace and stability have been felt especially strongly in the Indo-Pacific. The only major conflicts seen in the region in decades have been ongoing conflicts in Afghanistan and Pakistan, and major power conflict has not been seen since the end of the Korean War in 1953.[33] The only other state-based conflicts seen in the region today are the internal conflicts in Myanmar between Naypyidaw and its internal ethnic groups and between Manila and restive groups in the Southern Philippines—certainly disturbing events, but nothing near the scale of massive conflicts seen in the region in previous years and decades. Indeed, East Asia ranks just below Europe as one of the world's most prosperous and stable regions.[34]

Considering how much is going well in the Indo-Pacific, one may ask what the problem is. Although many appropriately point to the rise of China or North Korean belligerence as a cause of concern, there is a broader, more systematic dynamic at play that the United States must understand if it is going to maintain power and influence in the Indo-Pacific. The regional balance of power is rapidly changing, which historically has presaged a dramatic evolution to the existing regional order.

Mearsheimer argues that the distribution of power in a given system determines the type of order that emerges, and that when the system is unipolar, the political ideology of the sole pole matters greatly. "Liberal international orders," therefore, can arise only in unipolar systems where the leading state is a liberal democracy.[35] The coming decades will put this argument to the test, and this book argues that a liberal order can be sustained in an increasingly multipolar system if the order is sustained by strong institutions and by the coordinated efforts of like-minded allies and partners.

As new powers rise and American power (though still robust) grows increasingly diluted, the fundamental basis for the existing regional liberal order will come under threat. The next chapter describes recent changes to the balance of power in the Indo-Pacific— another tectonic shift—and explores how US allies and partners have reacted to their rapidly evolving strategic environment.

2
A REGION IN FLUX

Sophisticated US leadership is the sine qua non of a stable world order. However, we lack the former while the latter is getting worse.

—FINAL TWEET OF FORMER NATIONAL SECURITY ADVISER
ZBIGNIEW BRZEZINSKI, MAY 4, 2017

The previous chapter described the relationship between order and power in the Indo-Pacific, and surveyed how changes in the region's balance of power have driven significant shifts in the regional order. It described several tectonic shifts in the Asian order during the last two centuries, and argued that the postwar American order has been of tremendous benefit to the world.

This chapter argues that Asia is currently undergoing another tectonic shift in its balance of power and describes the potential implications of this shift for the existing regional order and for American interests. It concludes with an argument for the United States to shift its approach to the region to reflect these new strategic realities, and to look to its allies and partners as sources of strength to sustain regional stability and promote economic and political liberalism across the region.

THE INDO-PACIFIC'S CHANGING BALANCE OF POWER

The Indo-Pacific today is haunted by the twin specters of tremendous geopolitical change and a degree of strategic uncertainty unseen since the end of World War II. Although there is never a sure thing in international politics, the region has for decades experienced the closest thing to it: a stable environment free from major power wars and conducive to trade and integration has enabled the Indo-Pacific to emerge as the engine of the global economy, to the tremendous benefit of its people and American interests. Yet many in Asia, especially among US allies and partners, fear that the era of Pax Americana may be drawing to a close.

For decades, successive US administrations have believed that sustained American military, political, and economic dominance was essential to maintaining a liberal order across Asia. Indeed, American strategists have consistently deemed it a vital interest to prevent the rise of a hostile hegemonic power in the world's three key regions: Western Europe, the Middle East, and East Asia.[1] Yet somewhat ironically, the Indo-Pacific's success has also brought with it tectonic changes that threaten the very foundations of this success.

For decades, the Indo-Pacific has been rising in geopolitical significance at a remarkable pace. Recent decades have seen unprecedented economic development and stability for the region—a trend that began after the end of World War II in 1945, accelerated after the end of the Korean War in 1953, and really took off in the late 1970s with the embrace of market economics and (later) democratic governance by Taiwan and South Korea, and China's embrace of "reform and opening." From being a dysfunctional and unstable region during much of the Cold War, the region has emerged as the world's economic and geopolitical engine. Between 2001 and 2018 alone, the Indo-Pacific's combined gross domestic product (GDP)—not including the United States—exploded from $10.5 trillion to $20.5 trillion (for the sake of reference, the US economy grew during the same period from $10.6 trillion to $19.3 trillion) (figure 2.1).[2] Meanwhile, these countries' military expenditures more than doubled over the same decade, from $202 billion to $504 billion.[3]

Of course, the bulk of credit for this remarkable period of stability and prosperity belongs to the leaders of these countries, and to the countries' peoples themselves. Each took significant risks—both politically and personally—to encourage their countries to develop economically and socially and to establish an era of stability and prosperity. Yet it would also be a mistake to ignore the external environment that made these developments possible. The United States, and the liberal order it nurtured, served as a structural foundation for Asia's long peace. By establishing and sustaining alliances and partnerships that kept the peace—and by constructing an international framework of laws, norms, and institutions that promoted regional trade and the peaceful resolution of disputes—American power and the liberal order it supported created an external environment that several Asian nations adroitly utilized.

China's leaders have also in the past acknowledged the benefits of this peaceful external environment. In 2002, at the Sixteenth Party Congress, Jiang Zemin declared that the subsequent twenty years represented a "period of strategic opportunity" for China's growth and development.[4] This evaluation of China's external environment was later affirmed by Hu Jintao and Xi Jinping, though Xi did not put a time horizon on this period, stating somewhat ominously in his report to the Nineteenth Party Congress in 2017 that "both China and the world are in the midst of profound and complex changes. China is still in an important period of strategic opportunity for development; the prospects are bright, but the challenges are severe."[5] In other words, Xi sees China's external environment as still generally peaceful, but acknowledges the reality that changes under way in the region may threaten the foundations of this stability.

It would be unrealistic to expect such a virtuous cycle to not have geopolitical implications. As discussed in the preceding chapter, there has historically been a direct relationship between the balance of

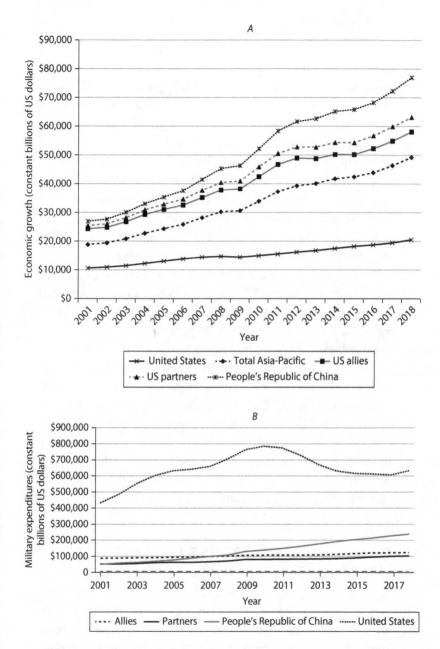

FIGURE 2.1 The Indo-Pacific's (A) economic growth and (B) military expenditures, 2001–18 (in constant billions of US dollars)

SOURCES: WORLD DEVELOPMENT INDICATORS; SIPRI MILITARY EXPENDITURE DATABASE.

power in Asia and the regional order. There is a tragic irony here: rapid economic growth and a remarkable period of stability have increased the region's significance, to be sure, but they have also set forces in motion that are dramatically changing the region's geopolitical dynamics and are threatening to undermine the stability and prosperity at the heart of its rise. Sustained stability and dramatic economic growth have allowed several countries in Asia to significantly enhance their military power and indigenous technological base. Because this development has occurred without any accompanying resolution of intraregional disputes and historical animosities, the risk of tension and conflict in Asia is growing.

Though still evolving, this new era in the Indo-Pacific appears to be driven by two overriding variables: China's rising power, and persistent questions about the sustainability and credibility of American power. Taken together, these two factors are breeding a profound sense of uncertainty across the Indo-Pacific and a threat to the existing liberal regional order. Although America's allies and partners have long been comfortable benefiting from the regional order without having the responsibility to preserve it, many are concerned that the region is trending in a direction that would be inimical to their interests and that the United States is unable or unwilling to effectively respond. To compensate for this situation, many are therefore beginning to acquire new military capabilities, and to pursue new economic and diplomatic initiatives.

CHINA'S CHALLENGE TO THE REGIONAL LIBERAL ORDER

It is easy to forget how far China has come.[6] When President Nixon and Henry Kissinger first reached out to Beijing, China was being consumed by the Great Proletarian Cultural Revolution. As described by US ambassador Chas Freeman, China's GDP at the time of that visit was only a bit larger than that of the District of Columbia today, and its 862 million people had an annual per capita income of about $132 (in current dollars).[7] If anyone expressed concerns about China and the role it might play in the world, such concerns grew out of Mao's ideology of perpetual revolution and his ambition to export revolution across the developing world.

Yet Nixon and Kissinger understood China's great potential, both as a check against the Soviet Union as well as an opportunity that went beyond Cold War competition. Writing in *Foreign Affairs* in 1967, Nixon stated "taking the long view, we simply cannot afford to leave China forever outside the family of nations, there to nurture its fantasies, cherish its hates and threaten its neighbors. There is no place on this small planet for a billion of its potentially most able people to live in angry isolation."[8]

At the time, few acknowledged the long-term geopolitical implications of engaging China and encouraging its rise. Those who did, however, believed that China's political system as well as its international orientation would gradually change. Indeed, in that same article, Nixon wrote, "The world cannot be safe until China changes. Thus our aim, to the extent that we can influence events, should be to induce change. The way to do this is to persuade China that it must change: that it cannot satisfy its imperial ambitions, and that its own national interest requires a turning away from foreign adventuring and a turning inward toward the solution of its own domestic problems."[9]

For a time, it seemed that history was moving in this direction. Deng Xiaoping's ascendance heralded the gradual embrace of economic liberalism and a marked shift in China's domestic politics away from one driven by Maoist ideology and his cult of personality to one driven by pragmatism. The experiences of other countries, such as South Korea and Taiwan, suggested that an embrace of economic liberalism would gradually but inexorably lead to political liberalism. Concurrently, it stood to reason that an increasingly integrated and market-oriented China would more and more identify its external interests with those of the broader liberal order.

With the end of the Cold War, the core raison d'être of the US–China relationship dissipated. In its place, Americans hoped that the relationship could be driven by efforts to shape China's decisions to be more supportive of the status quo, and to contribute more to the health and success of the liberal order. This hope was best expressed in 2005 by then US deputy secretary of state Robert Zoellick, who called on China to be a "responsible stakeholder."[10]

This approach of engaging China lasted in various forms through the Obama administration, with mixed results. In some areas—such as climate change and confronting Iran—China demonstrated a willingness to work with the United States and the international community on issues of global significance. Yet some in Beijing saw efforts to bring China into the tent and have it contribute to international public goods as a strategic trap and an indication of American geopolitical weakness.[11] On other issues, China has remained unwilling to cooperate—usually, because to do so would mean that it would be forced to restrict its options on issues of domestic political significance. Broadly speaking, China's willingness to cooperate on a given issue seemed to have less to do with strategic benevolence and more to do with Beijing's changing calculations of Chinese interests. In other words, for example, China likely agreed to work with the United States on climate change when the issue emerged as a significant factor in China's domestic politics and a popular challenge to domestic perceptions of the Chinese Communist Party's (CCP's) ability to govern.

For decades, it went unexamined whether China was actually identifying its national interests with the broader liberal regional order. China was too weak to figure largely in international politics. Throughout the 1990s, hope for political change and greater economic integration eclipsed hard-nosed considerations of how China's leaders were conceiving of China's interests and its role in the world. When President George W. Bush stated that the United States should "trade freely with China, and time is on our side," he was echoing his predecessor, Bill Clinton, who called the opening of China's political system "inevitable, just as inevitably the Berlin Wall fell."[12]

THE SOURCES OF CHINESE POWER

Today, China matters a great deal. Indeed, the rise of China since it began opening to the outside world in the late 1970s has been one of the most important geopolitical events of the first decades of the twenty-first century. China's economy has experienced a remarkable period of growth and development. Once a communist backwater, with a meager GDP of $154 billion in 1976, by 2016 China was the world's second-largest economy, with a GDP of $11.2 trillion (figure 2.2).[13] In all human history, the world has never witnessed economic growth of this speed or scale.

The export-oriented nature of the Chinese economy, and a stable and trade-nurturing external environment, enabled Beijing to emerge as the critical economic power in the Indo-Pacific. Indeed, China is now the top trading partner of 124 countries, more than twice the number of countries—52—for whom the United States is the most significant trade partner.[14] China's leaders have already begun to translate this newfound economic prosperity into

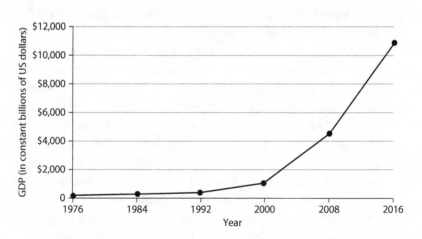

FIGURE 2.2 China's gross domestic product, 1976–2016 (in constant billions of US dollars)

SOURCE: WORLD BANK, WORLD DEVELOPMENT INDICATORS.

significant diplomatic and military power that is shaking the balance of power across the Indo-Pacific and around the world.

Militarily, China has consistently invested in its armed forces, with decades of regular, significant increases to its defense budget. In 2016, Chinese military spending accounted for $215 billion of the Asia-Pacific's $450 billion total.[15] These investments have greatly enhanced China's military capabilities. Once a so-called army of millet and rifles (小米加步枪 *xiaomi jia buqiang*), the People's Liberation Army (PLA) today is a large and effective military force that poses a significant challenge to every other military in the region, including that of the United States. China is now reaping the benefits of a more advanced military. For example, its fifth-generation stealth fighter—the J-20—recently entered service and poses a significant challenge to US air and naval power in the Western Pacific.[16] This means that the United States' presumed air superiority, which it has enjoyed in each conflict since the Korean War, may be coming to an end. China is also fielding large numbers of advanced naval assets, as well as a diverse array of ballistic missiles and advanced space and cyberspace capabilities. And the PLA has been reorganized along the lines of the American military to facilitate joint operations and centralized command and control.[17]

Although the PLA remains focused on scenarios related to Taiwan, China's expanding interests and geopolitical ambitions mean that the military is increasingly examining other contingencies, several of which lie far from China's shores.[18] And though China may be focused on East Asia and the South China Sea and East China Sea, Central and South Asia are beginning to figure more prominently in Chinese military ambitions. Indeed, in 2017, China established its first overseas military facility, in Djibouti, in order to help protect Chinese interests in the Middle East and, presumably, to begin the process of defending Chinese shipping lanes across the Indian Ocean. One should expect China to seek to establish additional facilities across East Africa and throughout the Indian Ocean Basin in the future.

With this power, China today has developed significant geopolitical influence across the Indo-Pacific and around the world—influence that is often exercised with little diplomatic subtlety. This has kindled a debate among China's neighbors about the stance they will take toward Beijing, and in the United States about competition for regional, and even global, dominance. Theorists like John Mearsheimer have asserted that China and the United States will inevitably come into conflict,[19] while Graham Allison has argued that the so-called Thucydides's Trap may be avoidable.[20]

The focus of this analysis is not to render an opinion on the likelihood of conflict between China and the United States. Instead, it assesses China's emerging approach to the world as a great power and its implications for the existing regional order.

WHAT BEIJING WANTS

China is emerging as a kind of world power never seen before: a wealthy, technocratic, and confident authoritarian state based on the strictures of Leninism, and with ambitions driven by a force that goes beyond nationalism.[21] China's ambitions blur the lines between domestic and foreign affairs, and seek to ensure that the CCP is able to pursue its interests and prerogatives without restriction. Although Beijing likely views its approach as benevolent and virtuous, a Chinese-led world order would nevertheless cast aside assumptions of liberal internationalism, and embrace a system founded on calculations of raw power, subtle influence, hierarchy, and great power spheres of influence.

China's ambitions for a revised regional order are rooted in its strategic motivations. A tremendous amount of ink has already been spilled by analysts attempting to describe the incredible rise to power of Xi Jinping. Although much has been made of Xi's recent success at removing term limits to his position, his equally significant bureaucratic successes have received much less notice. He has established himself as the chief decisionmaker in all critical political, economic, and military issues. Under his leadership, China has all but abandoned the idea of collective leadership and has centralized authority and power in a single individual.

So far in the international arena, Xi has demonstrated a penchant for decisive, opportunistic leadership that plays to China's strengths while minimizing its vulnerabilities. He has also demonstrated a greater willingness to tolerate risk and turbulence in international affairs, even going so far as to reportedly threaten military conflict with Vietnam over a dispute over maritime oil drilling.[22]

When the Nineteenth Congress of the CCP convened in Beijing in October 2017, it enshrined a new phrase into China's Constitution: "Xi Jinping Thought for the New Era of Socialism with Chinese Special Characteristics." This elevated Xi to the hallowed status of Mao and Deng, but also raised a critical question—what is this new era? To my mind, it was best described by an editorial published in Chinese media several weeks after the Nineteenth Party Congress, reflecting language used by Xi Jinping himself in his work report to the congress. It identified three phases of Chinese socialism: under Mao, China stood up; under Deng, China grew rich; and under Xi, China will become strong.[23]

Just a few days after becoming general secretary of the CCP, Xi Jinping gave a speech describing China's guiding ideology, in which he gives more specificity to his vision. In this speech—which was not published until June 2019 in the Chinese magazine *Qiushi*, the primary journal for party theory—Xi declared:[24]

Some foreign academics believe that the rapid pace of China's development has called Western theories into question. A new form of Marxist theory is overturning the traditional theories of the West! Yet from beginning to end, we have maintained that every country's road to development should be decided by the people of that country. The so-called China model, the road of socialism with Chinese characteristics, was created through the Chinese people's own struggles. We firmly believe that as socialism with Chinese characteristics develops further, our system will inevitably mature; it is likewise inevitable that the superiority of our socialist system will be increasingly apparent. Inevitably, our road will become wider; inevitably, our country's road of development will have increasingly greater influence on the world.[25]

Yet while Xi's role in explaining China's foreign policy behavior is essential, there are also broader institutional forces at work. Specifically, the CCP—as the source and conduit for all credible political power in China—is a critical force that must be understood. The CCP today is both the *driver* and the *purpose* of all political activity that is considered legitimate in China. Beijing has constructed a narrative that places the party at the center of modern Chinese history: According to its propaganda, it was the party that ended the so-called century of humiliation, consolidated power across China, stood up to the West, and enabled it to grow prosperous. And we would be remiss to ignore the role that the party itself plays as a driver and purpose of Chinese foreign policy.

In many ways, China today has become the apotheosis of Leninism, if not of Marxism-Leninism. Although the CCP certainly views itself as the revolutionary vanguard of the proletariat and thus as a prelude to the establishment of socialism, its objective has not been to overthrow capitalism. Rather, the party has embraced capitalism and harnessed it as a means to achieve its own end: the perpetuation of the party itself. And though the party may now be emphasizing a return to Marxist ideals, and Xi has emphasized the communist values of austerity and humility, an essential embrace of capitalism is now inextricably interwoven with China's economy.

In many ways, one of China's least-understood but most critical foreign policy objectives is about the CCP itself. On issues as diverse as attempts to influence foreign academics and forcing foreign companies to tow the party line, China's foreign policy is clearly used as a mechanism through which the CCP pursues its objectives.

This is just one indication that foreign observers of Chinese foreign policy need to abandon old preconceptions about China and its orientation toward the international order. Some of these preconceptions can still be seen within recent debates among American China watchers about an appropriate China strategy for the United States. In an open letter to the *Washington Post*, several top China watchers (including some deeply respected friends and colleagues of mine) argued that "although its rapid economic and military growth has led Beijing toward a more assertive international role, many Chinese officials and other elites know that a moderate, pragmatic and genuinely cooperative approach with the West serves China's interests. Washington's adversarial stance toward Beijing weakens the influence of those voices in favor of assertive nationalists. With the right balance of competition and cooperation, US actions can strengthen those Chinese leaders who want China to play a constructive role in world affairs."[26]

Inherent in this analysis is that these American scholars understand China's interests better than China's leaders, and that the United States has the ability to empower the moderate pragmatists among China's elite (who apparently share the same views as these American scholars) to guide China into a less assertive, more cooperative approach. It is a restatement of the argument, also made by former Treasury secretary Henry Paulson, that "if we treat China like an enemy, they might become one."[27] This approach is based on the assumptions that American hostility breeds hostility, and American acquiescence would encourage Chinese cooperation.

Unfortunately, in addition to absolving China of agency and responsibility for its own actions, this approach has not been reflected by recent Chinese behavior. The first years of the Obama administration, for instance, can partly be seen as an effort to engage China with respect and a genuine interest in cooperation. President Obama regularly highlighted China's power and its potential role in the world, and a United States–China joint statement in 2009 announced the two sides agreed that "respecting each other's core interests is extremely important to ensure steady progress in China–US relations."[28] Secretary of State Hillary Clinton stated in a 2009 speech to the Council on Foreign Relations that "first, no nation can meet the world's challenges alone," and "second, most nations worry about the same global threats."[29]

In September 2009, I was working as a fellow and director of the Asia Program at the Center for a New American Security, which had been established a few years earlier by Michèle Flournoy and Kurt Campbell and had rapidly emerged as a source for talent and foreign policy thinking for the Obama administration. Along with my friend and colleague Nirav Patel, I was launching a major report about the US–China relationship, titled "China's Arrival."[30] At the launch event, Deputy Secretary of State Jim Steinberg gave remarks titled, appropriately, "The Administration's Vision of the US–China Relationship." In his remarks, Steinberg described a concept of strategic reassurance:

> Strategic reassurance rests on a core, if tacit, bargain. Just as we and our allies must make clear that we are prepared to welcome China's "arrival," as you all have so nicely put it, as a prosperous and successful power, China must reassure the rest of the world that its development and growing global role will not come at the expense of security and well-being of others. Bolstering that bargain must be a priority in the US–China relationship. And strategic reassurance must find ways to highlight and reinforce the areas of common interest, while addressing the sources of mistrust directly, whether they be political, military, or economic.[31]

Taken together, it would be difficult to imagine an approach to China more in line with the scholars who wrote the 2019 open letter to the *Washington Post*. Yet the result from China was not a new era of great power cooperation. Despite the best of efforts of American diplomats to present the United States as respectful of Chinese interests and committed to a cooperative approach, the US–China security relationship and the Indo-Pacific region in the subsequent years grew far more tense and China's leaders grew increasingly assertive internationally. This was likely the result of Chinese confidence after the Great Recession as much as it was American diplomacy, but my conversations with Chinese scholars at the time suggested that Beijing interpreted such entreaties as evidence of Washington's weakness. Instead of meeting cooperation with cooperation, it seems Beijing's approach is guided more by Lenin's guidance to "probe with bayonets. If you encounter mush, proceed; if you encounter steel, withdraw."

Skepticism about past efforts to engage China has recently become something of conventional wisdom in Washington. Kurt Campbell and Ely Ratner coalesced this skepticism in the pages of *Foreign Affairs* thusly: "Nearly half a century since Nixon's first steps toward rapprochement, the record is increasingly clear that Washington once again put too much faith in its power to shape China's trajectory. All sides of the policy debate erred: free traders and financiers who foresaw inevitable and increasing openness in China, integrationists who argued that Beijing's ambitions would be tamed by greater interaction with the international community, and hawks who believed that China's power would be abated by perpetual American primacy."[32]

The debate in Washington has since coalesced into two rather extreme camps: one believing that engagement with China works, and one believing that engagement with China is a waste of time. My view—to be described later in this book—is somewhere between these two camps. Yet any evaluation of how the United States should approach China—a question that will fundamentally inform its approach to US allies and partners in Asia and around the world—should begin with a clear understanding of the challenge that China poses.

GREAT POWER WITH CHINESE CHARACTERISTICS

It is natural for political scientists to look to history for examples of other rising powers to give hints about the geopolitical implications of a risen China. In recent years, American scholars have proposed a host of potential progenitors, including Sparta and Wilhelmine Germany.[33] Although such analyses have varied in their narratives, the conclusions have been generally pessimistic: that rising powers often seek to change the rules of their external environment, and may come into conflict with other great powers depending on the roles that these rising powers define for themselves and how other great powers respond to their rise.[34]

Though valuable, historical analogies miss a critical aspect of understanding the implications of China's rise: as a great power, China will represent something completely new in the history of international relations. Though wealthy, technocratic, and confident like other rising powers have been, China's unique history and the ideology of the CCP mean that China's approach to foreign affairs will differ significantly from those of other great powers.

This should not be a surprise—every great power is different from another. For example, the United States did not re-create the British Empire as it rose to power, but rather pursued its own course in a way that reflected its own history, interests, and ideology. Similarly, it would be a mistake to assume that a rising China will mimic the actions and structures of other great powers. Beijing will undoubtedly pursue its own path. Our objective today is to better understand this path.

These differences clearly manifest when considering the long-term objectives of Chinese foreign policy. Although China's leaders have to date refrained from detailing a specific vision for a revised international order, a review of their statements and official Chinese state media suggests a fairly clear vision for the future—what Xi Jinping refers to as a "Community of Common Destiny." Much of the rhetoric surrounding this idea emphasizes equality, fairness, shared interests, and shared responsibilities. It seeks to describe a new model of international relations—as opposed to the old model associated with the West—that is premised on "win-win" relations and greater integration that transcends the self-interest of the past.[35] The Community of Common Destiny encapsulates Beijing's vision to transform international geopolitics to make it compatible with China's governance model and to enable its emergence as a global leader.[36]

Beijing's ultimate vision for the future mixes both domestic and foreign policy, envisioning a revitalized China that is stable and prosperous at home, dominant in Asia, and influential around the world in a way that ensures that the CCP is able to pursue its interests and prerogatives without restriction. Xi Jinping has encapsulated much of these objectives as the "Chinese Dream of National Rejuvenation." Tellingly, Xi's priorities are presented mostly in terms of domestic policy. This can be seen in Xi's adjustment of the so-called principal contradiction facing Chinese society to be "the contradiction between unbalanced and inadequate development and the people's ever-growing needs for a better life."[37] To achieve his objectives, Xi has laid out a two-stage development plan to realize socialist modernization between 2020 and 2035, and between 2035 and the middle of the twenty-first century to develop China into a great modern socialist country "that is prosperous, strong, democratic, culturally advanced, harmonious, and beautiful."[38] Again, these objectives are described almost entirely in domestic terms. Of the eleven characteristics Xi uses to describe these stages, only one relates to foreign affairs: that as a great modern socialist country, China will have "become a global leader in terms of composite national strength and international influence."[39]

This is the first key attribute of China as a great power: even as Xi has emphasized foreign affairs more than his predecessors, Chinese foreign policy is still primarily motivated by domestic considerations. There is no discussion in China of manifest destiny, noblesse oblige, or any other construction of a mandate for an active foreign policy beyond its utility in achieving domestic political, social, and economic goals or in realizing what Beijing sees as China's rightful place as a great power. This means that Chinese external behavior will likely be primarily a reflection and outgrowth of domestic priorities rather than an effort to reshape the world in its image or spread the ideology of Xi Jinping Thought.

Yet this is not to say that China's foreign policy is devoid of ideology or historical input. The second key attribute of China as a great power will be the influence of the CCP's unique ideology and its approach to history. Most important in this regard is the CCP's use of the so-called century of humiliation—the period from the mid-nineteenth century until 1949 during which China was repeatedly defeated militarily and forced to sign treaties that ceded territory and sovereignty—as a justification for its foreign policy behavior. According to the CCP's narrative, rapacious foreign powers caused China to fall from its rightful place as Asia's dominant power, and only the CCP has the ability to stand against hostile external forces and enable China to reassume its rightful place atop Asia's geopolitical hierarchy.[40] Thus, Chinese assertiveness over Taiwan, the South China Sea, and the East China Sea can be painted by Beijing as simply correcting an historical injustice.

Ideology also plays a role in shaping Chinese foreign policy behavior. For instance, Chinese leaders and scholars have long objected to the United States' global network of alliances—and especially its overseas military bases—as evidence of "hegemony" and a "Cold War mentality." As a result, China's approach to overseas bases and foreign alliances will likely differ significantly from the US approach. Although China has already established its first foreign military facility, in Djibouti, and it is likely to be pursuing opportunities for other bases around the world, its approach to these installations suggests a different stance than that of the United States. Chinese officials are careful to refer to the base in Djibouti as a "logistics facility," and its mission is focused on a narrow set of Chinese interests—defending Chinese maritime shipping and peacekeeping, and potentially assisting Chinese people in the region who are caught up in a disaster. There is little interest in Beijing of using these facilities to defend regional governments or deter conflict. Instead, China's limited aims suggest that these facilities will be used primarily to assert Chinese interests, with the provisioning of public goods a distant priority.

Another unique aspect of Chinese foreign policy behavior can be seen in the South China Sea. Beijing seeks to establish itself as the dominant power in the region, yet it has lacked the capabilities necessary to project and sustain military power far from its shores. The island reclamation and military construction that China has conducted in the South China Sea, as well as efforts to harass and intimidate neighboring countries' efforts to extract resources from their exclusive economic zones, can best be understood as a strategy by Beijing to enhance its ability to project power and coerce its neighbors while avoiding conflict or portraying itself as explicitly revisionist.

Similarly, China's approach to international trade and investment reflects a unique approach. Xi Jinping presents a very open and progressive public face when it comes to trade. In major speeches at Davos and again at China's Boao Forum, Xi expressed enthusiasm for open markets, regional economic integration, innovation, and the benefits of market forces. Yet at the same time, China's domestic economy is riven with protectionism and government subsidies.[41] Indeed, much of the economy remains dominated by inefficient state-owned enterprises, which in turn have distorted major sectors of the economy and limited innovation potential.

This highlights the third key attribute of China as a great power: its approach to international institutions, laws, and norms is highly exceptionalist. Beijing is no longer a revolutionary power, and it does not seek to rewrite the rules of the existing order wholesale, but rather has ambitions to carve out exceptions for itself when the rules limit its freedom of action or complicate the pursuit of its objectives. Beyond this, for the foreseeable future China's leaders seem comfortable with free-riding. Although this certainly cannot be applied universally, a version of Chinese exceptionalism can be perceived across a diverse swath of issues.

For instance, China's approach to freedom of navigation changes dramatically depending on whether Chinese vessels are involved. Although China objects to US military ships and aircraft sailing through its claimed territorial waters, it has exercised exactly the same rights in the undisputed territorial waters of the United States and many other counties. Indeed, a senior colonel for the PLA recently argued that China need not get permission from London before its naval ships sailed through the United Kingdom's territorial waters, but that London would need to get permission from Beijing before sailing through China's territorial waters.[42]

Chinese exceptionalism can also be seen in its approach to international trade laws, and especially the World Trade Organization

(WTO). When China joined the WTO in 2001, many expected that it would change China as it was bought into the same rules of the game for market-based trade that everyone else plays by. Indeed, Chinese premier Zhu Rongji argued that joining the WTO was necessary in order to force China to reform its economy.[43] Yet in the past seventeen years, China's economic reforms have remained aspirational, at best. Indeed, in recent years, Xi Jinping has reasserted the role of state-owned enterprises and the government's role in the economy even as he has rhetorically trumpeted the growing role of market forces.

China is neither entirely supportive of the status quo nor entirely dismissive of it. Instead, its approach changes issue by issue, according to how Beijing defines its interests. Although one may argue that this is similar to the approach of the United States, and that any criticism of China is therefore hypocritical, one must first acknowledge that Chinese exceptionalism is very different from American exceptionalism.

American exceptionalism is based on the idea that the United States has a special role to play in the world because, as Abraham Lincoln said, it is the "last, best hope of earth."[44] In the international sphere, the United States does not have a record of military restraint and an unflinching embrace of international laws and norms. In fact, the United States has sometimes flouted international conventions in the pursuit of its own policy objectives—at times to its own eventual regret. Yet the United States also has a tradition of adhering to international rules and norms, even when they restrict US freedom of action in specific circumstances, because US leaders have understood the broader liberal order to be in the long-term interests of the United States. This can be seen in the US approach to international maritime law as codified by the UN Convention on the Law of the Sea. The US Senate has not ratified the convention, yet the United States nonetheless operates under its strictures. Indeed, Chinese scholars and officials used to praise the United States for adhering to laws and norms that restrict its options. The rule of law and adherence to international rules and norms are critical aspects of a liberal order, and the sharp distinction between Beijing's and Washington's approaches to these issues is revealing.

For Chinese leaders, Chinese exceptionalism is based on a fundamental belief in China's inherent superiority—that China's historically appropriate role is to be Asia's dominant power and its primary source of culture and civilization. China's leaders therefore do not necessarily see Chinese exceptionalism as necessarily beneficial to its neighbors, but rather as its inherent right given its history and power.

The key difference is that American exceptionalism on the world stage, though at times problematic, has yet to fundamentally undermine the liberal order it helped establish. Yet Chinese exceptionalism will have significant implications for the existing liberal order.

Official Chinese statements are replete with criticisms that the established liberal order needs to be "democratized" and that China (e.g., the People's Republic of China, PRC) did not have a sufficient voice in its inception. Chinese diplomats also often say they seek 和而不同 (he er butong), which translates as "harmony, not uniformity." This is a reference to an aphorism of Confucius, who said that "the gentleman aims at harmony, and not at uniformity. The mean man aims at uniformity, and not at harmony." This is a way to emphasize the traditional Confucian relationship dynamics of benevolence and propriety.

In other words, from Beijing's view, China does not seek to explicitly dominate international relations, but only to ensure that the rest of the world can live in harmony with China as it pursues its interests. China's leaders believe it need not adapt to the world—it is the world that must adapt to China. Practically, this suggests that Chinese leaders do indeed have an implicit vision of global order in mind. At the heart of this apparent vision is a rejuvenated China resting at the center of an interconnected Asia, in which Beijing is able to shape every critical issue in the region and the ability to exercise influence globally. International laws, norms, and institutions can largely remain, but must be "correctly" shaped by, and deferential to, the needs and interests of the CCP. This means that

China's approach to international order, though piecemeal in its exceptionalism, would ultimately be revisionist.

This is the fourth key attribute of China's great power ambitions: it will eschew Western models of great power behavior and rather pursue a China-centric, hierarchical system. This system will involve a mix of formal and informal relationships and influence arrangements that China does not see as coercive, but rather based on a natural deference to Chinese preferences based on its economic, political, technological, and cultural dominance and superiority.

President Xi has presented the outlines of some aspects of this vision in several public forums for a China-centric regional order. When speaking to a summit of the Conference on Interaction Confidence-Building Measures in Asia in May 2014, Xi challenged the United States' continued leadership role in Asia, declaring his opposition to stronger military alliances in the region and arguing that "security problems in Asia should eventually be solved by Asians themselves."[45]

This vision necessarily involves a more circumscribed role for the United States in the Indo-Pacific. Chinese leaders, including Xi Jinping, regularly criticize the system of US alliances in Asia as a relic of the Cold War and as evidence of US intentions to encircle and contain China.

This is the appropriate context in which to view China's establishment of new mechanisms and institutions designed to promote China-centric economic integration, such as the Asian Infrastructure Investment Bank, and alternative security institutions like the Shanghai Cooperation Organization. Similarly, with China's Belt and Road Initiative, the clear geopolitical implications are to tie the region's economies more closely with China, ensuring that Beijing will sit at the heart of the region's economic destiny.

Thus, the fifth key attribute of China's great power ambitions: it will pursue its objectives using all elements of national power. Due to the nature of China's system, the CCP is able to employ and coordinate military, economic, informational, social, and political tools in the pursuit of its objectives. We have seen this acted out repeatedly in almost every Chinese foreign policy initiative—be it the South China Sea, expansion into South and Southeast Asia, and even in competition with the United States. China's leaders have the ability to identify national priorities and shift resources from across Chinese society to address them. And most important, China's political system enables Beijing to coordinate all its foreign policy tools into a cohesive, layered approach.

China makes significant use of its economic power as a tool of geopolitical statecraft. Although the idea that economic power can undergird strategic weight is not new, China leverages its economic relationships and potential in new and innovative ways. From development assistance and infrastructure support to free trade agreements and foreign direct investment, Beijing uses its newfound economic power as a geopolitical instrument in ways that challenge the traditional US approach to foreign policy.

Additionally, China employs both covert and overt tools of influence in its foreign policy. In September 2014, Xi Jinping gave a speech on the importance of political influence activities—referred to in CCP parlance as "united front work"[46]—using the Maoist term for it as one of the CCP's "magic weapons" (法宝).[47] China's political influence activities under Xi have accelerated significantly, and pursue four objectives:

1. Strengthen the CCP's efforts to manage and guide overseas Chinese communities and utilize them as agents of Chinese foreign policy;
2. Emphasize people-to-people, party-to-party, plus PRC enterprise-to-foreign enterprise relations, with the aim of co-opting foreigners to support and promote the CCP's foreign policy goals;
3. Promote and implement a global, multiplatform, and strategic communication strategy; and
4. Form a China-centric economic and strategic bloc.[48]

These activities occur all around the world. Although authoritarian regimes present China with a more straightforward avenue

of influence, the openness of democracies also represents opportunities for China's united front activities.[49] In recent years, the
countries belonging to the Association of Southeast Asian Nations
(ASEAN), Australia, Canada, France, Germany, Japan, New Zealand,
Taiwan, Singapore, and the United Kingdom have all been subject
to Chinese interference efforts.[50] Taken as a whole, China's foreign
influence activities seek to undermine the sovereignty and integrity
of the political systems of targeted states.

UNDERSTANDING CHINESE WEAKNESSES

With all this in mind, however, it would be inaccurate and unwise
to assess China's foreign policy ambitions without understanding
and acknowledging the tremendous challenges that Beijing must
address. Indeed, as I described above, China's top policy priorities
are almost entirely domestic. This is the direct result of the remarkable challenges that China must face.

Due to its size, there is no such thing as a small problem in China.
Even if an issue affects only 1 percent of its population, that is still
13.8 million people—greater than the population of Pennsylvania.
And China's problems are enormous in scale and intensity: urban-
ization, environmental degradation, economic inequality, informa-
tization, and the rising expectations of a burgeoning middle class
are just some of the challenges Beijing must confront. And it must
face all this in the face of an economy that is beginning to slow.

China also faces other challenges internationally. Although it
has tremendous influence, it has few allies. Its closest relationships, with countries like Pakistan and Laos, are complex and bring
little benefit to Beijing. China's soft power lags behind that of other,
smaller countries, despite Beijing's long-standing efforts to address
this shortcoming.

Similarly, China's military—the People's Liberation Army—faces
significant challenges. Although the PLA has enjoyed large budgets
for decades and has developed very impressive capabilities in significant quantities, it lacks experience. Moreover, China's military

continues to face challenges related to power projection, power sustainment, logistical support, and joint operations. And though many of the PLA's recent reforms have sought to address these shortcomings, the experiences of the US military suggest that they will take decades to overcome.

A fundamental challenge for China is that any effort to reorder an international system from unipolar to bipolar (or multipolar) will be necessarily seen as revisionist and aggressive. A key objective for China, therefore, is to delegitimize the global authority of the United States through cost-imposing practices and "salami-slicing" strategies (see below) that seek to undermine American credibility in the face of US allies and partners.[51]

Moreover, behind China's rapidly expanding power and ambition lie significant uncertainties about its future. Although the incredibly high rates of economic growth that it has previously enjoyed are clearly unsustainable, it is uncertain whether China's economy will be able to continue to grow at all. Indeed, some predict that China's economic and political system—as currently constructed—is brittle and unlikely to survive several major impending challenges.

The slowing of China's GDP growth rate since 2010 has set off a range of commentary on whether China's rise is ending.[52] In 2016, China's annual GDP growth rate had fallen to 6.7 percent from 10.6 percent in 2010; this weakening growth was attributed to dwindling catch-up and efficiency gains, an aging population, and declining productivity growth.[53] Some scholars have asserted that a lack of policy reform from the top will exacerbate continuing economic stagnation. David Shambaugh has predicted that a return to "hard authoritarianism" under Xi Jinping could stifle the innovation necessary for China to emerge from the middle-income trap, undermining the legitimacy of the CCP and increasing domestic instability and unpredictability.[54] Similarly, Nadège Rolland has argued that if China's leaders cannot drastically adapt to address new economic problems by abandoning their focus on keeping the CCP in power, China will not be able to encourage the economic growth necessary to maintain its strength.[55] Minxin Pei has asserted that China is "likely either to experience a regime transition at the upper-middle-income level," leading to the fall of the CCP, "or, if it fails to undergo a regime transition, to get stuck in the middle-income trap" as economic stagnation and elite disunity increase.[56]

The consequences of this uncertainty for the Indo-Pacific are profound. Although few expect an outright collapse of the Chinese system, an economic downturn is certainly possible. How Beijing may act in such a situation is impossible to predict, and that is exactly the point: China's future trajectory, and how its leaders may seek to use its burgeoning power, are critical but tremendously uncertain factors that will shape the geopolitics of the Indo-Pacific. Every country in the region, including the United States and its allies and partners, must account for this uncertainty and therefore be prepared for a range of potential contingencies.

IMPLICATIONS FOR THE UNITED STATES

These key attributes of a rising China, as well as uncertainties surrounding its weaknesses, should drive Washington to adjust its approach to Beijing. Specifically, there are five key implications from these attributes.

First, although China will formally subscribe to the inherent sovereign equality of all nations, in practice it will act under the firm belief in a de facto hierarchy of nations. Inherent in widespread beliefs that China's rise is merely a return to its rightful place of geopolitical preeminence is the assumption that other countries are inappropriate for regional leadership. When then foreign minister Yang Jiechi reportedly told a group of diplomats from across the Indo-Pacific that "China is a big country and other countries are small countries, and that's just a fact," he had conducted the classic diplomatic gaffe of openly stating an uncomfortable truth that everyone already knew. His statement was reflection of Beijing's hierarchical approach to foreign affairs, which already colors a great deal of its approach to the region.

Based on several conversations I have had with Chinese scholars and officials, both before and after my time in the Pentagon, many in Beijing believe that China deserves a great deal of deference in the region because of its economic strength, military power, and historical role as the center of regional authority. This was the true source of Chinese anxiety about the decision by Washington and Seoul to deploy the terminal high-altitude area defense system (THAAD) to the Korean Peninsula—it was not the interceptors or the radars, it was the fact that the United States and South Korea had acted in direct disregard for Beijing's preferences.[57] To many in China, South Korea should have known to not even consider such a decision out of deference to Chinese geopolitical sensibilities.

Second, China will seek to establish spheres of influence in the Indo-Pacific across multiple domains. Although it continues to benefit from globalization and economic integration, China also seeks to use its economic power and military might to establish itself as the dominant power in the region, out to the second island chain. And though Beijing will likely eschew imperial expansion and aggression, such as Japan pursued in the middle of the twentieth century, it will probably seek to gradually expand its control and sovereignty into the disputed waters along its periphery, using so-called gray zone tactics that raise tension yet do not engender an armed response. At the same time, Beijing will likely expand its political influence across the region, and eventually globally, to establish a new norm in which it is generally recognized as the critical voice on every issue of geopolitical significance in the Indo-Pacific. This will also necessarily mean a markedly constricted role for the United States, and especially its regional alliances, in order to make way for Chinese influence.

This will also essentially mean the eventual resolution to all of China's lingering territorial issues, including in the East China Sea, in the South China Sea, and especially with regard to Taiwan. Indeed, Xi Jinping drew an explicit connection between unification with Taiwan and the broader cause of "the great rejuvenation of the Chinese nation."[58] In other words, Beijing believes it cannot be dominant regionally if it continues to have lingering questions about its own sovereignty and territorial integrity.

Third, China will be a major power competitor unlike anything the United States has ever seen before. It is wealthy, powerful, Leninist, technocratic, authoritarian, ambitious, and increasingly willing to tolerate risk and external turbulence in the pursuit of its goals. Although the relative priorities Beijing pursues may evolve as Xi Jinping transitions China from collective leadership to one-man rule, the fundamental nature of China's power is likely to linger.

Fourth, the distinction between domestic and foreign policy will grow increasingly blurred. One of the driving features of Chinese foreign policy will be to ensure that the CCP has the ability to pursue its interests and assert its priorities without hindrance—and this applies both domestically and internationally. Consider Chinese efforts to influence domestic politics in Australia and New Zealand through traditional and nontraditional means. This has been largely coordinated by the United Front Work Department of the CCP, whose mission is to manage relations with nonparty elites, both inside and outside China, to ensure that these groups are supportive of and useful to party rule. This is remarkable behavior for a country that, for decades, has championed noninterference in internal affairs as one of the five principles of peaceful coexistence.

It should be noted that China is not conducting these activities in a way similar to other great powers. It is not seeking to overthrow existing governments and install a Chinese-style regime, or even seeking to inject instability and chaos. It merely seeks to ensure that foreign governments are sympathetic to the priorities and interests of the CCP—priorities and interests that know no traditional international boundaries.

And fifth, China will implicitly undermine some international institutions, laws, and norms that it finds to be counter to its interests, even as it relies on and promotes others. All policies must serve Beijing's interests, and it will support or ignore these laws and norms on that basis. Liberal internationalism, upon which much Western foreign policy has been based, will come under increasing challenge as raw calculations of power overtake legalistic interpretations and normative constraints. In this, the United States may be unique as a great power that largely—if imperfectly—has restrained itself in order to support a broader system of laws and norms that it has found to be in its interests.

This approach to foreign affairs by China represents a profound challenge to the liberal order generally, and to several critical American interests in particular. From an international community guided by laws and norms about freedom of navigation and the peaceful resolution of disputes, to a broader responsibility to defeat threats to global stability like terrorism and proliferation, China's approach will have profound implications for a system that has promoted stability and prosperity for generations.

More specifically for the United States, China's ambitions to be the dominant power in the Indo-Pacific have obvious implications. In recent years, the region has grown increasingly important to the American economy and American geopolitical interests. Add to this that the United States is historically a Pacific power with deep roots and responsibilities across the region. If Washington's role in the Indo-Pacific is successfully circumscribed by Beijing, the negative effects on key US interests and principles will be significant.

The Trump administration has clearly indicated its intent to compete with this rising China, and to win this competition. The National Security Strategy states that "China and Russia challenge American power, influence, and interests, attempting to erode American security and prosperity. They are determined to make economies less free and less fair, to grow their militaries, and to control information and data to repress their societies and expand their influence."[59] The National Defense Strategy is even more explicit, stating that "the central challenge to US prosperity and security is the reemergence of long-term, strategic competition by what the National Security Strategy classifies as revisionist powers."[60]

The Trump administration's acknowledgment of the ongoing strategic competition between China and the United States is a welcome indication that Washington is taking this challenge seriously.

Indeed, these views have spread across Washington's China-watching community. Yet there is a significant difference between identifying the challenge and actually addressing it—the Trump administration has yet to describe, or even enact, a strategic framework for competition along the lines one would expect from such a broad and dramatic declaration of competition as a top national priority. The strategy documents that the Trump administration has produced, such as the Department of Defense's *Indo-Pacific Strategy Report*, are generally well considered and well argued, yet they lack a crucial element: support from the president.[61] Throughout his first three years as president, Donald Trump has routinely criticized US allies and partners, has questioned their value, and has been pursuing strategies that undermine the ability of the United States to successfully compete with China. These actions, it should be noted, are in direct contradiction to several strategies published by the US government during his administration.

In fact, there still remains a great amount of uncertainty about the contours and aims of US–China competition: What are we competing over? Why? What would constitute success? Even across the Trump administration, there has been significant disagreement over how to answer these questions.

IMPLICATIONS FOR REGIONAL ORDER

As discussed in the previous chapter, significant changes to the balance of power in the Indo-Pacific have historically coincided with concomitant changes to the regional order. Historically, rising powers generally prefer to free-ride globally while pursuing revision regionally. This is because their power, interests, and focus begin as fundamentally regional, while those of an established power are perceived globally. Thus, rising states need not grow their power to be equal to that of established powers on a global scale. Instead, they need only build enough power to challenge an established power and its order on a regional scale.[62]

Tang Shiping of Fudan University in Shanghai has identified three Chinese schools of thought regarding the existing liberal order. The first school of thought is based on the idea that the existing order was established as fundamentally hostile toward non-Western states, and that China should lead the way in fundamentally restructuring it. The second school of thought argues that the existing order is acceptable but needs reform under China's lead. And the third school of thought has the same perception as the second, but prefers a coalition with other countries to modify the order.[63] Tang argues that current Chinese leaders are torn between the third and the second schools, and they see a need to lean toward the second one as a result of the Trump administration's more confrontational approach. Tang predicts that "China will likely invest heavily in two key issue areas: (1) regionalism in East Asia and Central Asia; and (2) interregional cooperation and coordination. Perhaps unsurprisingly, China's ambitious One Belt and One Road initiative seeks to integrate these two issue areas."[64] For "East Asia," Tang highlights the strategic significance of the proposed Regional Comprehensive Economic Partnership—free trade agreements among the ASEAN+6—for China to form a non-US-centric, regional economic grouping.[65]

A rising China with ambitions to dominate Asia and reconfigure the regional order to better accord with the interests of the CCP threatens to undermine the liberal character of the Indo-Pacific order and the stability and prosperity it has achieved. This is a challenge that crosses multiple domains and geographic locations, yet the theme is consistent: Beijing seeks to rewrite the existing order, and will challenge any country it perceives to be unsupportive of its ambitions. This can be seen in its coercive tactics that seek to assert expansionist territorial and maritime claims with no basis in international law, and by its efforts to weaken the bonds between the United States and its allies, which have underpinned this order in terms of both power and legitimacy.

In the East China Sea, a dispute between China and Japan over the Senkaku/Diaoyu Islands continues to fester, even though Japan has administered the islands since 1895 as a result of its victory in the First Sino-Japanese War. Although tensions between China and Japan over the islands have ebbed and flowed, particularly since the early 2000s, recent years have seen the dispute grow ever more strident. In 2010, a Chinese fishing vessel rammed two Japanese Coast Guard ships. Japan held the captain for seventeen days, prompting demonstrations in both countries. In 2012, as a result of burgeoning nationalism across sectors of Japan's politics, the mayor of Tokyo announced a plan to purchase three of the islands. To prevent this, the Japanese government purchased them instead. Large protests erupted in major cities across China,[66] and Chinese incursions into the islands' territorial waters spiked dramatically,[67] raising the odds of a collision or other military incident in the vicinity. Chinese vessels routinely operate within close proximity of these vessels, and suggest ambitions from Beijing to eventually bring the islands under its administration.

Similarly, the South China Sea has been a locus for regional tensions wrought by Chinese ambitions. Although China, Taiwan, Vietnam, the Philippines, Malaysia, and Brunei all claim features in the Spratly and/or Paracel Islands, the most geopolitically significant claim is that of China, which has drawn a large "nine-dash line" across most of the sea itself, cutting across the claims of every other nation involved. And though Beijing has not clarified the specific nature of its claims (e.g., whether it claims all the waters or just the land features within the line), the US State Department has argued that China's position is incompatible with established international law.[68]

Nevertheless, in December 2013, China began reclaiming land to build up the features under its control. By June 2015, the PRC had constructed over 2,900 acres of artificial islands in the Spratlys—seventeen times more land in twenty months than the other claimants combined over the past forty years, accounting for about 95 percent of all reclaimed land in the Spratly Islands.[69] The Philippines filed a 2013 case against China with an arbitral tribunal constituted under Annex VII of the UN Convention on the Law of the Sea (UNCLOS). In the tribunal's 2016 decision, it ruled that China's claimed features in the Spratlys were incapable of generating exclusive economic zones (EEZs) and that its nine-dash line had no basis in international law. The tribunal also declared illegal Chinese fishing and other activities in the Philippines' EEZ and around other land features, along with Chinese military installations on seven Spratly formations. Philippines president Rodrigo Duterte has softened his country's position on China since taking office in 2016, just before the tribunal's decision, though there have been instances since when Duterte has taken a less conciliatory approach to Beijing. Meanwhile, ASEAN has likewise omitted references to Chinese land reclamation in its official statements.[70]

Instances of Chinese exceptionalism can be seen in several other arenas as well. An insightful study from the Center for a New American Security, for instance, detailed China's exceptionalist approach to several UN organs and functions, in which Beijing sought to advance its interests by

- promoting an exceptionalist view of human rights, in which governments can cite "unique" local conditions to justify disregard for individual or minority claims;
- redefining democracy in terms of so-called economic and social rights, rather than inalienable civil or political rights;
- making state sovereignty inviolable and reestablishing states as the only legitimate stakeholders, with the purported aim of "democratizing" international relations and setting developing countries on equal footing in the global governance system;
- infusing consensus global goals with Chinese ideological terms and foreign policy strategies, such as the Belt and Road Initiative; and
- resolving political issues through bilateral negotiations, where China can use its full panoply of leverage to get its way, rather than through rules-based approaches. [71]

The implications of China's exceptionalist efforts are profound. China's use of maritime forces and economic sanctions to pressure those in a maritime dispute with Beijing also represents a challenge to long-standing international norms against the use of force or the threat of force to change territorial borders or to resolve disputes. Further, the existing liberal order, and the prosperity that it has brought to billions around the world (including in China), requires unfettered peaceful access to the maritime commons. The free movement of trade and access to sea-based resources rely on the security of the maritime commons, which in turn depends on the unconstrained flow of military forces through international waters. EEZs are especially critical to this system; 42 percent of all oceans lie within an EEZ, including all key international waterways (see figure 2.3). Any restriction on the free flow of vessels through EEZs—either military or civilian—would have disastrous implications

FIGURE 2.3 Maximum EEZ claims by country

SOURCE: MARITIME AWARENESS PROJECT, NATIONAL BUREAU OF ASIAN RESEARCH, HTTP://MARITIMEAWARENESSPROJECT.ORG/INTERACTIVEMAP/.

for global stability and prosperity. The picture becomes especially murky in the South China Sea, where restrictions on freedom of navigation in EEZs could potentially be used to shut down the sea as an international waterway.

Of course, the implications of China's rise go far beyond questions of maritime security and international laws and institutions. Indeed, China has broadened the scope of its efforts to impose its political preferences on a wide variety of issues. For example, Beijing has pressured foreign airlines and hotels to adjust how they refer to Taiwan on their websites.[72] The United Front Department of the CCP has sought to influence the societies and politics of several US allies to bend their views on controversial issues to align more with Beijing.[73] China has also employed economic coercion to press its geopolitical preferences, as in the case with Japan when Beijing cut off exports of essential raw earth materials as a tactic to pressure Tokyo to relent over a dispute in the East China Sea,[74] or when it halted fruit imports from the Philippines over a dispute in the South China Sea.[75]

Finally, Beijing has sought to drive wedges in US alliances and partnerships across the Indo-Pacific. For example, after Washington and Seoul agreed to deploy the THAAD missile defense system in response to the North Korean ballistic missile threat, Beijing imposed major—if unofficial—sanctions on South Korea that cost that country $4.7 billion in lost tourism alone.[76] As Australian foreign minister Julie Bishop described the situation that many other in the Indo-Pacific share, never before has Australia's chief ally and top economic partner existed in a highly competitive relationship.[77]

Still, China has an opportunity to work with the existing order—from which it has derived such incredible benefits—and to contribute to it. This would not require China to be weakened or its influence to be circumscribed; indeed, China's power would likely increase dramatically if it chose to work within the existing order rather than in opposition to it. China has in the past acceded to certain aspects of the liberal order, such as international arms control arrangements.[78]

Developments like these raise concerns over China's respect for international laws and norms and its willingness to employ its growing power to change these norms in ways that further enhance its power and influence. Although China has benefited greatly from the stability, free trade, and international rules that the existing liberal order have provided, as has already been discussed, China seeks to adjust the established order to better accommodate its interests and those of the CCP.

In the minds of many in Beijing, its dependence on the existing liberal order makes it dependent on the United States—an unacceptable arrangement, considering what Beijing sees as Washington's determination to prevent China from assuming its "proper" place in the regional and global order.[79] When discussing the liberal order itself, Chinese scholars and officials often object to its highly unipolar quality and call for it to become "more democratic" by giving added weight to emerging powers.[80]

China's objections to the global order often seem to be primarily focused on objections to American preeminence itself. For Chinese scholars, the key features of the liberal order they find most problematic are the continued existence of US alliances and global military presence; American ideological hostility to China's political system; and an assessed belief that the United States is determined to undermine China's rise to global geopolitical power.

Although still not detailed, statements by Chinese leaders suggest the outlines of a Chinese vision for revising the global order. In his work report to the Nineteenth Party Congress in October 2017, President Xi Jinping said that the world is entering a "new era that sees China moving closer to center stage and making greater contributions to mankind." He noted that "the path, the theory, the system, and the culture of socialism with Chinese characteristics have kept developing, blazing a new trail for other developing countries to achieve modernization. It offers a new option for other countries and nations who want to speed up their development while preserving their independence; and it offers Chinese wisdom and a Chinese approach to solving the problems facing mankind."[81] At the heart of this vision is a revitalized China that is stable and prosperous at home, is the dominant power in the Indo-Pacific, and is able to shape events around the world through an informal hierarchical system with China at the center. Chinese leaders do not appear to see this vision as a coercive arrangement; rather, they paint this system as founded upon tight economic integration and dependence on China, as well as the region's eventual recognition of China as the natural, and rightful, dominant regional power.

Taken as a whole, Beijing seems to envision an international system in which China's geopolitical power is widely represented and respected. Beyond that, Beijing seeks a region where American power and freedom of action in the Indo-Pacific are circumscribed, American alliances are weakened or dismantled, and China sits at the heart of the regional economic, security, and political order. International institutions and laws would only be applied or utilized when they are seen to be supportive of Chinese national interests; otherwise, they would be disregarded or only given lip service. China has also sought to promote institutions, such as the Asian Infrastructure Investment Bank and the Shanghai Cooperation Organization, that may serve as alternatives to more established international institutions, while also promoting initiatives that support China's national interests.

China's actions in recent years have also demonstrated a preference for avoiding conflict and tension, but a willingness to accept strategic turbulence and risk in the pursuit of its interests. This has been most apparent in the South China Sea, where China has gradually emplaced several military installations that will support power projection and sustainment far from the shores of mainland China. China has preferred to operate below the threshold of conflict and actively avoids direct confrontation, yet has steadfastly refused to acknowledge the concerns and claims of other countries and the findings of an international tribunal.[82] Moreover, China reportedly threatened war with Vietnam if Hanoi were to continue oil exploration in disputed waters.[83] The lesson is clear: Beijing would prefer that other countries simply defer to its preferences, but is willing to ignore international laws and norms, and threaten the use of force, if confronted with direct opposition. Yet paradoxically, China's use of so-called gray zone tactics reflects an acknowledgment of some norms against the use of force, or a recognition that its military and society may not yet be prepared for the shocks and costs of conflict. I expect it is a mix of both, but also a reflection that Beijing perceives it may be able to achieve its objectives without conflict if it remains patient, careful, and persistent.

Such an approach represents a fundamental challenge to America's continued power and influence in the Indo-Pacific, and to the long-term health and success of the region's existing liberal order. Rules and norms against the use of force for access to resources and territorial aggrandizement would be weakened, as would the fundamental basis for a fair and predictable rules-based liberal order. Washington's access would be highly proscribed, and the region's stability, economic rules of the road, and political dynamics would all be subject to Beijing's interests. This is clearly not a future that the United States, nor many of the rest of the countries in the Indo-Pacific, would welcome.

China's rising power and expanding ambitions are challenging the laws and norms that sit at the foundation of the regional order. Freedom of navigation in international waters is being questioned by arguments from Beijing (among others) that an exclusive economic zone should convey the same rights and restrictions as territorial waters. China has also begun to undermine international norms against the use or threatened use of force to pursue aggressive territorial ambitions. Through a strategy commonly referred to as "salami-slicing," China has used small-scale initiatives in the East China Sea and South China Sea that, individually, are provocative but do not rise to the level of a major confrontation or crisis. Yet considered collectively, these actions have begun to dramatically reshape the dynamics of the East China Sea and South China Sea, making them more contested and more prone to major power crises than any time since the end of World War II. In some cases, Chinese actions have literally reshaped the physical map of these locations, and have advanced China's territorial claims at the expense of Japan, the Philippines, and Vietnam.

China's interest in expanding its regional power and influence is best encapsulated in the Belt and Road Initiative (BRI), which is Xi Jinping's driving foreign policy concept and the capstone of his vision for China's role in the world. Described as a twenty-first-century Silk Road,[84] BRI aims to shape and influence foreign policy through a wide comprehensive network of infrastructure projects crisscrossing Eurasia, Europe, and Africa. Such a show of force and influence tempts other states with investment and infrastructure development. Of course, as with many aspects of China's rise, there is also a significant amount of marketing involved in BRI. A great deal of the initiative is likely instances of Chinese entrepreneurs pursuing business opportunities. Overall, it would be as much of a mistake to see BRI as a grandiose challenge to the existing Bretton Woods economic architecture as it would be to dismiss it as simply propaganda concocted by Beijing to make normal economic behavior appear to be a master foreign policy plan.

The realities, in all likelihood, are that BRI is a mix of both strategy and circumstance. Yet its impact, and scale, should not be ignored. Nor should US strategists ignore the BRI brand and the message it conveys to the world—China is engaged, active, and looking to do business. With the United States struggling to make a case for its role in the world, and with many in the United States being deeply skeptical of free trade as a concept, the United States is falling behind China in the minds of middle powers across Asia as the region's driving economic force. As one Indo-Pacific official told me in mid-2019, "China offers to the region what it offers to its people: political acquiescence in exchange for economic development. It is a tricky decision for most, but it is far more attractive than what many believe the United States offers: political acquiescence in exchange for no economic development."

Chinese assertiveness and exceptionalism cannot be successfully countered by appeals to international laws and norms or shifts in military posture alone. Although such actions may have been successful in the past, they apparently have not risen to the level of threatening what Beijing's current leadership holds dear. Although Beijing's current calculations require further analysis that is far beyond the scope of this study, it is clear that military engagement and balancing will be an element of any US strategy.

The challenge for the United States in this case is that the use of military power as a tool of political influence is fairly inflexible, at times counterproductive, and could significantly diminish the attractive power of the United States in regions that are deeply skeptical of foreign military power. Although the American military is an incredible fighting force and works brilliantly with American allies and partners, it is not America's most effective or efficient diplomatic tool. To be sure, global military dominance is tremendously beneficial to American interests and global stability. Yet it is of limited utility in a regional context if aspects of this power are inflexible or if the issues involve nonmilitary aspects of national power. Surely, in a time of major crisis or conflict, the United States could feasibly send several aircraft carrier battle groups to the region and thus overwhelm China's ability to project power. Yet military power alone cannot address the region's economic or development challenges, and it cannot sustain a liberal order.

The United States therefore cannot rest on its laurels in the Indo-Pacific. Regional exceptionalism and assertiveness from China, made real by efforts to annex territory and exert political will through the use or threatened use of force, can only be thwarted by countries that can utilize all elements of national power—including international laws and norms, information and public diplomacy, economic sanctions, and military initiatives—as a cohesive whole in a way that undermines interests that Beijing holds dear.

UNCERTAINTIES ABOUT US POWER AND COMMITMENT TO THE INDO-PACIFIC

As China's power has risen and the threat from North Korea has intensified, US allies and partners have increasingly looked to the United States to balance the negative implications of these trends. Concurrently, the region has also begun to question the long-term sustainability and viability of American commitments to the Indo-Pacific.

It is natural for allies and partners to routinely express anxiety about the will and capability of the United States to come to their defense in a time of crisis and conflict (abandonment), while at the same time remaining fearful that they may be dragged into a war against their national interests (entrapment).[85] Such concerns are a predictable and normal result of an unequal alliance relationship, in which the smaller power is dependent on the larger power for its security and national survival. Any country, no matter how confident, would seek regular reassurances from its security guarantor—and this is especially true when security threats are manifest and growing.

Nonetheless, recent years have witnessed a marked increase in the pace and force of such concerns from US allies and partners. This growth in the allied crisis of confidence can be traced to two developments that, for the first time since the end of World War II, have raised the specter of a world where relative American power is substantially diminished. The first trend was America's seemingly unending wars and crises in Afghanistan and across the Middle East in the wake of the September 11, 2001, terrorist attacks. Many US allies, especially those in Asia, worried that these conflicts would drain American attention and resources while also shaping an American military force structure tailored to fighting insurgents rather than the massive, high-end threats extant in the Indo-Pacific.[86]

These fears were not entirely unjustified. In 2017, the Pentagon estimated that US military operations in Iraq, Afghanistan,

Syria, and Pakistan since 2001 have cost $1.5 trillion. An independent study included costs not addressed by the Pentagon—including recurring expenses such as long-term medical care for veterans, war costs incurred by the State Department, and related spending by the Department of Homeland Security, the Department of Veterans Affairs, and others.[87] Over 2.7 million US service members have been to the war zones of Iraq and Afghanistan since 2001, and over half of them have deployed more than once. US allies and partners in Asia are keenly aware of these commitments, and fear that the US focus and investment in these areas is coming at the expense of US attention and resources to the Indo-Pacific. Moreover, several Asian allies and partners have contributed resources, military personnel, and civilians to US efforts in these areas to demonstrate the value of the relationship—decisions that have at times generated a significant domestic backlash.

The second trend driving regional concerns about American staying power has been America's declining share of global economic power, which was announced by the global financial crisis of 2008–9. The American economy had been severely damaged to a degree not seen since the Great Depression, while the Chinese economy was able to insulate itself from the crisis and sustain record levels of growth.[88] Couple this with the subsequent government shutdowns that took place and sequestration's cut of $500 billion over ten years to the US defense budget, and many US allies and partners learned that American geopolitical power was mortal and vulnerable to existential crisis.

When considering these fears, however, it is important to recall that the United States continues to possess significant strengths and advantages. Although China has become the top trading partner with most of the region's major economies, the United States is still by far the largest source of foreign direct investment. Moreover, the United States retains a significant military presence in the region, which includes its most advanced capabilities, such as aircraft carriers, F-35 and F-22 aircraft, and advanced destroyers, cruisers, and submarines.

American power in Asia is founded upon its economic strength and resilience, and (barring some major, unexpected shock) this foundation will remain strong for the foreseeable future. Between 1991 and 2016, nominal US GDP tripled, from $6.2 trillion to $18.6 trillion, while global GDP rose only slightly faster, from $24 trillion to $75.8 trillion.[89] The American economy has also proven remarkably resilient. After suffering its worst economic crisis since the Great Depression, the United States regained much of its strength and vitality in five years. Few in China would likely expect such remarkable social or economic resilience from their system (figure 2.4).

This tremendous prosperity and remarkable resilience have enabled robust and sustained investments in American military power—to the tune of $11.8 trillion over the same period—making the US armed forces by far the world's largest, most advanced, and most capable.[90] The US military remains the only force in the world that can project and sustain significant military power across the

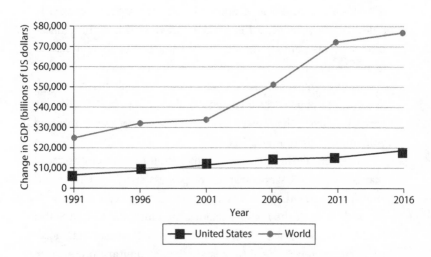

FIGURE 2.4 Change in the United States' and the world's gross domestic product, 1991–2016 (in billions of US dollars)

SOURCE: WORLD BANK, WORLD DEVELOPMENT INDICATORS.

globe indefinitely. Even China's much-discussed aircraft carriers are far behind their American counterparts in terms of capability, effectiveness, and sustainability.[91] Although China has made great strides in recent decades, it still has a long way to go.

Barring a major shock or strategic incompetence, American power is clearly resilient and sustainable over the long term.[92] Yet potential national power is insufficient if it is not successfully and efficiently harnessed to achieve national objectives. For a nation of global responsibilities that has been embroiled in conflict for eighteen years (and counting), the critical question for American policymakers is how to prioritize American objectives and interests, and how to properly allocate resources to align with these priorities.

Recognizing these dynamics, strategists in the Obama administration sought to reassure US allies, partners, and potential adversaries alike that the United States remained committed to the region and was fully capable of acting if necessary, despite the complexities of American politics and continuing needs for American power elsewhere in the world. The result was "the pivot," later rechristened "strategic rebalancing"—a whole-of-government effort announced by President Obama to ensure that American influence and presence in the region would be sustained despite changing strategic dynamics in the region and political difficulties at home.[93] In his account of the formulation of "the pivot," former assistant secretary of state Kurt Campbell describes it as a course correction after years of Asia's relegation to secondary theater status.[94] During the first term of the Obama administration, the pivot took on a "two-pronged approach" to bolster America's hub-and-spokes system in Asia by strengthening bilateral alliances and directly linking alliance partners.[95] This also included a leadership role in the Trans-Pacific Partnership (TPP), which was intended to buttress US economic links to the region and define regional economic relations along preferred American lines.[96]

The Obama administration's "rebalance" toward the Indo-Pacific was successful, in that it greatly strengthened US engagement with the region and maintained high-level attention toward the region throughout President Obama's two terms, despite intensifying crises elsewhere in the world and domestic political and economic challenges at home.[97] It was also a success in the sense of making policy progress, in that America's diplomatic position in the region was greatly strengthened, its military posture and access were significantly enhanced, and its economic engagement with the region deepened.

Still, by the end of the Obama administration, the rebalance remained unfinished. The balance of military aid, for example, is still heavily weighted toward other regions of the world. For cultural and historic reasons, crises in the Middle East and Europe continue to garner more attention from senior American leaders. Most egregiously, the Obama administration's failure to secure American entry into the TPP, and the Trump administration's decision to withdraw from the TPP soon after assuming power, constituted major setbacks to what was perhaps the most geopolitically consequential aspect of the rebalance.

To date, the Trump administration has largely failed to reassure US allies and partners. In fact, President Trump's statements and policies have created a third source of concern in the region about the future of American power in the Indo-Pacific: that the United States may no longer see itself as a regional leader and may no longer be a reliable stalwart of liberal internationalism. Upon taking office, the Trump administration's first policy shot in the heart of American credibility in the Indo-Pacific was the decision to withdraw from the TPP, which several US allies and partners had already sold to their respective publics and policy establishments as necessary to reform their domestic economies and solidify US engagement in the region.

Due to the critical role of economics in driving the region's geopolitics, many—both across the Indo-Pacific and within the Obama administration—saw the TPP as a necessary pillar in enhancing US engagement in the region. Moreover, many saw the TPP as a critical vehicle for the United States to lead the way on establishing updated laws and norms for global trade. As President Obama wrote in 2016, "The Asia-Pacific region will continue its economic integration, with or without the United States. We can lead that process, or we can sit on the sidelines and watch prosperity pass us by."[98] Yet President Trump views international trade very differently, describing the TPP as a "bad deal" that "will squeeze our manufacturing sector," "lead to even greater unemployment," "increase our trade deficits & send even more jobs overseas."[99]

Further inflaming regional uncertainties about the reliability of American power across the Indo-Pacific were several public statements by the president himself. During his campaign, Trump stated that the United States could no longer remain the "policeman of the world" and further emphasized the "unfair" and one-sided international security relationships throughout the world, creating deep unease among US allies and partners globally.[100] At the beginning of his presidency, Trump insisted that South Korea should pay for the missile defense system, stating, "I informed South Korea it would be appropriate if they pay. . . . That's [THAAD] a billion dollar system. . . . We're going to protect them. But they should pay for that, and they understand that."[101]

Just a few months into the Trump administration, the effects of such statements could already be felt across the region. According to the Pew Research Center, global "confidence in the US president" dropped from 64 to 22 percent at the beginning of Trump's time in office, while the percentage reporting favorable views of the United States fell from 64 to 49.[102] Among the respondents in the Indo-Pacific region—from South Korea, Japan, Australia, Indonesia, Vietnam, the Philippines, and India—a median of 57 percent reported no confidence in President Trump "to do the right thing regarding world affairs." In a survey of Southeast Asian scholars, government officials, business leaders, and others by the ASEAN Studies Centre at the ISEAS–Yusof Ishak Institute, 71.7 percent of respondents expressed a perception that the global image of the United States had deteriorated over the first four months of 2017.[103] Among that group, 25.4 percent indicated that the United States' global image had "deteriorated immensely."

Five hundred days into the Trump administration, the president had evinced a clear pattern of sparring with allies and questioning their utility, while at the same time advocating for closer relationships with nondemocratic countries with interests inimical to those of the United States, such as Russia, China, and even North Korea. Indeed, by May 2018, the Trump administration had imposed more tariffs on US allies than on China.[104] Moreover, Trump's campaign-era skepticism about the utility of alliances continued into his time as president. He has reportedly expressed deep skepticism about the strategic necessity of US troops in South Korea, and he thinks the United States gets nothing back from maintaining a robust military presence on the Korean Peninsula.[105]

Fundamentally, President Trump has called into question the implicit pact that the United States had offered to its allies and partners in Asia: security in return for market access and geopolitical alignment. By hinting that security could be contingent on economic gains, he casts alliances and partnerships as mere protection rackets.[106]

Yet US allies and partners have yet to find an answer to a critical question: Do President Trump's nontraditional views represent a fundamental change in how the American people view the role of the United States in the world? Is Trump the effect or the cause of populist nationalism in America? Once his administration is over—either in 2021 or 2025—will the United States return to its traditional foreign policies, or is Trump an indication of what may come? Although these questions may be impossible to answer until President Trump's administration has actually come to an end, there are some data to suggest that this may be more of an aberration than a harbinger.

A 2017 survey by the Chicago Council on World Affairs found that "the American public continues to support many aspects of the traditional US alliance system in Europe and Asia, including US commitments to their defense." It further found that President Trump's views on alliances were not broadly shared by the American public, and were only held by the president's core political supporters. In fact, the survey found Americans to be more convinced in 2017 than they were in previous surveys about the efficacy of US alliances. Specifically, the survey found that public support in the United States between 2015 and 2017 rose from 58 to 64 percent for Japan, 36 to 42 percent for South Korea, and 34 to 36 percent for India. Six in 10 Americans (62 percent) supported defending South Korea from a North Korean invasion, up from 47 percent in 2015. Moreover, support for defending Japan in a confrontation with China over disputed islands rose from 40 to 33 percent over the same time period, although 58 percent of Americans still opposed US military involvement in that dispute.[107] Overall, polling suggests that the American people continue to support an active and engaged United States that is committed to its allies, although support for military involvement in regional disputes remains limited.

The consequences of these perceptions are manifold. As US allies and partners continue to doubt US commitment and power in the region, they will be forced to develop strategies to cope with these uncertainties. At the same time, power differentials between states will vary, depending on the dimension of power in question. Moreover, the interconnectedness of states—which also varies with respect to trade, military ties, immigration, and other dimensions—combined with great power competition and tension in the region, will make the Indo-Pacific a complex strategic environment for years to come.

UNDERSTANDING THE EMERGING INDO-PACIFIC HETERARCHY

The balance of power in the Indo-Pacific will be increasingly measured via a continually evolving assessment of hierarchies of relative levels of existing and potential national power. These multiple, interrelated hierarchies will inform great power competition in the Indo-Pacific and likewise drive the development of strategies by the region's middle powers to hedge against tremendous strategic uncertainty. States will perceive a series of power hierarchies among various measures of national power, be it overall economic strength, the resilience of domestic politics and economics, per capita income and innovation, defense budgets, qualitative assessments of military capabilities, geography, and/or soft power. These overlapping hierarchies—which can be collectively referred to as a heterarchy (*heterarchy* can be defined as a system of organization where the elements of the organization possess the potential to be ranked in a number of different ways)—will drive competition, hedging, cooperating, and balancing between states along multiple axes and based on calculations of relative national power across multiple hierarchies.[108]

Between 1991 and 2016, the US economy tripled in size, from $6.2 trillion to $18.6 trillion, and the collective size of regional allied and partner economies grew substantially as well, from $5 trillion to $12.68 trillion.[109] Overall, the United States and its allies and partners in the Indo-Pacific saw their combined GDP increase 88 percent between 1991 and 2016, collectively representing $31.3 trillion in 2016. Most remarkably, China's economy grew during this period from $383.4 billion in 1991 to $11.2 trillion in 2016.[110] The proportion of global GDP that these economies (the United States, its allies and partners, and China) occupy also rose during this time, collectively increasing from 48.5 percent to 56 percent of global GDP.[111]

China has invested some of its newfound prosperity in its military with decades of double-digit budget increases, rising over eightfold between 2001 and 2017, from $27.8 billion to $228.2 billion.[112] Other Asian powers have also seen significant expansion in their economic and military power, as the next chapter discusses in greater detail (figures 2.5 and 2.6).

Short a major disruption, the Indo-Pacific's future balance of power is trending toward a far more complex dynamic than what has been seen previously. The Lowy Institute's Asia Power Index—a terrific source for details about the current and future Asian heterarchies[113]—rates the United States as the dominant overall

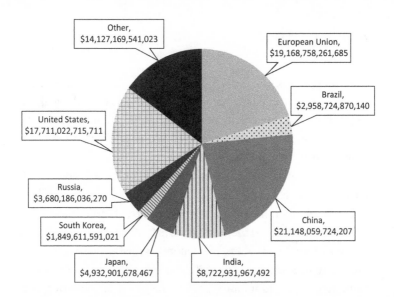

FIGURE 2.5 The global economy, by gross domestic product

Note: "Other" includes Australia, Canada, Indonesia, Iran, Mexico, Turkey, and the United Kingdom.

SOURCE: WORLD BANK, WORLD DEVELOPMENT INDICATORS DATABASE,

FEBRUARY 2017.

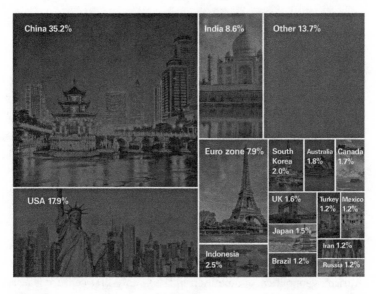

FIGURE 2.6 Percentage of estimated global growth (2017–19) in real gross domestic product

SOURCE: JEFF DESJARDINS, "CHART: WHERE IS GLOBAL GROWTH HAPPENING?,"

VISUAL CAPITALIST, JUNE 2, 2017, HTTP://WWW.VISUALCAPITALIST.COM

/CHART-GLOBAL-GROWTH-HAPPENING/. USED BY PERMISSION.

regional power today, though the index rates China as the country with the most diplomatic and economic influence. Looking ahead, the United States will likely remain the region's dominant military power, while China is expected to overtake the United States in economic size by about 2030.[114]

Yet the United States, Japan, and South Korea will continue to be primary sources of technological innovation and high standards of living, while China will face significant structural economic and political difficulties in the coming years that will challenge its ability to sustain robust rates of economic growth. Other countries, especially in Southeast Asia, will likely also become loci of significant economic and military power. The result of these dynamics will be a complex muddle of middle powers, with the United States and China far more powerful than the rest, while others (e.g., North Korea) will remain far behind their neighbors in most respects.

EARLY INDICATIONS OF LIFE IN THE ASIA HETERARCHY: OVERLAPPING SPHERES OF INFLUENCE

Geopolitical competition between the major powers will likely be the defining characteristic of power dynamics in Asia in the coming years, which will pose a significant challenge to the United States and its ability to sustain and strengthen a liberal order in the region. This competition is reminiscent of the great power competition that defined Europe in the nineteenth century, yet it involves far more complex calculations of national power.

Although great power competition in previous centuries focused on the relative military might of major powers, and understood national economies primarily as engines to support military adventurism, geopolitical competition in the twenty-first century is a far more complex dynamic. The spread of nuclear weapons and the interlinkage of national economies have greatly raised the potential costs of outright conflict between major powers. Concurrently, the spread of decentralized information dissemination technologies, persistent tension over territorial disputes, concerns about changes to the regional balance of power, and the rising expectations of increasingly wealthy and educated populations are intensifying interstate tension and driving the region closer to crisis and conflict.[115]

As a result of these complex dynamics, military power is no longer the only relevant measurement of national power. Strategists across Asia today must consider the relative economic, military, and soft power of several nations—both near and far—and determine which measures of national power are most consequential for their nation's interests and ambitions.

Great power competition between China and the United States is playing out in the maritime and territorial disputes between Beijing and Washington's allies and partners, primarily over arcane claims to small rocks and islets that are, in and of themselves, of minimal importance to the United States. Claims are being asserted and fought over using coast guard and fishing vessels, with naval ships often stationed nearby but keeping their distance so as to avoid provoking a direct armed conflict.

Great power competition is also playing out in the economic and political realms. China is the largest trading partner for most of the Indo-Pacific's major economies—according to China's Ministry of Commerce, China is the largest trading partner for sixteen Asian countries, with trade between China and twenty-five other Asian countries reaching $1.17 trillion in the first eleven months of 2017, representing a third of all regional trade.[116] For its part, the United States remains a significant trading partner for much of the region and is the dominant source of foreign direct investment.

Yet this competition has mostly come in the form of competing visions for international trade. Beijing has promoted a series of mechanisms designed to solidify its position at the center of the region's economic destiny while also marginalizing the role of the United States. Although a great deal of attention has been played to Beijing's Belt and Road Initiative, China has also promoted the Regional Comprehensive Economic Partnership (RCEP), which would include the ten member states of ASEAN and the six Indo-Pacific states with which ASEAN has existing free trade agreements (Australia, China, India, Japan, South Korea, and New Zealand). The RCEP was in competition for the region's future economic structure with the TPP—a mechanism that would include the United States but did not include China and India. Yet the Trump administration's decision to withdraw the United States from the TPP changed this dynamic, and negotiations surrounding the RCEP have since accelerated.[117] If the United States continues to fail to join regional trade mechanisms, it will exacerbate an economic power vacuum that will represent a strategic opportunity to expand its influence across the region.[118]

Such complexities pose significant challenges for US allies and partners, which themselves harbor serious concerns about China's intentions as well as American staying power. In fact, real and perceived indications of American retrenchment and China's rise have resulted in significant shifts in the strategic calculations of other nations. The result has been a complex hedging strategy whereby allies work with all sides, and one another, to maximize benefits and minimize risk in an increasingly complicated and uncertain world. For the United States, this means that its approach toward Asia must include all elements of national power—military, economic, and political—if it seeks to compete in the increasingly complex Asian heterarchy.

As this dynamic progresses, the region's heterarchy is likely to develop into a series of overlapping spheres of geographic and functional influence.[119] Although some countries across Asia may fall into either a Chinese or American camp, it is likely that several will straddle both and seek to sustain positive relations with Washington and Beijing simultaneously. Yet if China and the United States develop competing functional systems—including economic trade blocs (RCEP or TPP), telecommunications and cybersecurity standards, and infrastructure development mechanisms—countries are likely to pick and choose between the American and Chinese systems according to which brings them the greatest benefit. These overlapping functional mechanisms of cooperation could eventually become functional spheres of influence, in which China and the United States exert outsized influence in a particular realm of national power but a given nation does not explicitly fall into either geopolitical bloc.

ALLIES AND PARTNERS REACT

As a result of these trends, US allies and partners find themselves in a very problematic position. This feeds existing insecurities about the future and drives their leaders to employ a complex mix of different strategies to address the dilemma. In dissimilar ways and to varying degrees, all US allies are pursuing complex hedging strategies that

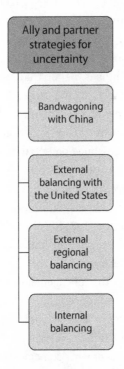

FIGURE 2.7 US allies' and partners' strategies for uncertainty

include a mix of four different responses to this uncertainty: band-wagoning with China, external balancing with the United States, external intraregional balancing, and internal balancing (figure 2.7).[120]

BANDWAGONING WITH CHINA

Many countries across the Indo-Pacific have sought to strengthen their ties with China in order to avoid conflict and enjoy the benefits of China's rising prosperity. This has occurred in three ways—some states (e.g., Laos and Cambodia) have been essentially drawn into China's geopolitical orbit, while others (e.g., Malaysia and Sri Lanka) have lost some autonomy in exchange for major investments from Beijing. Still others have sought to enhance their relationships with China across a wide variety of issue areas, but have maintained a ceiling on those engagements to preserve their autonomy and not make themselves vulnerable to pressure and coercion from Beijing.

For decades, the most attractive aspect of China's rise has been its economy. Today, China is the top trading partner of almost every Indo-Pacific nation (including the United States) and is a major destination for foreign direct investment.[121] This attraction has been primarily due to the low costs to multinational corporations of industrial production, and the huge potential market that China has represented as its people have begun to move up the economic ladder. Countries around the world have wanted to benefit from China's rise, which has put China at the center of the global economy and given it the world's second-largest GDP after that of the United States.

Although the motivations for countries to engage with China have been primarily economic on their face, there has also been a geopolitical aspect to this engagement. This has enabled Beijing to attempt to use its economic relationships to pressure its neighbors on political issues.[122] This dynamic has played out all around the world, where, for example, certain countries have received significant economic inducements coincidentally with their switching of diplomatic recognition from Taipei to Beijing, while others have been punished for their positions on sensitive subjects like the Dalai Lama or the Nobel laureate Liu Xiaobo.[123]

China's most recent grand economic enterprises, such as the Belt and Road Initiative, have been the locus for regional economic bandwagoning. As of this writing, more than three dozen countries have signed a memorandum of understanding with China to join BRI. They include nearly all of Eastern Europe, eight countries in the Indo-Pacific (including South Korea and New Zealand), and fourteen countries in the Middle East, Central Asia, South Asia, and Africa.[124] Yet it is important to note that BRI has yet to translate into greater political or strategic influence. To the contrary, concerns about Chinese economic practices within BRI have already created problems in Beijing's relationships with its neighbors.[125]

For America's Indo-Pacific allies, economic ties have been used by Beijing as a tool of both attraction and coercion. Japan, for example, was unable to import rare earth materials from China after an intensification of tensions with China over the disputed Senkaku/ Diaoyu Islands in the East China Sea.[126] The Philippines also saw its economic interests with China affected when some of its agricultural exports to China were left to rot on the dock during a tense moment in their dispute over parts of the South China Sea.[127] Yet this dynamic was most clear with the deployment of THAAD in South Korea, a decision that China firmly opposed because of its concerns that the missile defense system's radar could see into China.[128] As a result of this decision, China imposed a swath of economic sanctions against South Korean economic interests, ranging from banning popular South Korean entertainment to banning the sale of South Korean products such as food and automobiles. Lotte, a major South Korean conglomerate, faced the harshest economic pushback from China after giving the South Korean government one of its golf courses to use as a THAAD deployment site in exchange for a plot of military-owned land. In response, China began closing Lotte Marts located in mainland China over safety violations and denouncing the company in state media, while Chinese hackers attacked Lotte's webpage.[129]

With regard to increasing security cooperation with neighboring countries, Beijing built a strong relationship with Manila while it was led by President Gloria Macapagal-Arroyo by becoming one of the most important investors in and financiers of the country's infrastructure and mining sectors—a positive economic bond juxtaposed to steadily growing tension in the South China Sea and a cooling relationship with the United States.[130] Since the end of Arroyo's term in 2010, tensions between the PRC and the Philippines have increased as a result of China's aggressive island building in the Spratlys. However, President Rodrigo Duterte's 2016 election win revealed a leader who aims to decrease dependence on the United States and rebuild fallen bilateral communication channels with China, rather than the aggressively anti-Chinese politician he had seemed to be during his presidential campaign.[131] In fact, in 2016, Duterte stated that the Philippines would be willing to find a resolution to territorial disputes if China provided aid for domestic infrastructure.[132] Duterte has also mused about a "post-American" future for the Philippines in which China would play a major role.[133]

This is only one example of the sway China's economy has with its neighbors, seeking to draw them closer to China and making the long-term durability of security relations with the United States seem questionable. Malaysia has maintained a close security relationship with the United States, even allowing US planes to launch from its bases as they conduct surveillance in the South China Sea. However, a landmark 2016 defense deal with China heightened security ties with the PRC to a new level. The deal entails Malaysia purchasing four Chinese littoral mission ships and was reached a year after the countries began conducting joint military exercises.[134] The deal also comes amid tension in US–Malaysia relations after the US Department of Justice began investigating money laundering by high-level officials using the 1Malaysia Development Berhad state fund, established by Prime Minister Najib Razak. During Najib's visit to the White House in September 2017, however, President Donald Trump avoided raising the issue.[135]

Interestingly, China's attempts at economic coercion have so far failed to make a decisive geopolitical impact. China's disputes with Japan and the Philippines did not disappear, and the new government in Seoul has repeatedly stated its support for THAAD deployment (though South Korean president Moon Jae-in strongly questioned the process by which the THAAD deployment was decided). Indeed, economic coercion at this point seems less like an effective tool of leverage for Beijing and more like a means by which Beijing can express displeasure. For the purposes of this discussion, China's attempts at economic coercion have, to date, been tactical failures and strategically unhelpful for Beijing's interests.

Instances of China's economic coercion have had the strategic effect of driving its Asian neighbors to look askance at the possibility of bandwagoning with it. Such coercion demonstrates that China's leaders are only concerned with their own national interests, and that they expect China's neighbors to disregard their own legitimate interests or security concerns out of deference to Chinese prerogatives. This is one reason why, for the most part, bandwagoning has not been an attractive option for America's Asian allies and partners. Although they seek to maintain positive relations with Beijing, this has not translated into an explicit alignment with China among US allies and partners in Asia.

EXTERNAL BALANCING WITH THE UNITED STATES

Strengthening relations with the United States has, for most of the Indo-Pacific, presented a more attractive option. Only the United States has the economic heft and military capability to serve as a plausible balancer against China, and the distance of the United States means that allies and partners have enjoyed a great deal of strategic independence from Washington—even over issues of great importance to the United States.

The Obama administration correctly perceived this demand signal as an opportunity to pursue its rebalancing strategy. This strategy demonstrated the continued will and commitment of the United States to remain engaged in the region, even as challenges in the Middle East and Eastern Europe intensified. The rebalance also provided a platform for countries to enhance their security relationships with the United States, and US alliances and partnerships made terrific progress in this area. From a new set of alliance guidelines with Japan to new agreements for access and cooperation across Southeast Asia, the United States greatly diversified its political and military ties with the Indo-Pacific under President Obama.

Yet the Obama administration's "rebalance" lacked a critical aspect: intensified economic engagement. Failure to pass the Trans-Pacific Partnership significantly handicapped the ability of the United States to comprehensively engage the region, allowing China to fill the strategic void with its own vision. This problem was greatly exacerbated by the decision of the Trump administration to withdraw the United States from TPP negotiations altogether, paving the way for China to set the rules of the road and forcing US allies and partners to explore other options.

Despite these setbacks, several Asian nations have continued to engage Washington in an effort to further tie the United States to themselves. Preeminent in this strategy has been Japan, whose prompt, high-level engagement with President Trump paid early reassuring dividends. Though less immediately successful than Japan, other allies and partners have similarly redoubled their efforts in an attempt to strengthen the embrace of the United States. Taiwan made international headlines when President Tsai Ing-wen spoke with president-elect Trump in the days after the presidential election—breaking decades of noncontact between leaders from Taiwan and the United States. Australian prime minister Malcolm Turnbull likewise traveled to Washington for a summit with President Trump, despite an early phone call that reportedly grew heated. In all cases, allies emphasize interoperability, jointness, and integrated alliance coordination mechanisms in order to ensure that they stay closely lashed to Washington and the US military.

The geopolitical significance of these attempts at high-level engagement rises when considering that Asian nations are starkly divided in public confidence in president Trump. According to the Pew Research Center, Trump's greatest support comes from the Philippines, where 69 percent say they have confidence in him.

A majority in Vietnam (58 percent) also expressed confidence in Trump, whereas confidence in Trump is remarkably low in Japan (24 percent) and South Korea (17 percent). Compared with Chinese president Xi Jinping, greater shares of people in the Philippines, Vietnam, and Japan are confident in Trump. (In Asia, the Philippines had the highest confidence in Xi, at 53 percent, while the Japanese had the lowest, at 11 percent.) In contrast, people in South Korea were more than twice as likely to have confidence in Xi than in Trump regarding world affairs (38 vs. 17 percent).[136]

EXTERNAL REGIONAL BALANCING

In the face of rising security threats and burgeoning concerns about US will and capability, several American allies and partners have begun to work together to expand their economic opportunities beyond China and their security opportunities beyond the United States. Although Japan has been the most visible in its efforts to supplement American leadership, India and Australia have also begun to consider strategies to further bind the Indo-Pacific—sans China and the United States—into a more cohesive, cooperative whole. Although there is little to no chance that such efforts will in themselves fundamentally change regional geopolitical dynamics, replace the United States, or constitute an effective balance against China, they nonetheless represent an important aspect of how US allies and partners are adjusting to new strategic realities.

Talks among the remaining eleven nations involved in the Trans-Pacific Partnership deal have rekindled without the United States, after President Trump took the United States out of the deal at the beginning of his term and made any trade deal seem impossible. Japan—a country that relied strongly on the US economy while growing from its postwar state into a global economic power—spearheaded the deal, which was signed in March 2018 as the Comprehensive and Progressive Agreement for Trans-Pacific Partnership. This points to a realization that other democratic countries must initiate the kinds of diplomatic and mutually advantageous agreements that the United States has presided over since the end of World War II, and that they are in fact doing so.[137]

Beyond efforts to keep the TPP on life support, several US allies and partners have sought to enhance intraregional economic connectivity to check Beijing's efforts to establish a Sinocentric regional economic structure. In Taiwan, President Tsai Ing-wen initiated the New Southbound Policy to strengthen Taipei's relationships with the ten countries of ASEAN, six states in South Asia (India, Pakistan, Bangladesh, Nepal, Sri Lanka, and Bhutan), Australia, and New Zealand in order to leverage Taiwan's cultural, educational, technological, agricultural, and economic assets to deepen its regional integration.[138] Similarly, India, South Korea, and Australia have pursued similar initiatives designed to diversify their countries' economic relationships beyond China.

In parallel with these economic initiatives, US allies and partners have pursued stronger security relationships between each other. For example, the military relationship between India and Vietnam is an increasingly close and underappreciated driver of regional military engagement. Likewise, Japan and Australia have also sought to enhance defense ties across the region and with one another. Finally, US European allies—especially France—have recently examined options to play a larger role in the Indo-Pacific.[139]

INTERNAL BALANCING

Finally, America's Asian allies and partners have begun to expand investments in their militaries while also adjusting these investments to focus on the areas necessary to enhance their ability to respond to emerging security threats from China and North Korea.

Predictably, an intensified threat from North Korea and China is driving fears of war and crisis, and these fears are at least partly behind efforts in South Korea and Japan to enhance their self-defense capabilities. After North Korea's second launch of intercontinental ballistic missiles in July 2017, South Korean president Moon Jae-in made the decision to deploy the US THAAD missile defense system as a necessary defense measure; during his presidential campaign, he ran on a platform fervently opposed to the system and frequently cited plans to focus on increasing peaceful dialogue with North Korea.[140] Moon has also expressed an interest in accelerating the long-delayed transfer of wartime operational control (OPCON) of the South Korean military from the United States to South Korea—a process that will require significant investments by Seoul to improve South Korean capabilities in several areas.

In Japan, Prime Minister Shinzo Abe has pointed to the intensifying threat from North Korea and China as a reason to expand the capabilities of Japan's Self-Defense Force and amend the Constitution's Article 9 in order to strengthen the Self-Defense Force's constitutional foundation and expand its mandate. Specifically, Tokyo is examining options to improve Japan's ability to conduct offensive strikes and enhance missile defense capabilities. Although Japan's leaders have repeatedly stressed that such capabilities would make the US–Japan alliance stronger, these investments would nonetheless enhance Japan's ability to operate with greater effectiveness and greater independence.

The Japanese Ministry of Defense requested a ¥5.26 trillion ($48.1 billion) fiscal year budget for 2018, setting a record in defense spending.[141] Similarly, South Korea is set to also raise its military budget to support President Moon's campaign to grow South Korean defense capabilities in response to increasing belligerence from the North. The budget will be 43.2 trillion won ($39.7 billion), a growth of 7 percent for the year and the largest annual increase since 2009.[142] In India, Prime Minister Modi announced an ambitious $250 billion plan to modernize India's military—a very ambitious program that is already being stymied by the country's own rules and bureaucracy.[143] Australia is also boosting its defense budget over several years, and is using the additional funds to acquire more advanced submarines, aircraft, and surface ships.

Even in Southeast Asia, countries are investing more in security capabilities despite significant resource constraints. Between 2007 and 2017, military spending among Southeast Asian nations adjacent to the South China Sea rose by nearly 80 percent.[144] Much of this investment has gone toward maritime capabilities—both in the shape of navies and in building coast guards.

These investments will gradually help US allies and partners to defend their interests and resist coercion, to various degrees. This is especially true for allies and partners that are already quite advanced technologically, like Japan and Australia, as they have the infrastructure and resource base necessary to sustain and maintain advanced capabilities. Yet for less developed allies and partners, there is a significant limitation to the capabilities they can support. Even if they could afford the acquisition of significant advanced capabilities, they would not have the infrastructure, resources, or know-how to maintain them for an extended period of time. Thus, for less developed allies and partners, initial investments will likely focus more on building infrastructure and sustainability rather than the acquisition of new technologies, thus limiting their ability to resist coercion from a high-end adversary like China.

Finally, US allies and partners in the Indo-Pacific know that they can only do so much against potential Chinese aggression. Although geography and inexperience will likely continue to be a barrier for Chinese power projection for several years, the scale and increasingly modern quality of China's People's Liberation Army capabilities will pose a significant challenge for any ally and partner to resist directly and on their own. Rather, smaller partners like Taiwan are pursuing innovative and asymmetric strategies to counter potential coercion or aggression from Beijing.[145] Moreover, the realization that China poses a potentially overwhelming military threat will likely drive US allies and partners to see internal balancing as complementary to their strategy to externally balance with the United States. In this way, some allies are pursuing another hedging strategy to enhance their ability to contribute to joint operations with the US military while at the same time enhancing indigenous capabilities to operate independently should the United States fail to come to their aid.

WANTED: A NEW APPROACH TO THE INDO-PACIFIC

Clearly, Asia is changing rapidly. Economic, military, and political power is more distributed than ever before. China has grown prosperous and powerful, and other major powers (e.g., India) have seen remarkable growth as well. Although US preponderance remains, uncertainty about the sustainability and reliability of American engagement in the region raises questions about the long-term viability of the regional liberal order.

In this new regional heterarchy, major powers are likely to compete for an advantage across all aspects of national power. The middle powers, meanwhile, will pursue hedging strategies that maximize their flexibility and minimize vulnerability to coercion or domination. The capabilities and ambitions of US adversaries are increasing, US allies and partners are working together in new ways and fielding new military capabilities, and the region is gradually coming to believe that the role of the United States in the Indo-Pacific will be far more circumscribed than it has been since the end of World War II. As a result, Asia today is unstable, unpredictable, and increasingly well-armed—dynamics that will test the ability of the United States to sustain a regional liberal order.

The time has come for US strategy toward the Indo-Pacific to enter a new phase. The United States has an opportunity to revitalize its alliances and partnerships across the region, to harness their growing capabilities, and to empower them to play a more significant regional role in sustaining a liberal regional order.

The fact that most US allies and partners in the Indo-Pacific have to date emphasized balancing—both external and internal—represents an opportunity for the United States. One somewhat surprising lesson over the past three years has been the resilience of US alliances and partnerships in the face of rising threats from China and North Korea and perceptions of decline, distraction, and outright hostility from the United States. Despite concerns that allies and partners may abandon the United States in the face of such turbulence, they instead have continued to see the United States as the only major power that can check a rising China and help them maintain autonomy and sovereignty. It seems that these relationships may be more robust and resilient than some in Washington—and Beijing—had assumed. This means that these allies and partners still generally see the United States as largely a geopolitical asset, and at the same time they want to do more in the region. Washington should not discourage this hedging; rather, it should harness it and channel these energies into a concerted strategy toward commonly defined ends.

At the end of World War II, the United States saw that the world had fundamentally changed, and it was able to adapt its foreign, economic, and national security policies to the requirements of that changed world. As international dynamics reach another inflection point, it is incumbent on the United States to lead the liberal order into the twenty-first century. No other power has nearly the same combination of wealth, military might, and geopolitical influence. America did it before, and can do it again.

3

EMPOWERING US ALLIES AND PARTNERS IN THE INDO-PACIFIC

History is clear: nations with strong allies thrive, and those without them wither.

—JAMES MATTIS, FORMER US SECRETARY OF DEFENSE

Strategic trends currently under way in Asia will alter the fundamental power dynamics of the region, threaten its long-term stability and prosperity, and drive greater demand for American power. Yet the availability of this power will be relatively circumscribed by domestic economic and budgetary forces and diminished by the rise of other Indo-Pacific powers.

Several scholars and former senior American officials have written about the catastrophes that would result from the loss of American power in the world.[1] Although this analysis is instructive in highlighting the importance of American power in the preservation of a liberal international system, the improbability of a complete American withdrawal from the Indo-Pacific requires considerations of more realistic scenarios.

Scholars have often examined the so-called patron's dilemma, which deals with the question of how a major power (or "patron") can best provide security to its allies without becoming trapped in unwanted conflicts. The dilemma is that strong commitments worsen the risk of entrapment but improve deterrence against attack, whereas a weaker commitment reduces the potential for entrapment but diminishes the deterrent effect of the overall relationship. As described by the scholars Keren Yarhi-Milo, Alexander Lanoszka, and Zack Cooper, great power patrons primarily make such decisions on the basis of the extent to which their leaders believe that they and their ally share common security interests, and whether the patron believes that its client has sufficient military capabilities to deter its main adversary without the patron's assistance.[2]

Therefore, if the United States remains engaged in the region but is not able to convince its allies and partners to play a greater strategic role, three broad scenarios are possible.

The first scenario is ever-expanding unilateralism. Washington could choose to continue the robust investments needed to unilaterally address the many security challenges facing the Indo-Pacific. Without substantial contributions or adjustments from its allies and partners, its basing structure and logistical infrastructure will become increasingly costly, and vulnerable. The Indo-Pacific will likely require a significant portion of American defense spending and deployments, which would likely have the dual effect of expanding budget deficits while reducing the American military presence (and increasing strategic risk) in other parts of the world.

The second scenario is a diminished role. Isolationist sentiments within the United States have gained ascendance in many circles in Washington, and threaten to substantially limit the ability of the United States to address challenges and maintain power in the Indo-Pacific. The likely result would be weakened confidence in the reliability of American commitments, diminished stability and prosperity in the Indo-Pacific, a gradual fading of American leadership on several issues of strategic importance, and a weakened liberal order. This will tacitly leave other issues to the whims of an anarchic international system or another power looking for a strategic vacuum to fill—namely, China. A Sinocentric Asia would operate in a fashion that would be highly problematic for the United States. Established rules and norms, like freedom of the seas and the peaceful resolution of disputes, would be pushed to the wayside in the face of Beijing's preferences. The region would become more corrupt and less democratic, and it would be consumed with intraregional tension.

And the third scenario is hollow leadership. It is possible that the United States can continue to rhetorically expand its regional commitments but fail to provide the necessary resources to do so. Indeed, great powers often initiate risky military and diplomatic interventions in far-off regions because of the refusal of their leaders to accept losses in their state's relative power, international status, or prestige. Instead of cutting their losses, leaders often continue to invest blood and money in failed excursions into the periphery.[3] Allies and partners, as well as adversaries, will be fully aware of the expanding gaps in America's rhetoric and its capabilities and will likely react accordingly. The result would probably be little different than if the United States were open about accepting a diminished regional role. Confidence in American power would be diminished, regional stability and prosperity would be threatened, and the liberal order would be weakened in the face of a rising and increasingly ambitious China.

To effectively address these challenges and preserve the stability and prosperity that the regional order has enabled for the past several decades, the United States must adjust its strategies and policies toward the Indo-Pacific. To counteract changes to the regional balance of power and China's exceptionalist objectives, the United States should enhance its own geopolitical strength and empower its allies to contribute more to the health and success of a twenty-first-century regional liberal order—a de facto arrangement of primus inter pares. At the same time, the United States should focus its energies, and those of its allies and partners, on preserving the key principles that have made the liberal order so beneficial for its own interests and for the entire Indo-Pacific.

This chapter proposes a framework for the United States to buttress its own power, while at the same time approaching its alliances and partnerships in the Indo-Pacific as geopolitical platforms for cooperation and the coordination of efforts across all aspects of national power in order to address shared challenges and build a twenty-first-century regional liberal order.

SHAPING THE TWENTY-FIRST-CENTURY REGIONAL ORDER

It is reasonable for the United States to seek to preserve the gains that the existing regional order has brought. However, sustaining the old order is insufficient; it must find a way to also evolve that order to reflect geopolitical realities. As convincingly argued by Rebecca Friedman Lissner and Mira Rapp-Hooper, "International affairs experts cannot resign themselves to simply critiquing the seared remains of the liberal order. . . . The task at hand is formidable: a twenty-first-century vision of liberal order, advanced through an American strategy that properly couples foreign policy objectives with material and political resources."[4]

Although most American strategists appropriately focus on strategies and investments to sustain and advance American power in the region, far less analysis has been devoted to strategies for building and harnessing the power of US allies and partners themselves. Yet to give this latter aspect of US Indo-Pacific strategy greater attention would not diminish American power and influence in the region itself. It is US allies, after all, that have enabled and supported America's leadership in the Indo-Pacific for decades.

America cannot do this alone. As its allies and partners in the Indo-Pacific rise in geopolitical power, the United States has an opportunity to harness the power of like-minded nations to evolve the regional system in a way that sustains and strengthens the key attributes of the past. This chapter describes such a strategy, arguing that, instead of ignoring or attempting to reverse these strategic trends, the United States should build and employ the tremendous geopolitical power of its allies and partners in order to shape the future direction of the Indo-Pacific order in a way conducive to America's interests and those of its allies and partners.

Each US ally and partner has its own unique history, strategic culture, interests, threat perceptions, and ambitions. Each alliance and partnership will likewise require unique approaches and arrangements that reflect these differences. Nevertheless, they also have a vital unifying commonality: the United States. American interests require that each alliance and partnership exhibits some degree of continuity across various issues. To this end, the United States should work with its Indo-Pacific allies and partners to develop a shared vision for the twenty-first-century liberal order of the Indo-Pacific.

DEVELOPING A SHARED VISION FOR REGIONAL ORDER

Either out of fear or ambition, America's allies and partners require a positive vision for the future, and a strong argument about how working with the United States will help them realize their own national objectives.[5] As such, a critical aspect of an initiative by the United States to enable its allies and partners is to build a common vision for the future of Asia. Although the Trump administration's "Free and Open Indo-Pacific" is potentially a good start, the contours of this strategy remain unclear and require further elucidation.

This chapter proposes a positive vision whereby the United States should work with its allies and partners to enhance the power of America and that of its friends, and work collaboratively to strengthen and evolve the regional order to sustain the key liberal principles of the postwar order that enabled the region's stability and prosperity.

As it stands today, the United States and its allies and partners share the same primary challenges in the Indo-Pacific: a rising China, an uncertain United States, and an alternately belligerent and engaging North Korea. Yet there are significant disparities in whether these trends are seen as positive or negative, and severe or manageable. These are significant, but not insurmountable, differences. The key for the United States will not be to convince its allies and partners that they are wrong, but rather to listen to their concerns and find a common ground on which to build.

The development of a twenty-first-century liberal regional order would be in the interest of the United States and its friends in the Indo-Pacific, but it will not come naturally. Many US allies and partners, left to their own devices, will narrowly focus on their own national interests, with considerations of the broader regional order being left to academics or seen as a problem for larger powers. Moreover, US allies and partners in the region will have a limited ability to marshal disparate powers into a common cause—although some are beginning to try. It is the necessary role of the United States to provide this vision and demonstrate that its allies and partners can advance their own interests while simultaneously contributing to the health and success of a regional order that they, indeed, count on. Fundamentally, this approach transforms the regional order from one that is primarily based on American power to one in which the United States is the leader of a more distributed, networked force to maintain the regional order.

This approach was suggested by then–US secretary of defense Ash Carter's speech at the 2016 Shangri-La Dialogue in Singapore. Secretary Carter described the US role in the Indo-Pacific as providing, with its network of allies and partners, the "oxygen" of regional stability that has underwritten rapid economic growth and the development of security ties.[6] He advocated for the further development of the increasingly interconnected region into a "principled security network." Such a network would entail "nations building connections for a common cause, planning and training together, and eventually operating in a coordinated way." The United States would continue to serve as the primary provider of regional security and as a leading contributor to the region's principled security network, while at the same time empowering its allies and partners in the region to do more for themselves.

Although a strategy to empower allies and partners to contribute to the health and success of the regional liberal order is clearly in the interest of all involved, few are likely to express their strategy in such a way. Rather, they are far more likely to focus on, and be motivated by, issues closer to home—such as managing territorial disputes, protecting freedom of navigation, and building the ability to resist coercion and aggression. Yet strategies to address these motivations could, if properly conceived and implemented, also be constituent parts of a broader effort to strengthen the regional order. The next subsections give primary examples of how common concerns could be used as the driver of cooperation between the United States and its allies and partners to fortify the liberal regional order.

SUSTAINING CRITICAL PRINCIPLES

Considering the challenges it faces, the foundation of the United States' engagement with its allies and partners should be to preserve the key principles that have enabled the region's stability and prosperity, while also adapting its approach to reflect the requirements of a changed world. At a geopolitical level, this will mean sustaining the key attributes of the liberal order that it has trumpeted since the end of World War II, which were described by Henry Kissinger as "an inexorably expanding cooperative order of states observing common rules and norms, embracing liberal economic systems, forswearing territorial conquest, respecting national sovereignty, and adopting participatory and democratic systems of government."[7]

A key challenge for American foreign policy professionals seeking to sustain aspects of a liberal order will be a striking ambivalence about the liberal order among some Asian partners, and even in the United States itself. Indeed, the Trump administration has evinced disdain for aspects of the liberal order, by questioning the utility of alliances and undermining the legitimacy of the World Trade Organization's appellate function. Yet at other times, such as its call for a "Free and Open Indo-Pacific," the Trump administration has demonstrated an implicit embrace of aspects of liberal internationalism. The reality is that there has likely been a significant debate about these issues within the Trump administration itself, with the president potentially falling on either side of the debate depending on the issues involved.

Similarly, as sovereign nations, the United States and its allies and partners may not always entirely agree on the specifics of these principles or how they may be applied. Such disagreements are natural in international relations, and should not be seen as an impediment to cooperation and coordination. Indeed, one of the most critical norms of a liberal order is the peaceful resolution of disputes. This is why so many mechanisms, institutions, and international laws have been established, and why the United States should work with its allies and partners to buttress the legitimacy of international laws and norms.

An important way strategists could navigate potential allergies to a "liberal regional order," be they foreign or domestic, would be to focus less on the concept of a liberal order and more on the principles of the order and their tangible effects. Couching issues of order building in terms of values and interests is more likely to attract support, especially from leaders who have professed a deep suspicion of liberal internationalism. Thus the utility of Kissinger's formulation above—it will likely be more advantageous for policymakers and thought leaders to focus on substance and specifics rather than concepts of order.

In this vein, buttressing international laws and norms can be especially useful for the United States and its allies and partners as they seek to navigate the complex disputes in the East China Sea and South China Sea. The 1982 UN Convention on the Law of the Seas (UNCLOS) clearly identifies the rights of coastal states and transiting vessels through international waters and territorial waters, as well as exclusive economic zones. A diplomatic effort to harmonize regional interpretations of the rights, and coordinated programs to exercise these rights by employing freedom-of-navigation operations, would significantly buttress the relevance, power, and credibility of UNCLOS.

Similarly, the United States and its allies and partners have an opportunity to clarify the status of various disputed land features in the East China Sea and South China Sea by employing the dispute resolution mechanisms established by existing international institutions. For example, the Philippines initiated a tribunal under Annex VII of UNCLOS against China regarding the status of various features in the South China Sea and the legality of China's "nine-dash line" claim. In July 2016, the Permanent Court of Arbitration published the tribunal's ruling that China's nine-dash line claim was contrary to UNCLOS, and it ruled on the status of several land features. Yet this ruling has not had a significant impact on the dynamics of the South China Sea itself, and the United States has largely ignored the ruling. This is a missed opportunity, because the ruling could be used by the United States and its allies and partners to reassert the critical role of international laws and norms in peacefully addressing disputes. Washington should therefore work with its allies and partners to buttress the legitimacy of this ruling, encourage other states to use this mechanism to address disputes, and operate according to its findings.

Embracing liberal economic systems is another aspect of a twenty-first-century regional order that the United States should pursue with its allies and partners. The Trans-Pacific Partnership (TPP) would have been an obvious way to advance economic liberalism across the region, as it would have forced several illiberal economic systems in the region—especially Vietnam—to substantially reform major sectors of their economies. Yet even beyond the TPP, bilateral economic agreements have the potential to expand liberal economic principles across the region. With Taiwan, for example, the United States has an opportunity to help Taipei reform its financial and agricultural sectors by finally concluding a much-delayed bilateral trade and investment agreement.

Another critical principle of a liberal order that should be strengthened is the sovereignty of nation states. In this, a great deal of work needs to be done. Several US allies—especially Australia and New Zealand—have come under increasing attack by Chinese influence operations. Entities as disparate as politicians, companies, and universities have come under increasing pressure from the United Front Department of the Chinese Communist Party (CCP) to adopt policies conforming with Beijing's preferences.[8] The United States has also not been spared such efforts, including the well-documented efforts by Russia to influence the 2016 presidential elections,[9] and also Chinese initiatives to force American companies to change how they list Taiwan and other areas on their websites.[10]

Although the Trump administration publicly criticized Beijing for these efforts, more can be done.[11] Because they face a common threat, and because preserving sovereignty is one of the most commonly shared principles across the region, the United States should establish a mechanism to share information and coordinate responses to efforts to interfere in democratic processes. To demonstrate solidarity with smaller states that are under increasing pressure from abroad, the United States would be able to greatly strengthen its regional ties.

US officials should also be cognizant of the challenges inherent in discussing issues of sovereignty. China will routinely use sovereignty issues to push back on US policies toward Taiwan, the South China Sea, and Tibet. Furthermore, authoritarian regimes routinely cite sovereignty to deflect international concerns about human rights abuses. This is not to say that sovereignty is an issue to be ignored; rather, it is to highlight the complexities of this issue as a principle for the United States and its allies and partners.

Finally, a critical principle for the United States to promote with its allies and partners is the adoption and strengthening of participatory and democratic systems of government. Democracy is not an American value, per se. It is a human value, and one that has been embraced across the Indo-Pacific region to great success. Yet there has been some evidence of a democratic decline in Southeast Asia in recent years, as some previously democratic states have grown more illiberal, and some authoritarian states have receded further away from liberalism.[12] There is a danger that the United States and its democratic allies may turn their backs on these countries, and give their competitors an opportunity to displace the United States, tolerate further authoritarianism, and engage in corrupt practices to enrich themselves and expand their power.

COMPETING WITH A RISING CHINA

The most significant geopolitical development in the Indo-Pacific since the end of the Cold War has been the rise of China from one of the region's poorest and most dysfunctional nations into a major power that has the potential to challenge the United States for regional (though not global) dominance.[13] As described above, China has gained significant political influence across the region and built an advanced military capability that may soon challenge American military primacy in Asia. China has also begun to construct alternative political and economic architectures that circumvent established institutions and reflect Beijing's interests and prerogatives.

China today is a confident economic and political power that is charting its own path in both domestic and international affairs. It is increasingly assertive in international affairs and is willing to tolerate turbulence and risk in the pursuit of its interests. It is investing in advanced technologies and military capabilities that will put it in the economic driver's seat for the coming decades, and it has demonstrated an ability to use all elements of national power in the pursuit of its goals. It has identified its objectives and how it plans to achieve them, and it follows through by devoting significant resources to these ends.[14]

The United States' competition with China will be a defining geopolitical aspect of the twenty-first century, and future historians will certainly write that the first years were slow going. It has taken the United States far too long to explicitly recognize that it was in a great power competition that has significant implications for its own interests, prosperity, and security. But recognizing that one has a problem and understanding its scale is the first step toward finding a solution.

The rise of China poses a vexing challenge for all the nations in the Indo-Pacific, and especially US allies and partners. Although they certainly seek to benefit from China's economic growth and they are not keen to be used as pawns in a great power competition between Beijing and Washington, they are also wary of the implications of a powerful China for their own independence. Leaders and scholars across the Indo-Pacific have expressed profound concern that a rising China will seek to constrain their freedom of action and demand greater degrees of deference on issues of disagreement. In Japan, policymakers and scholars continue to debate the best strategy for engaging China and hedging against its rise, but most now agree that China's increased military spending and activities pose a challenge to the region.[15] Conservative leaders advocating for increased military spending, including Prime Minister Shinzo Abe, have expressed their concerns over China's economic strength and expanding military capabilities. In remarks made in New York City in 2013, Abe hinted at this concern by contrasting the annual 0.8 percent increase in Japan's defense budget with China's annual increase of over 10 percent.[16] South Korean policymakers and academics also increasingly view a rising China as a challenger to the region's order, despite a "charm offensive" from China.[17] South Korean leaders have voiced concern particularly over China's willingness to use economic leverage to obtain security concessions.[18]

Such fears are not solely theoretical. China has repeatedly demonstrated a penchant for using leverage in order to press for its own interests across the region. Indeed, the estimable Evan Feigenbaum of the Paulson Institute (formerly of the State Department) usefully identified five typologies of leverage utilized in Chinese foreign policy: passive, active, exclusionary, coercive, and latent.[19]

As has happened between great powers multiple times in the past, geopolitical competition between China and the United

States is likely to occur in their strategic periphery. In Asia, this means that the Korean Peninsula, Taiwan, the East China Sea, and the South China Sea will likely be the theater for the United States, China, and (in the case of the South China Sea) India to compete with one another for relative power and influence. Yet such competition is unlikely to be played out on the battlefield as it had been in the nineteenth and twentieth centuries—the potential for all-out war between the great powers remains low, though smaller-scale conflicts and peripheral interventions are more likely possibilities. Instead, competition will occur in the functional spheres of influence of the emerging regional heterarchy—international laws and norms, trade and investment flows, freedom of the seas, maritime gray zones, technology standards, regional architecture, and culture.

It should be made clear, and repeated often, that the goal of the United States and its allies should not be to undermine China's domestic stability. Such an objective would be foolhardy on its face, if for no other reason than that making China a hostile or unstable power is counter to the interests of the United States and the rest of the Indo-Pacific. Yet this does not mean the United States and China are not locked in a geopolitical competition. Rather, it means that the contours of the competition are different from previous, more existential rivalries.

It would also be equally foolhardy, however, to pretend that competition between China and the United States does not exist. Too often, scholars and officials have tried to demonstrate their commitment to maintaining positive and constructive relations with China by claiming that the United States is not competing with China or that some actions taken by the United States in the Indo-Pacific have nothing to do with China's rise. This is not to say that everything the United States does in Asia is about competition with China, but to deny that China motivates major aspects of US strategy toward the Indo-Pacific is difficult. Such statements can actually damage American credibility in the region, because they send a message (however inadvertently) that the United States does not appreciate the implications of China's rise or, even worse, that it *does* understand the implications of China's rise and simply does not care. This is why the Trump administration's acknowledgment of US competition with China is actually helpful.[20] It recognizes a dynamic on which Beijing has been focused for years, and it opens space for discussion about *how* the United States can best compete with China.

The United States and its allies and partners should work together to ensure that China's actions support, rather than undermine, key aspects of the liberal order. Ensuring that China does not undermine international laws and norms that preserve stability and prosperity is in the common interest of the entire region, and should be a unifying objective in this endeavor. This should apply to all aspects of geopolitics, including issues as varied as freedom of navigation, the peaceful resolution of disputes, and the rules of the road for economic engagement and interaction. As such, cooperation with China should also be pursued in areas where US and Chinese interests converge. Yet Washington— as well as its allies and partners—should be careful to not allow promises of cooperation to be used by Beijing as leverage in other issue areas. Cooperation should never be seen as a favor granted by Beijing as a reflection of a generally friendly relationship, but rather as an action undertaken because cooperation is in the mutual interests of each side.

Overall, it is in the interest of the United States that its Indo-Pacific allies and partners balance, rather than bandwagon, in response to China's rise. Although Washington should not oppose efforts by any country to engage Beijing—indeed, engagement is a critical aspect of any strategy toward Beijing—it should ensure that such engagement does not transform into a more general strategy of bandwagoning and acquiescence to Beijing's coercion and suzerainty.

Yet encouraging allies and partners to balance against the rise of China is, in itself, insufficient. The United States also has an interest in the *type* of balancing that its allies and partners pursue. Although intraregional balancing would be beneficial to the United States if it contributes to regional cohesion and enables enhanced trilateral or multilateral cooperation, Washington should be wary of efforts at intraregional balancing that could be used to take care of their own security through regional self-help strategies, the aggregate of which would amount to a challenge of the basis for American leadership in Asia and would likely foster an uncoordinated, indecisive, and potentially illiberal approach that will not sustain stability over the long term. Although such efforts would likely fail—multilateral cooperation without a dominant power is a recipe for indecision and floundering—they would send a clear signal to China and the rest of the region about American weakness.

Instead, Washington should focus on strategies that bolster American power and engagement in the region and encourage both external and internal balancing among its Asian allies and partners in a way that strengthens their ties to the United States, and encourages them to contribute more to the health and success of the liberal regional order. More specifically, US allies and partners should be empowered to better defend themselves and assert their interests in ways that strengthen key principles of a liberal regional order, such as freedom of navigation, political and economic liberalism, and the peaceful resolution of disputes based on international laws and norms. With this approach, the United States has an opportunity to build a confederated effort to strengthen the liberal order that has made the region increasingly peaceful, democratic, and prosperous.

To these ends, the United States should empower its allies and partners to more effectively assert their own rights, defend their sovereignty, and preserve their geopolitical independence from potential Chinese coercion. This will require a comprehensive strategy of cooperation and coordination across economic and diplomatic spheres to ensure that the United States and its allies and partners remain linked in a common cause, as well as a concerted military effort to enable allies and partners to more effectively understand their external environment and contribute to security operations that defend the liberal order.

NAVIGATING A MULTIPOLAR ASIA

Although the rise of China has been the Indo-Pacific's most dramatic strategic event in recent memory, the expansion of the region's middle powers will also have significant implications. In the coming decades, the United States will need to manage an increasingly multipolar Indo-Pacific that is riven by historical animosities and simmering territorial disputes.

In recent years, growth rates in the Indo-Pacific have been heavily weighted toward developing economies, while America's Asian allies (Australia, Japan, South Korea, Thailand, and the Philippines) have remained relatively stagnant. In recent decades, the combined gross domestic product (GDP) of the countries belonging to the Association of Southeast Asian Nations (ASEAN) exploded, from $383 billion in 1991 to $2.15 trillion in 2011 (in 2011 dollars).[21] Similarly, India's economy expanded significantly over the same period, from 3.1 percent of global GDP to 5.6 percent. The economies of America's allies, by contrast, have not changed appreciably as a portion of global GDP, and Japan's has collapsed, from 10.2 percent to 5.6 percent.[22]

An increasingly multipolar Indo-Pacific will pose both a challenge and an opportunity for the United States. On one hand, the relatively stagnating power of America's allies suggests that the relative power of these allies will continue to decrease over the coming years. This will be especially problematic if Asia's rising powers use their newfound strength to assert territorial claims, redress historical grievances with their neighbors, or undermine fundamental tenets of the liberal order (e.g., freedom of navigation or the strength of international institutions). On the other hand, many of Asia's rising powers are democracies, are generally friendly to the United States, and/or evince growing anxiety regarding Chinese assertiveness. Indonesia and India are the best examples of rising democracies that are concerned about rising Chinese power; some even believe that Myanmar's recent reforms have been partially driven by concerns about China's influence and an attempt to reach out to the United States. Although these countries are certainly not interested in becoming official American allies, and many harbor significant suspicions about the United States, deft engagement could expand areas of potential cooperation that would help the United States sustain its regional access and presence.[23]

Additionally, an important feature of geopolitics in a multipolar Indo-Pacific is its various subregional institutions—most significantly, ASEAN. Although Washington has already recognized that a robust and unified ASEAN would likely be an important bulwark for regional stability and economic integration and could help check Chinese assertiveness, ASEAN's tendency toward dialogue over action will routinely frustrate American policymakers who are focused on results over dialogue and process.

In addition to the strategic dynamics described above that are changing the balance of power *between* Indo-Pacific states, significant changes *within* the polities of America's allies and partners themselves are shaking some of the key foundations of America's network of Asian alliances. For example, America's developed Asian allies today are far more prosperous than they were when the relationships were first established at the outset of the Cold War. As a result, allied governments are (at least theoretically) better able to afford greater investments in military capabilities. Yet economic stagnation, along with looming demographic challenges, will likely drive investment toward domestic social programs and away from the military and foreign affairs.[24]

These dynamics are already playing out in regional defense budgets. Military investments by several rising regional powers have expanded dramatically in recent years, while those of Asia's established powers have stagnated. For example, while Indonesia's defense budget tripled between 2001 and 2011, and India's grew from $26 billion to $42 billion, the defense budgets of America's allies remained largely stagnant, and declined relative to total regional defense spending, from 43 to 31 percent.[25] Although the budgets of America's allies remain large in an absolute sense, growth rates suggest the beginning of a fundamental shift in regional power that mirrors regional economic trends. This suggests that the US military will need to focus on capacity building and interoperability with its allies and partners, and that considerations of economic and demographic outlooks should inform US outreach efforts over the long term.

Additionally, popular sentiment within America's Asian allies and partners—in which support for the United States is generally robust, but large segments of the population are often opposed to a large American military footprint and significant investments in defensive capabilities—can complicate relationship management and development.[26] These dynamics can be clearly seen in attempts by the United States and Japan to adjust the terms of American basing arrangements in Okinawa, where agreements to shift American military forces have been left unimplemented because of determined political opposition in Okinawa. Similarly, popular sentiment in South Korea over historical issues forced Seoul to scuttle a proposed intelligence sharing agreement with Tokyo, and has recently inflamed bilateral tensions over disputed islands. Clearly, the Pentagon's goal of a force posture that is "politically sustainable" will only be accomplished if it addresses the internal dynamics of each ally and partner.[27] Recent enhancements to the US force posture in Japan and Australia suggest that the United States has been relatively successful in some areas, while persistent challenges in the Philippines and with Vietnam also suggest that it still has a long way to go.

As a result of these and other trends occurring *within* US allies and partners, Washington's ability to convince its Asian friends to play a more significant role in the region will be fraught. Asking too much will likely breed resentment and distrust, while threats to withdraw support will raise fears of abandonment.[28] The United States therefore requires a nuanced understanding of the calculations affecting each of its allies and partners, what is possible, and what is a bridge too far.

Overall, navigating a multipolar Indo-Pacific will pose a significant challenge to regional stability and intensify demand for American leadership. Although opportunities exist for the United States to harness rising powers to buttress the international system, such an effort cannot substitute for American power and leadership. The United States will therefore require a framework that increases burden sharing with like-minded Asian nations in a way that also reinforces American leadership. Accomplishing this difficult task will require a nuanced approach that is grounded in a deep understanding of regional dynamics and that has significant input from America's regional allies and partners.

PROVIDING PUBLIC GOODS

In the past, American power and influence in the Indo-Pacific were derived principally by providing key global public goods that overlap with the United States' vital interests: regional stability, a vibrant global economy, and fair access to the global commons. Joseph Nye has argued that recognizing the relationship of American power to global public goods helps unveil "an important strategic principle that could help America reconcile its national interests with a broader global perspective and assert effective leadership."[29] Viewing America's Indo-Pacific strategy through this prism reveals how American leadership can be sustained not with preeminence alone but also by enabling like-minded countries to contribute to public goods.

Such leadership can be exercised in a wide variety of areas, utilizing multiple elements of national power. For example, US allies and partners—both in the Indo-Pacific and around the world—could contribute to the openness and stability of the maritime commons by contributing their own maritime forces for counterpiracy operations and sea lane patrols, by facilitating the presence of American maritime forces, and by supporting international laws and norms that protect the openness and stability of the global commons in international forums. Although allies and partners may be able to conduct these activities on their own, collective action among several states will require continued leadership from the United States.

This also applies to the space and cyber commons, in which China and Russia have sought to promote illiberal norms that would undermine their openness and stability. Beijing, for instance, has expressed ambitions to establish international laws and norms that would limit military-related freedom of action in space for its adversaries while concurrently allowing China to continue to develop and use ground-based antisatellite weapons. This is not to say that China today has violated existing international laws; in fact, China largely follows existing legal principles and norms to the same extent that the United States and other major powers have done.[30] Yet at the same time, Beijing has joined Moscow in pushing for new agreements on space weapons that would prohibit the "first placement of weapons in space" while still allowing land-based antisatellite weapons to remain—an arrangement generally seen as conducive to Chinese interests at the expense of those of the United States.[31]

The United States therefore has an opportunity to work with its allies and partners in the Indo-Pacific on establishing and strengthening international laws and norms based on liberal principles. This is also a potentially fruitful area of potential cooperation with Europe, as geographic proximity is less of a concern in space than it may be in other domains. For example, international law on space is not nearly as developed as it is for other domains, and is largely governed by treaties from the 1960s and 1970s.[32] This is the case despite the dramatic technological changes that have made space far more accessible for smaller nations, as well as the critical role that space plays in the global economy, modern military operations, and global communications and media.

The development of new laws and norms that sustain access to space, and address emerging challenges such as the proliferation of orbital debris, would be a highly productive way for the United States, Europe, and like-minded countries in the Indo-Pacific with interests and capabilities in space to work together to buttress liberal principles in space and push back against illiberal ambitions from Moscow and Beijing. From the distribution of resources to governance over the development and use of weapons in space and the management of space debris, Washington and its allies and partners share significant interests in coordinating their diplomatic approaches.

Similarly, in cyberspace, efforts by China and Russia to institute laws and norms at the United Nations would presumably sideline the Budapest Convention—which is supported by the United States and its allies—and would give Beijing greater input on the new laws' parameters.[33] There have been some early indications of what Moscow and Beijing would seek: Russia has recently circulated a draft treaty that would empower countries to solidify their hold over information and communications technology within their borders—a clear effort to monitor and restrict activities and speech online.[34] Clearly, cyberspace is another area where the United States and its allies and partners in Europe and the Indo-Pacific have an opportunity to coordinate their activities and develop new laws and norms that support shared liberal principles.

Similar opportunities for collaboration and integration to help alleviate demand for American power exist in humanitarian relief and disaster response after natural disasters. The earthquakes and tsunamis that struck the Indian Ocean in 2004 and Japan's Tōhoku region in 2011, which cost a combined 240,000 lives and hundreds of billions of dollars in damage, demonstrated the Indo-Pacific's vulnerability to natural disasters.[35] Such threats will likely intensify in the coming years, as populations in the region's coastal areas expand dramatically.[36]

This situation is driving Asia's maritime powers to focus more on investments associated with humanitarian relief and disaster response—both as key capabilities for their own militaries and civil societies and as a vital element of their engagement with external powers.[37] Efforts by the United States to build the capacity of its allies and partners to respond to natural disasters would have multiple benefits for American leadership and regional stability.

CONFRONTING A BELLIGERENT NORTH KOREA

North Korea threatens more nations than just South Korea and Japan—it poses a danger to the stability and prosperity of the entire Indo-Pacific. Although the threat had for decades been primarily confined to the Korean Peninsula, North Korea's development of ballistic missiles at increasingly greater ranges has expanded the threat to include Japan and, now, the American homeland as well. So far, efforts by the United States to address the North Korean challenge have been broadly seen by the region as detracting from its overall strategy to the Indo-Pacific.

Since taking office, President Trump has veered wildly in his approach to North Korea, between threats of military attack to flattery and blind expressions of trust. Despite President Trump's claim that his mid-2018 summit in Singapore with North Korean leader Kim Jong Un had removed the North Korean nuclear threat, the reality is that North Korea remains as vexing and dangerous a threat as ever. To date, the diplomatic process begun by President Trump in Singapore appears to be less an effort aimed at achieving North Korea's complete, verifiable, and irreversible denuclearization and to more an effort to normalize relations with Pyongyang as a de facto nuclear weapons state without a strategy to address the ramifications of this emerging reality.

It is unknowable how long diplomacy may last, if North Korea's complete denuclearization is achievable, and what may happen if and when diplomacy collapses. What we do know, however, is that North Korea is likely to remain a significant threat to the stability of East Asia—and to the security of American allies—for the foreseeable future. Addressing North Korean belligerence will therefore require a broad, comprehensive, long-term strategy, in which US allies and partners should play a critical role. Such an approach will be necessarily focused on East Asia, given that it is the locus of the North Korean threat. Although the United States should continue to ensure that it maintains the ability to defend itself and its allies from North Korean threats, working to enhance the capabilities of South Korea and Japan should also be a top priority for the United States.

Although the focus of this monograph is not on what form a strategy toward North Korea may take, American policymakers must understand the role that the North Korean threat plays in shaping US alliances with South Korea and Japan. Indeed, the North Korean threat has already become a driver for South Korea and Japan to invest in new military capabilities and expand the authorities of their defense forces in order to defend against a potential North Korean attack. After domestic debate and months of protest from China, the Moon administration fully deployed the Terminal High-Altitude Area Defense (THAAD) missile system on a "temporary" basis in September 2017.[38] During President Trump's trip to Asia in November, the two presidents also agreed to eliminate the previous limit on South Korean missile payloads and discussed the potential acquisition or development of nuclear-powered submarines by South Korea.[39] In December 2017, Japan approved the purchase and installation of two American Aegis Ashore systems, a land-based version of the Aegis missile defense system, which are expected to be operational by 2023.[40]

In addition to this focus on Northeast Asia, US efforts to maximize pressure on Pyongyang should also include allies and partners across the Indo-Pacific and around the world. The Philippines, for example, has extensive economic ties to North Korea; effective diplomacy with Manila could help cut off a vital source of capital for Pyongyang.[41] Japan can also greatly contribute to efforts by the United States and South Korea to enhance military capabilities to defend against and respond to North Korean aggression.

Finally, US allies and partners, and their diplomatic personnel in particular, can contribute to efforts to further isolate North Korea by cracking down on illicit activities and forced labor. Additionally, sending home North Korean officials who act more like members of organized crime than the diplomats they purport to be—even to the point of closing down entire North Korean embassies—would contribute to efforts to maximize pressure on Pyongyang.

Ultimately, efforts to maximize pressure on North Korea cannot be accomplished without US allies and partners, especially in the Indo-Pacific. Although doing so will be in the interests of most allies and partners, successful coordination of this effort will require American leadership. Washington cannot focus on one to the cost of the other—its strategy toward North Korea must be integrated as part of a broader regional strategy. Such an approach will not only be more effective; it will also help counter efforts by Beijing to use the North Korea issue to drive wedges between Washington and its allies and raise questions about US reliability.

To implement a shared vision for the future of the Indo-Pacific and to empower US allies and partners in the region, the United States should adopt a policy framework composed of six elements: bolstering American power and leadership, maximizing US engagement and influence, building up military capabilities, expanding economic interconnectivity, deepening diplomatic coordination, and networking alliance and partner relationships.

BOLSTERING AMERICAN POWER AND LEADERSHIP IN THE INDO-PACIFIC

A critical aspect of strengthening the United States' relations with its allies and partners will be strengthening American power itself. This has long been the key ingredient for regional stability and prosperity, and the United States remains the most vital actor in the Indo-Pacific.

There is an irony to these dynamics that could pose a significant dilemma for American strategists. Foreign interest in forming partnerships or allying with the United States is, in part, driven by the perceived reliability and effectiveness of American power. Foreign powers will be more likely to align themselves with the United States when they see Washington as powerful, capable, and dependable. Yet, conversely, Washington's need for allies and partners diminishes as Washington perceives itself as more powerful.

This dynamic was demonstrated two weeks after the terrorist attacks of September 11, 2001, when then US deputy secretary of defense Paul Wolfowitz made it clear that the United States would not seek collective NATO action and preferred to ask for contributions from individual states, reiterating then secretary of defense Donald Rumsfeld's statement that the mission would determine the coalition.[42] This approach came in the context of post–Cold War American triumphalism and the George W. Bush administration's more unilateral approach to foreign affairs—an approach that many in NATO believed represented "a fundamental misjudgment about the nature of the Alliance that devalued the importance of strategic solidarity."[43]

Conversely, efforts by the United States to shift defensive responsibilities to its allies and partners during a time of perceived American weakness could result in intensifying foreign concerns about the reliability of the United States. For example, after President Richard Nixon announced his "Nixon Doctrine" during a speech in Guam in 1969,[44] the United States reduced its military presence in Asia from 727,300 in 1969 to 284,000 in 1971, and in South Korea from 63,000 to 43,000.[45] This greatly intensified fears of US abandonment across the region. In South Korea, for example, then president Park Chung Hee wrote that "this series of developments contained an almost unprecedented peril to our people's survival," which drove Park to pursue a clandestine nuclear weapons program and impose his Yusin reforms, which involved the imposition of martial law, dissolution of the National Assembly, and the banning of all antigovernment activity.[46]

However, the changing realities today across the Indo-Pacific, and within the United States, demand an updated approach. The United States cannot simply seek to sustain the postwar order that worked for so many decades—it must update its approach to economic, diplomatic, and defense policy toward the Indo-Pacific if it hopes to keep its leadership and influence across the region.

DOMESTIC INVESTMENTS IN FOUNDATIONS OF NATIONAL POWER

Complicating efforts to enhance America's international position is the reality that many of these issues bring with them large consequences for America's domestic politics. Trade is by far the most obvious such issue: Many Americans fear that expanding global economic integration will threaten American jobs, although support for international trade remains generally high. In fact, in 2017 a record high 72 percent of Americans saw foreign trade as an opportunity.[47] Yet a failure to pursue further economic integration—either in the form of the now-rejected TPP or under some other rubric—will have the effect of shutting the United States out of an increasingly integrated global economy and, over time, threatening America's leadership in global economics. Of course, considering the current state of American politics, it will be incumbent upon American political leaders to find a path forward on international trade that both deepens US economic connections to the world and also advocates for the interests of American workers.

Other issues—from education to infrastructure and immigration—will also have profound implications for the long-term sustainability of American power. Though not often discussed in national security terms today, these issues are fundamental. The GI Bill, for example, provided unemployment compensation, home and business loans, and tuition support to veterans of World War II and subsequent wars. By 1947, veteran students made up more than 50 percent of the overall college population. This was undoubtedly a major contributor to the incredible growth of the American economy of the 1950s and helped lay the foundation for American technological and economic progress in the second half of the twentieth century, for the simple reason that an educated and skilled population is more productive and creates a more prosperous economy and a more vibrant society. Similarly, major investments by the US government in science and technology through the military, space program, and universities paved the way for the nation's future as the global economic and technological powerhouse.

For too long, questions of domestic economic policy have been divorced from considerations of foreign policy in US political discussions. Although both presidents Obama and Trump have identified a link between economic performance at home and American power abroad, political debates about domestic economics rarely touch on their implications for American geopolitical power. From issues like the national debt and infrastructure to funding for education and science, technology, engineering, and mathematics research in areas like artificial intelligence and robotics, American power cannot be sustained globally if it ignores the foundation of its economic vitality and innovation.

INVESTING IN TOOLS OF AMERICAN FOREIGN POLICY

Additionally, a highly consequential determinant of the sustainability of American power in the Indo-Pacific will be investing adequately in the most critical aspects of American foreign policy: its diplomats, foreign aid, and the military.[48] In 2017, the Trump administration proposed drastic cuts in funding for diplomacy, foreign aid, and foreign military financing for Asia. For the 2018 fiscal year, the administration requested $37.6 billion for the combined budget of the State Department and the US Agency for International Development (USAID), a reduction of about 32.4 percent from the $55.6 billion requested for fiscal year (FY) 2017.[49] This included $15.4 billion for USAID-managed programs, down from the $22.7 billion requested for FY 2017.[50] The administration has cited a need to make the State Department and USAID leaner and more efficient.[51] Such efficiency would be achieved by "streamlining State Department and USAID administrative costs, particularly those attributable to travel, office support contractors, and other support activities" and eliminating "programs that can draw on other private and public resources."[52] House and Senate members have voiced concern over these proposed reductions, with Chairman Ed Royce of the House Committee on Foreign Affairs noting during the foreign affairs budget hearing that "sufficient resources are needed for our military, for sure, but also for our diplomats working to end the many conflicts impacting our security."[53]

When it comes to military expenditures, no country comes close to the United States. In 2018, US military spending reached $700 billion, more than the entire Indo-Pacific combined and more than triple the estimated $228 billion spent by China in 2017.[54] Critically, however, the significant imbalance in global military spending is only eclipsed by the tremendous imbalance in the utilization of military power. No other military has more responsibilities, against a greater range of extant and potential challenges, across more widely distributed geographies, than the US military. It has kept America safe for decades, and it has defended US allies and preserved stability and prosperity in the world's most critical regions. It is also the most active military in the world, having fought for nineteen of the twenty-nine years since 1989.

Such broad responsibilities have diminished Washington's ability to prioritize. As a result, the United States has found itself embroiled in an increasingly long set of international crises and challenges; thus, a host of situations compete for resources and national attention—ongoing instability in the Middle East, ongoing military operations in Afghanistan with no end in sight, counterterrorist operations in Sub-Saharan Africa, a potentially renewed nuclear crisis with Iran as a result of the US withdrawal from the Joint Comprehensive Plan of Action, and a burgeoning crisis in Central and Eastern Europe in the face of a revanchist Russia. Yet there is little discussion in Washington about prioritizing such responsibilities, strategic restraint, or even an acknowledgment that focus in one area necessarily diminishes the ability of the United States to operate in another. Instead, national leaders often act as if American power and resources were infinite.

At times, when American power is unchallenged and the international system is stable, such "operations of choice" could be seen as acceptable, if unfortunate. Yet, during a time when American power is increasingly called into question, when it is challenged by a variety of rising powers, and when the liberal order is increasingly under pressure, decisions to dilute or weaken American power—when such actions are of limited value to American strategic interests—are nothing short of an abdication of leadership by the United States.

If the Indo-Pacific is truly going to be a long-term priority for the United States, Washington will need to devote significant resources to its presence and actions in the region. In January 2017,

Senator John McCain proposed the creation of an "Asia Pacific Stability Initiative," with $1.5 billion in designated annual funding in future defense budgets.[55] McCain has stated that the initiative would include "targeted funding to realign US military force posture in the region, improve operationally relevant infrastructure, fund additional exercises, preposition equipment and munitions, and build capacity with our allies and partners."[56] The proposal gained some traction in 2017, when bipartisan groups of Senate and House members sent letters of support for such an initiative to then secretary of defense James Mattis.[57]

Although $1.5 billion may sound like a significant amount, it actually pales in comparison with other military initiatives. The ongoing war in Afghanistan, for example, costs roughly $45 billion annually.[58] A similar initiative in Europe—dubbed the "Europe Deterrence Initiative"—was requested to be $6.5 billion for fiscal year 2019. One may note that this represented a $1.7 billion increase from the previous year—more than the entirety of Senator McCain's original proposal for Asia.[59] This suggests that even the Pentagon, which arguably has been the most active in realigning its focus toward the Indo-Pacific, still has a long way to go in terms of reprioritization.

As the military challenges from China and North Korea continue to evolve, the United States must continue to evolve as well, if it seeks to sustain conventional military deterrence, maintain its technological advantages, and successfully compete with China. This will require significant investments in emerging military technologies, while also adjusting US military force posture across the region to account for new capabilities and new threats. Though the US military services are already evolving their operations and doctrine—take, for instance, the US Marine Corps Commandant's "Planning Guidance"[60]—the Department of Defense will also need to work closely with allies and partners across the region to ensure that necessary adjustments and investments can be implemented smoothly and effectively.

Yet the tools of American foreign policy most desperately in need of greater support and funding are those that exist outside the

Pentagon. The State Department, for example, was severely diminished by a hiring freeze that was in place from President Trump's inauguration in January 2017 through May 2018; a congressionally mandated report from the Office of the Inspector General found that "several bureaus charged with protecting security, health, and life safety reported to [this office] that the hiring freeze had significant detrimental effects on their operations." Experienced diplomats have left in droves, and morale is reported to be gutted.[61] At the same time, China in 2019 surpassed the United States with the most diplomatic posts in the world.[62] This is a time when the United States needs more diplomats—not fewer.

PROTECTING AGAINST DISENGAGEMENT

Unfortunately, the several months of the Trump administration further fueled regional perceptions of American distraction and decline, in three related ways. First came the Trump administration's decision to withdraw from the Trans-Pacific Partnership, which opened the door for Beijing to attempt to assert leadership over regional economic dynamics with its Belt and Road Initiative and the Regional Comprehensive Economic Partnership.[63] US allies, partners, and adversaries alike all saw the US withdrawal from the TPP as a major signal of US economic disengagement from the region.

Also a cause of concern for US allies and partners were the multiple statements by President Trump both before and after he took office criticizing US allies and partners in the region. As noted in the previous chapter, Trump stated before his election that the United States could no longer remain the "policeman of the world" and decried the United States' "unfair" and one-sided international security relationships, creating deep unease with allies and partners globally.[64] At the beginning of his presidency, Trump insisted that South Korea should pay for the THAAD missile system, stating, "I informed South Korea it would be appropriate if they pay. . . . That's a billion dollar system. . . . We're going to protect them. But they should pay for that, and they understand that."[65]

Finally, America's adversaries and allies across the Indo-Pacific have noted President Trump's transactional approach to China. Trump expressed a willingness to explicitly set aside important issues related to Taiwan, trade, and currency (for example) in order to gain Chinese assistance in dealing with North Korea. Officials from Taipei, Tokyo, and elsewhere were unanimously concerned that such a transactional relationship would open the door for China to drive a wedge between Washington and its allies.[66]

These challenges must be addressed if the United States is to sustain its leadership position in the Indo-Pacific and maintain regional peace and prosperity. As has been argued by a wide variety of scholars and other former officials, the world needs the United States. It has been the driver of prosperity, the ultimate guarantor of international stability, and a vital advocate for international law and human rights. Without American leadership, the world would be far more dangerous, unstable, and poor. As then secretary of state Madeleine Albright said in 1998, America is "the indispensable nation," which "stand[s] tall . . . and see[s] further than other countries into the future."[67]

Sustaining American power and leadership are not only important objectives in themselves; they are also essential to any strategy for strengthening allies and partners. These relationships are founded on the calculation by allies and partners that American power is resilient and reliable. If the United States were to diminish its power and leadership role—especially through self-inflicted wounds—US allies and partners would likely turn away from Washington and pursue a different strategy. Tying calls for American retrenchment to calls for allies and partners to do more is therefore a recipe for strategic disaster.

MAXIMIZING US ENGAGEMENT AND INFLUENCE

For the United States, its allies and partners in the Indo-Pacific are essential to its regional power and access. Although some provide operational bases for the US military, all (in varying ways) provide entry points for the United States to influence the region, shape the decisions of its leaders, and promote its interests and values across a region of critical geopolitical significance.

A key, though often overlooked, strategic advantage for the United States in the Indo-Pacific is that the United States and its allies and partners share many of the same objectives. Though priorities and goals are not uniform across the region, several states (and especially US allies and partners) perceive American power, and the regional order it sustains, as tremendously beneficial to their own interests and ambitions. All seek to avoid conflict, and most enjoy the economic benefits of integration and access to global commons, though the different nature of the region's political regimes means that the embrace of political and economic liberalism is not held universally. This means that empowering US allies and partners would be a net benefit for the strength of the regional liberal order and for the advancement of US interests.

US initiatives toward allies and partners must therefore focus not on simply sustaining and expanding American power, but rather on maximizing US engagement and influence in the region and pursing a common strategy based on shared interests and objectives. This will require an expanded understanding of the nature of alliances and partnerships, and greater ambitions about the role they can play in contributing to the region's liberal order—even if they do so out of their own self-interest.

ALLIANCES AS A COMPREHENSIVE PLATFORM FOR COOPERATION

A broader and more ambitious approach to alliances and partnerships in the Indo-Pacific will help ensure the health and success of the region's liberal order while simultaneously enhancing the ability of the United States to compete in the more complex Asian heterarchy described in the previous chapter. If accompanied by efforts to enhance US unilateral power and influence in the region, a strategy to empower America's Asian allies and partners will greatly buttress the liberal regional order and help preserve stability and prosperity across the region.

Most fundamentally, the United States should no longer see alliances as essentially military in nature, with a focus on deterrence. Instead, the United States should transform these relationships in to platforms for cooperation and collaboration across all elements of national power.[68] Although the military component of alliances will remain vital in an increasingly competitive strategic environment, the United States should ensure that diplomatic and economic engagement with its allies and partners is pursued just as vigorously.

The United States made great strides in enhancing its diplomatic engagement with the region under the Obama administration. For example, acceding to the Treaty of Amity and Cooperation in Southeast Asia in 2009 paved the way for US participation in the East Asia Summit in 2010 and enabled enhanced engagement with ASEAN. This was followed by a greatly accelerated pace of top-level engagements, with heads of state from across the Indo-Pacific visiting the United States, and vice versa, at an unprecedented pace. Under the Obama administration, heads of state of ASEAN member nations visited the United States for summits and official, working, and state visits thirty times, as compared with the twenty-one visits made under the George W. Bush administration. During President Trump's first year in office, ASEAN officials made four visits.[69] In turn, whereas President Bush made three trips to the region, President Obama traveled to Southeast Asia nine times and added Malaysia, Myanmar, Cambodia, and Laos to the list of ASEAN countries that Bush had visited.[70] To date, President Trump has made one trip to the region.[71]

Through these engagements, the United States empowered its allies and partners to assert their own interests and, at times, push back against Chinese assertiveness. Whereas the smaller nations in the Indo-Pacific had previously gone along with Chinese efforts to paper over regional disputes during multinational forums, the sustained and high-level pace of US engagements allowed the region to push back. This dynamic was evident in the 2015 assembly of the ASEAN Defence Ministers' Meeting–Plus, in which the various nations refused to agree to Chinese demands for a joint statement that ignored the very evident regional tensions stemming from China's actions in the South China Sea.[72] Although many saw a failure to issue a joint statement as a failure of regional diplomacy, it was actually a success for the United States and its allies, demonstrating that with steady and focused engagement by the United States, China would not be able to dictate the terms of regional diplomacy.

Of course, sustained and high-level diplomacy requires continued engagement for several years across successive US administrations, which is no small feat. Sustaining this engagement by the Trump administration, and its successors, will be essential to the future success of US strategy in the Indo-Pacific. Yet, as difficult as this will be, it is not the most challenging aspect of US Indo-Pacific strategy. That distinction belongs to the economic realm.

ROBUST ECONOMIC ENGAGEMENT

Economic engagement with the world is fundamentally connected with geopolitics. Yet, lately, domestic debates about foreign economic engagement have focused on domestic political implications. Arguments that the vigorous pursuit of economic engagement with the world is critical to sustaining America's place as the dominant global power have lost to a focus on the implications of such agreements for jobs at home. This is how the two leading candidates in the 2016 presidential election both announced their opposition to the Trans-Pacific Partnership, even though top experts from both Democratic and Republican foreign policy circles highlighted the criticality of the TPP for America's continued leadership in the Indo-Pacific.[73]

Instead of the TPP, the Trump administration has stated a preference for bilateral trade agreements, which, it argues, will achieve the same geopolitical effects of the TPP without sacrificing critical American economic interests.[74] Although this argument is questionable, what is clear is that when it comes to bilateral trade agreements in the Indo-Pacific, more is better.

The United States should therefore vigorously pursue robust economic agreements with its allies and partners in the Indo-Pacific. Beyond the economic imperatives of such agreements, there is a compelling geopolitical argument for them as well. By finalizing a swath of bilateral economic agreements with its allies and partners, the United States will have a much greater say in the economic dynamics of the world's most economically critical region. Moreover, such engagement will demonstrate to its allies and partners that the United States has skin in the game, which will do more to strengthen perceptions of US commitment and resolve than any number of talking points and, even in peacetime, military deployments.

Beyond agreements related to trade and investment, the United States should invest more in development assistance for its less-developed allies and partners. For its allies and partners to have the ability to successfully govern themselves and defend their interests, many require significant assistance in the development of their economies. Moreover, economic development has emerged as a critical front in China's geopolitical competition with the United States, as Beijing has poured billions of dollars into development assistance across the Indo-Pacific.

The Trump administration has emphasized private-sector initiatives as the primary focus of its regional economic strategy. In July 2018, Secretary of State Mike Pompeo stated that "American companies have been a force for prosperity and good throughout the Indo-Pacific region," and he announced $113 million in new US initiatives to support foundational areas of the future: the digital economy, energy, and infrastructure. He described these funds as "just a down payment on a new era in US economic commitment to peace and prosperity in the Indo-Pacific region."[75] Although certainly a modest amount when compared with the hundreds of billions of dollars in infrastructure projects announced by Beijing, recognition that Washington needed to do more in this area was welcome, and hopes are high that these policies will pave the way for significant US investment and focus.

Yet more needs to be done. Although the private sector is certainly an area of significant comparative advantage for the United States, in order to compete with China in the geo-economic realm, the US government's structural inability to direct these investments toward geopolitical ends or to coordinate them with similar allied efforts will make such efforts less effective and less efficient than would broader trade agreements.

In October 2018, President Trump signed the Better Utilization of Investments Leading to Development—BUILD—Act, which seeks to better utilize private-sector funding for development. It established the US International Development Finance Corporation (DFC), through which the United States can make loans and limited equity investments, allowing the DFC to better form partnerships with allies and partners for greater development impact. The BUILD Act established the total investment limitation for the DFC at $60 billion, and empowered it to provide technical assistance and conduct feasibility studies specific to development finance projects.[76] Though certainly a promising initiative, the government will be challenged to ensure that development initiatives are allocated and directed in a way that supports broader national interests. Indeed, though the private sector should rightly retain the ability to make decisions based on specific business calculations, the US government should develop the ability to set geopolitical objectives as it enables enhanced private-sector engagement.

ENHANCING GOVERNANCE AND FIGHTING CORRUPTION

Ineffective and insufficient governance has been a longtime inhibitor of the ability of several US allies and partners to stabilize, grow prosperous, and build national power. A critical aspect of governance deficiencies has been corruption, which is endemic across much of the Indo-Pacific. According to Transparency International, New Zealand and Singapore are among the least corrupt countries in the world, while the Philippines and India "score high for corruption and have fewer press freedoms and higher numbers of journalist deaths."[77]

Corruption not only depresses the effectiveness of governance; it also represents an opportunity for Beijing to exert outsized influence. This is especially problematic within the smaller countries in the Indo-Pacific, for which Chinese investment has represented an increasingly significant source of capital. For these countries, the concern is less about Chinese government interference and more focused on the corruption that often accompanies Chinese investment.[78] Initiatives to fight corruption and enhance governance across the Indo-Pacific will therefore be essential both to empower US allies and partners and to shape China's influence across the region.

A critical aspect of any effort to improve governance across the Indo-Pacific will involve efforts to counter China's efforts to interfere in the domestic politics of its neighbors. Beijing's efforts are supplemented by its efforts to export a high-tech version of political illiberalism, which it hopes will both sustain nondemocratic governments and serve as a pathway for enhanced Chinese political influence. As described earlier in this book, this is a challenge that affects the entire region—and especially US allies and partners. Inoculating democratic systems from Chinese interference efforts, therefore, should be a shared objective for the United States and its democratic allies and partners across the Indo-Pacific. As such, the United States should take the lead in establishing a mechanism to share information, defend democratic political processes, protect and promote freedom in both the real world and in the digital domain, and sustain liberal ideals of freedom and openness while also avoiding policies that lead to discrimination against immigrants from China or people of Chinese descent.[79]

ENHANCING MILITARY CAPABILITIES AND PRESENCE

Even without significant efforts by the United States, its allies and partners in the Indo-Pacific have already begun to strengthen their military capabilities in what has become a modest form of a regional arms race.[80] In the Indo-Pacific, US allies and partners increased their military expenditures by 30 percent between 2007 and 2016 (figure 3.1).[81] Yet the pace of expansion did not keep up with Beijing; during the same decade, China's military spending is estimated to have more than doubled (figure 3.2)—resulting in a sizable imbalance of power.[82]

The United States and its allies and partners retain the advantages provided by interoperability among their forces, which train and exercise together regularly, but China's expanding numbers and its close geography require the United States to address this imbalance of power. Efforts to date, though certainly laudable, have been too piecemeal and too small in scale to have a significant impact on the maritime balance of power. The Obama administration pursued this

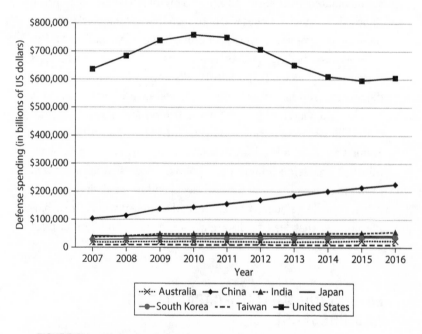

FIGURE 3.1 Defense spending in the Asia-Pacific region, 2007–16

Note: The defense budget is calculated in constant 2015 US dollars.

SOURCE: STOCKHOLM INTERNATIONAL MILITARY RESEARCH INSTITUTE, "MILITARY EXPENDITURE DATABASE," HTTPS://WWW.SIPRI.ORG/DATABASES/MILEX.

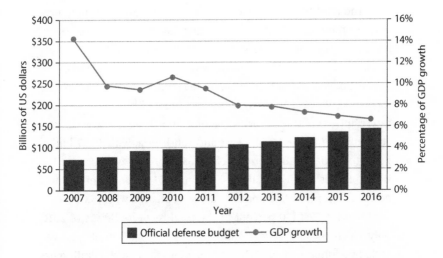

FIGURE 3.2   China's official defense budget in billions of US dollars (adjusted for inflation), 2007–16

SOURCE: US DEPARTMENT OF DEFENSE, "MILITARY AND SECURITY DEVELOPMENTS INVOLVING THE PEOPLE'S REPUBLIC OF CHINA 2017," HTTPS://WWW.DEFENSE .GOV/PORTALS/1/DOCUMENTS/PUBS/2017_CHINA_MILITARY_POWER_REPORT.PDF.

objective through several initiatives, including with a series of free-dom-of-navigation operations and allocating more than $250 million over FYs 2015 and 2016 toward building maritime capacity in Southeast Asia.[83] Additionally, the Department of Defense began to implement the Southeast Asia Maritime Security Initiative, which allocated $425 million to train, equip, supply, and conduct small-scale construction in cooperation with Indonesia, Malaysia, the Philippines, Thailand, and Vietnam.[84] Unfortunately, such efforts were insufficient to substantially change the Asian balance of power.

STRENGTHENING AND REFORMING SECURITY ASSISTANCE

A large, focused, and sustained initiative from Washington to responsibly build the capabilities of its allies and partners is sorely needed. US allies and partners in Asia would benefit tremendously from the kind of military support that Washington routinely provides in the Middle East. Reprioritizing Asia to receive a more significant percentage of US defense assistance would be extremely valuable in bolstering the capabilities of US allies and partners.

The Obama administration requested minimal security assistance for Asia in its FY 2017 budget, as compared with other areas. The top recipients of US security assistance in that request were largely concentrated in the Middle East and South Asia, with $3.67 billion going to Afghanistan.[85] In 2015, of the $5.64 billion requested for the United States' Foreign Military Financing (FMF), $67.4 million was designated for East Asia and the Pacific, compared with $5.09 billion for the Near East (90 percent of the total requested).[86] As of 2016, only 1 percent of FMF was annually sent to Asian countries, even including funding given to Indonesia, Vietnam, and the Philippines as part of the Maritime Security Initiative.[87] This trend continued into the Trump administration; as part of reforms to the FMF program included in its FY 2018 budget, the administration proposed a reduction in grants of $1 billion, with the exception of the top three recipients—Israel, Egypt, and Jordan—which constitute 93 percent of the overall budget for FY 2018.[88] The administration also put forward a shift of remaining foreign military assistance to both a $200 million FMF "global fund" and other loans in order to reduce costs.[89]

Some have argued that this change would push some countries to shift their weapons purchases to Russia or China, which offer less expensive options.[90] Indeed, some US allies have grown so frustrated with attempts to acquire military drones from the United States that they have already turned to China.[91] For its part, Taiwan has also begun to look beyond the United States in its efforts to acquire affordable and effective military capabilities.[92]

Secretary Pompeo's August 2018 announcement of plans to provide nearly $300 million in FMF to Asia suggests that the tide may be turning.[93] The United States should also consider conducting more of its foreign military assistance in the form of grants rather than loans. This would greatly help many countries in Southeast Asia, especially those with fewer resources to devote to defense.

In addition to adjusting how funds are allocated, the United States will also need to reform its overall security assistance programs. The current US system is excessively bureaucratic and legalistic, and is not nearly responsive or strategic enough for the demands of the twenty-first century. Within the State Department, the roles of two separate entities in planning and decisionmaking—the Bureau of Political-Military Affairs and the Office of US Foreign Assistance Resources, respectively—as well as the involvement of regional and functional bureaus in deciding on the allocation of funds, have led to a disjointed, confusing process with no clear leader.[94] Legal constraints on State Department security assistance include Section 660 of the Foreign Assistance Act of 1961, which prevents security assistance from being used to equip, train, or advise law enforcement forces.[95] FMF funds are also specifically prohibited from going to nonmilitary entities within the governments of military partners, constraining the United States' ability to assist in sectors like cybersecurity.[96]

Central to reforming these security assistance programs will be enhancing the ability of the United States to provide its allies and partners with affordable, reliable, and effective drones. Such capabilities are essential in Southeast Asia, where countries with limited resources but significant swaths of sea to monitor would greatly benefit from such capabilities. Despite this reality, the United States continues to classify drones as missiles rather than as aircraft, severely limiting what US allies and partners are able to acquire. In the past, the United States followed the strict guidelines of the Missile Technology Control Regime (MTCR), which pushed some partners to instead purchase drones from countries like China, depriving the United States of opportunities to deepen relationships with them and shape global norms regarding unmanned aerial vehicles.[97] The MTCR, though a valuable aspect of international arms control, has yet to adapt to the reality that drones are fundamentally different from cruise missiles, and should be treated as such.[98]

In April 2018, the Trump administration announced new rules that would somewhat relax US export controls on drones; these rules allowed some drones to be sold through the direct commercial sales process (a far more rapid process than the foreign military sales process), and reclassified drones with strike-enabling technology as unarmed, which will make export easier. Moreover, the Trump administration was reportedly considering proposing changes to the MTCR itself, to no longer classify drones as cruise missiles.[99] As with other types of weaponry, the United States and the rest of the international community will need to find a way to balance military necessities against counterproliferation objectives. Drawing a line between unarmed and armed drones seems to be a workable way forward, especially in the Indo-Pacific, where most US allies and partners (especially in Southeast Asia) primarily need unarmed drones for intelligence, surveillance, and reconnaissance missions.

There are other authorities that could be adjusted to better position the United States to build the capabilities of its allies and partners. The current division of foreign military assistance authorities between Title 22 funds (State Department) and Title 10 funds (Defense Department) means that foreign assistance often reflects the culture and priorities of the department providing the assistance, resulting in a stovepiped approach that raises inefficiency and limits the effectiveness of these efforts.[100] Centralizing these authorities, and placing them under a single department that can make decisions about prioritization and military need, would go a long way toward fixing what has become a highly bureaucratic process that can be slow to recognize changes in American strategy or the geopolitical environment.

Similarly, the US government should follow through on longstanding pledges to accelerate FMF and foreign military sales. Although significant progress has been made in recent years, more needs to be done to make processes more efficient, less bureaucratic, and more responsive to the needs of US allies and partners. This is not just a Pentagon issue—Congress and the State Department both have roles to play, and should work together to develop a more efficient and streamlined process.

America's allies and partners, especially those in Southeast Asia with significant maritime security challenges but limited resources, should be prioritized in the US Excess Defense Articles program, in which US military and coast guard platforms are offered at reduced or no cost in support of US national security and foreign policy objectives. Moreover, the US government should encourage US defense companies, and those of its more advanced allies around the world, to develop effective, sustainable, and affordable platforms that could be used by US allies and partners to enhance maritime security.

These efforts should be focused and calculated, however, to ensure that such capabilities actually contribute to the needs of US allies and partners and respond to the challenges they face. The United States should therefore focus on two areas where military assistance would be of greatest benefit to its Indo-Pacific allies and partners: maritime security and missile defense.

BUTTRESSING REGIONAL MARITIME SECURITY CAPABILITIES

The bulk of competition in Asia will take place in international waters. Unlike Europe and the vast plains of Central and Eastern Europe that beguiled American and Soviet military planners for generations, the major powers of Asia are predominantly divided by water. Thus, maritime power has become the sine qua non of military capability in the Indo-Pacific.

This arms race is leading to a significant imbalance in Asian maritime forces, with Beijing gaining the upper hand. China has the ability to flood a zone with fishing vessels, coast guard ships, and naval vessels to a degree that no ally or partner can match, despite advantages the latter may enjoy due to geographic proximity. Before 2012, it is estimated that Japan invested slightly more than China in its coast guard. Since then, Beijing has made a heavy investment and outspent Tokyo in 2015 by $500 million.[101] In the meantime, China has also rapidly increased its naval forces. According to the Department of Defense's estimate, China has deployed forty-six more ships in the past six years.[102] During the same period, Japan has decreased the number of its naval forces but increased their displacement by 28,000 tons. The US Seventh Fleet has deployed an additional ten ships, for a total of thirty, in Japan and Guam since 2016.[103] Most of the US Pacific Fleet's assets are deployed in the Eastern Pacific, which is managed by the Third Fleet, and would take much longer to reach the area in the event of a conflict (figure 3.3).

An example of how this dynamic has evolved can be seen in the dispute between China and Japan over the Senkaku/Diaoyu Islands, which lie some 80 nautical miles north of Japan's Yamayoe Islands in the Okinawa Prefecture, 90 nautical miles northeast of Taiwan, and 200 nautical miles east of China's Fujian Province. Although China is farthest from the island group, it has demonstrated its capacity to mobilize overwhelming numbers of government and fishing vessels to the area, while using its air force to pose a simultaneous threat from above.[104]

China's expanding maritime advantage in relation to its neighbors has fueled intensified tensions around its periphery. In addition to

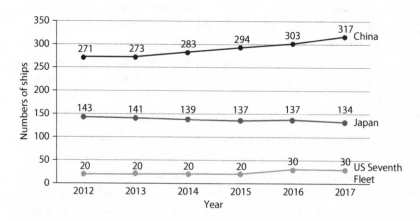

FIGURE 3.3 The naval balance in East Asia, 2012–17

SOURCE: DAVID LAGUE AND BENJAMIN KANG LIM, "RULING THE WAVES," *REUTERS*, APRIL 30, 2019, HTTPS://WWW.REUTERS.COM/INVESTIGATES /SPECIAL-REPORT/CHINA-ARMY-NAVY/.

the dispute in the East China Sea described above, China has greatly expanded its maritime presence in the South China Sea, where its claims overlap those of five other governments. And the size and capabilities of these other claimants pale in comparison with China's. Figure 3.4 shows the size of Chinese and some Southeast Asian naval forces, as documented by the International Institute for Strategic Studies.

These disparities have enabled China to profoundly change East Asia's geopolitics, and even the physical landscape of the South China Sea. As noted in the previous chapter, in December 2013, China began reclaiming land to build up the features under its control. By June 2015, it had reclaimed over 2,900 acres in the Spratlys—"17 times more land in 20 months than the other claimants combined over the past 40 years, accounting for approximately 95 percent of all reclaimed land in the Spratly Islands."[105] In March 2017, the United States estimated that China had reclaimed 3,200 acres on seven former rocky outcrops and reefs in the previous three years—more than ten times the size of the National Mall in Washington—creating major military edifices on that land.[106] According to the Department of Defense's 2017 "China Military Report," China has built three airfields on the Mischief Reef, Subi Reef, and Fiery Cross Reef, as well as one port facility on each of the seven occupied land features.

Washington should therefore dramatically expand its efforts to provide its Indo-Pacific allies and partners with maritime capabilities, including building regional coast guards and developing a regional maritime domain awareness network. Although there may be a lack of political will in Washington to make this happen, allies like Canberra and Tokyo should be consulted to assist and supplement these initiatives—potentially to the point of concluding a trilateral memorandum of understanding to formalize alliance collaboration toward these ends.

In pursuing this objective, the United States and its more advanced allies and partners will be confronted with the realities that many Southeast Asian partners lack the resources to

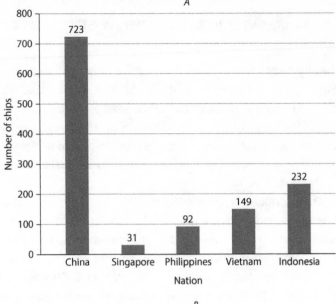

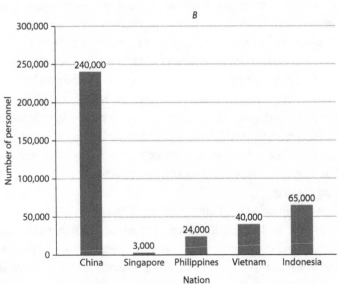

FIGURE 3.4 Comparisons of (A) naval ships and (B) personnel, 2018

Note: The International Institute for Strategic Studies includes small coastal patrol boats, landing craft, and logistics and support ships in its report. This explains why the number of Chinese naval ships documented is lower in the US Department of Defense annual report. Using different data here is for the purpose of unity, as the International Institute for Strategic Studies has a comprehensive investigation of Southeast Asian naval forces.

SOURCE: INTERNATIONAL INSTITUTE FOR STRATEGIC STUDIES, "THE MILITARY BALANCE 2018," FEBRUARY 14, 2018, HTTPS://WWW.IISS.ORG/EN/PUBLICATIONS /MILITARY PERCENT20BALANCE/ISSUES/THE-MILITARY-BALANCE-2018-545F.

adequately fund such initiatives, and may otherwise be focused on internal security challenges that distract from those presented by China.[107] Such challenges are normal in Southeast Asia, yet can be addressed—though not entirely overcome—with sufficient financial assistance and persistent diplomacy to encourage Southeast Asian partners to appreciate the challenges and opportunities involved.

BUILDING REGIONAL COAST GUARDS

Through its rampant use of Chinese Coast Guard (CCG) vessels to assert its maritime claims in the East China Sea and South China Sea, China has radically transformed the role of coast guards in East Asia. Traditionally used to fight narcotrafficking and maritime population flows, coast guards today are at the vanguard of interstate tensions across East Asia. States have made coast guards the tool of choice for asserting their maritime claims for two reasons: they are generally seen as a less aggressive tool than traditional navies, and their use demonstrates the view that the area in question is not in international waters—the traditional domain of navies—but is in domestic waters, and is therefore subject to domestic civilian jurisdiction.

The RAND Corporation's Lyle Morris conducted a thorough study on the evolution of East Asian coast guards and found that several East Asian nations have vastly increased the size of their coast guard fleets in recent years, with China leading the way with the largest coast guard in the world, at an estimated 190,000 tons of ship power (table 3.1).[108] Other countries have also greatly expanded the sizes of their fleets, though not on a scale comparable to China.

The sophistication of coast guard vessels has also increased in recent years. Chinese Coast Guard ships are typically larger and more capable than their East Asian counterparts, often because many of the CCG vessels were formerly part of the People's Liberation Army Navy and had been painted white and transferred to the CCG.[109]

TABLE 3.1 TOTAL COAST GUARD TONNAGE INCREASES OF SELECTED COUNTRIES IN EAST ASIA AND SOUTHEAST ASIA, 2010–16

COUNTRY	TOTAL TONNAGE, 2010	ESTIMATED ADDED TONNAGE, 2010–16	TOTAL TONNAGE, 2016	TOTAL PERCENTAGE INCREASE
China	110,000	80,000	190,000	73
Japan	70,500	35,000	105,500	50
Vietnam	20,500	15,000	35,500	73
Philippines	10,000	10,000	20,000	100

SOURCE: LYLE J. MORRIS, "BLUNT DEFENDERS OF SOVEREIGNTY: THE RISE OF COAST GUARDS OF EAST AND SOUTHEAST ASIA," *NAVAL WAR COLLEGE REVIEW* 70, NO. 2 (2017): 75–112, AT 78, HTTPS://USNWC2.USNWC.EDU/GETATTACHMENT /EAA0678E-83A0-4C67-8AAB-0F829D7A2B27/BLUNT-DEFENDERS-OF-SOVEREIGNTY —-THE-RISE-OF-COAST.ASPX: "AUTHOR ESTIMATES BASED ON OPEN-SOURCE MEDIA REPORTING AND ON US NAVY, *THE PLA NAVY*, P. 45."

Note: As Lyle J. Morris explains in the source given above, "Estimated added tonnage column takes into account vessels that are either under construction or anticipated to be delivered by the end of 2016. China's coast guard calculations do not include vessels from the MSA, which is not considered part of China's reformed coast guard fleet and typically does not patrol disputed areas in the East and South China Seas. Vietnam's coast guard calculations do not include vessels from the VFSF, VINAMARINE, or the VBG. The Philippine Coast Guard calculations do not include vessels from the PNP-MG, Customs, or the BFAR. Overall estimates of total tonnage are rough approximations of the total capacity and are meant for illustrative purposes only."

Despite their best efforts, US allies and partners have not been able to keep up with the rapid expansion of CCG capabilities. They need America's help, and Washington should answer the call by greatly expanding its efforts to build the coast guards of its allies and partners, especially in Southeast Asia. This should include provisioning ships and support craft, as well as providing the training and support that are necessary to sustain such a capability over the long term.

DEVELOPING A REGIONAL MARITIME DOMAIN AWARENESS NETWORK

A critical gap in the capabilities of many US allies and partners, especially in South and Southeast Asia, lies in maritime domain awareness. Their radar installations and other surveillance capabilities are so limited that they often have no idea what is happening in their immediate vicinity. This gap was clearly demonstrated after the 2014 disappearance of Malaysia Airlines Flight 370, when several countries grudgingly admitted that their radar coverage did not cover significant swaths of airspace.

More directly, several Southeast Asian officials related to me in 2014 that their maritime domain awareness capabilities were spotty, unreliable, and highly vulnerable to the seasonal monsoons that sweep through the region. In fact, one official stated that it was often the case that, after they got their limited radar capabilities up and running after a monsoon, it sometimes took them *months* before realizing that Chinese forces had significantly shifted their position and disposition without their knowledge.

Critical to building maritime security for US allies and partners will be building their ability to understand what is happening in their immediate vicinities. This will require strengthening their command, control, communications, computers, intelligence, surveillance, and reconnaissance capabilities, largely by establishing new information sharing centers and infrastructure, as well as providing sea- and air-based collection platforms.

The United States should also establish a network for allies and partners to share information they collect through a common operating picture available to all participants, specifically in the form of a maritime domain awareness network. The United States is uniquely positioned to broker such a network. It is not party to any of the intraregional rivalries and disputes that roil the region, and it shares the basic interests of its allies and partners in maintaining regional stability and checking Chinese assertiveness and expansionism. The United States should therefore establish a network system in which members provide their maritime domain awareness information to a central location where information is sanitized and distributed to all members. This would require the establishment of multiple information-sharing agreements that address the security concerns of partners, the procurement and distribution of hardware and software to enable the collection and distribution of information, and the establishment of criteria that would allow allies and partners to join and participate.

Such a network could help build cooperation and trust between allies and partners, establish patterns of cooperation, and enable the United States to push its diplomatic priorities. For example, participation in the network could be contingent on the member country recognizing the UN Convention on the Law of the Seas and the 2016 arbitral tribunal ruling on disputes in the South China Sea. This would help establish the legal and diplomatic foundation for such a network and contribute to the more esoteric objective of maintaining critical aspects of the liberal order, such as the rule of law and the peaceful resolution of disputes.

EXPANDING MISSILE DEFENSE

Both China and North Korea present significant missile threats to US allies and partners that, in the case of North Korea, also entail the potential use of chemical or biological weapons. The February 2017 assassination of Kim Jong-un's half-brother, Kim Jong-nam, in Kuala Lumpur International Airport with VX nerve agent thrust North Korea's stockpile of chemical weapons back into the spotlight.[110] North Korea also appears to be investing in education in microbiology, as well as factories, equipment, and laboratories that could be used to launch an advanced biological weapons program. *Asahi Shimbun* reported in December 2017 that North Korea has begun test loading anthrax onto intercontinental ballistic missiles.[111]

The United States, as well as its allies and partners, have the absolute right to defend themselves from such threats. Ballistic missiles not only threaten their civilian populations; they also threaten the ability of US and allied military forces to effectively respond to armed aggression. Although cost and effectiveness are certainly issues to consider, it is clear that theater-level ballistic missile defenses are a key component of any significant military capability in the Indo-Pacific.

The United States and its allies have already established a moderate missile defense presence in the region. Although the most prominent capability in recent years has been the deployment of the Terminal High-Altitude Area Defense missile system to the Korean Peninsula in 2017, the United States has also emplaced THAAD in Guam. There are Patriot and PAC-3 batteries in Japan, Taiwan, and South Korea, as well as the Aegis-equipped ships of the US Navy, the South Korean Navy, and the Japan Maritime Self-Defense Force that can identify incoming missiles and, in the case of the American and Japanese ships, attempt to shoot them down.

Yet much more should be done to enhance missile defense capabilities in the region. Japan is already considering acquiring THAAD or Aegis-ashore, either of which will be necessary to contribute to the defense of missile threats from North Korea and China and help free up Aegis-equipped destroyers to conduct other missions. The United States and its allies should look at other capabilities that could enhance missile defense, such as the introduction of additional Aegis-equipped ships to Japan and other places around the region, and—most important—enhance trilateral missile defense cooperation.

The United States, South Korea, and Japan made significant strides in improving trilateral missile defense cooperation in 2015 and 2016. In June 2016, the three countries participated in their first joint ballistic missile defense exercise, Pacific Dragon, off the coast of Hawaii. A second joint exercise was held in November of that year.[112] In 2017, four sets of trilateral missile defense drills were conducted in January, March, October, and December; the last of these drills focused on ballistic missile tracking and information sharing.[113]

Such cooperation was based on the fundamental judgment from all sides that information sharing and enhanced cooperation were necessary for the defense of Japan, South Korea, and the United

States. Networking in missile defense is critical, and more progress in this area must be made between the United States, South Korea, and Japan if they are to succeed in the face of significant ballistic missile threats.

ENHANCING ISLAND AND SHORE DEFENSES

Much of the military threat that China will pose to allies and partners in the Indo-Pacific will be maritime. Specifically, China's naval capabilities will threaten the security of islands and features that are administered by US allies and partners. Whether the threat be invasion or blockade, the threat of Chinese naval power must be addressed.

Specifically, the United States should provide selected allies and partners with survivable and affordable capabilities that would challenge China's ability to threaten the security of their islands and features. These capabilities could be in the form of mobile antiship cruise missiles, advanced mines, and other capabilities that would increase the risks of efforts by China to coerce and invade its neighbors. In this, other allies and partners could also have an important role to play in building the capabilities of other powers that face a threat from China's maritime power. Japan and Taiwan are especially well positioned to both enhance their island defense capabilities and to assist others in the development of their own capabilities.

Yet such an initiative should be pursued cautiously. The irresponsible proliferation of these capabilities could have a deleterious effect to regional stability and the freedom and openness of maritime commons. After all, once the capabilities are in hand, there would be nothing to stop an irresponsible ally or partner from using these capabilities offensively. Because the United States has no interest in triggering an arms race, the provision of such advanced capabilities should only come after thorough assurances have been made that these capabilities will only be used defensively and will not be proliferated. Moreover, the United States should insist that allies and partners seeking to receive these capabilities first affirm that they share US interpretations of international law, and demonstrate such a commitment with policies, activities, and confidence-building measures. Finally, the United States should reserve the option to regain control of these capabilities if they are found to have been used offensively or in ways incompatible with international law.

COORDINATING WITH ALLIES AND PARTNERS

Across all elements of military power, the United States should emphasize establishing mechanisms and habits of cooperation and coordination between its allies and partners. Brokering stronger partnerships between allies and partners, specifically focusing on expanding the relationship between Seoul and Tokyo, should continue to be a priority for Washington. Additionally, enhancing cooperation in missile defense and interoperability among the defense industries could better position regional partners to pursue meaningful cooperative and security measures throughout the region.

Missile defense cooperation between the United States, Japan, and South Korea is an example of how allies and partners can contribute to one another's security. Although enthusiasm for expanded trilateral cooperation in missile defense has stalled as the political relationship between Seoul and Tokyo has soured, military cooperation has remained somewhat inoculated from these vicissitudes. Reviving enthusiasm in trilateral missile defense cooperation should be a priority for Washington, as should be the reduction in tension between Tokyo and Seoul. This would give political space for expanded ambition in trilateral missile defense cooperation, which has tremendous potential to enhance the security of all involved. Information sharing, joint exercises, and (eventually) collective self-defense against North Korean ballistic missiles may be possible.

Enhancing cooperation between the defense industries of the United States, India, Japan, South Korea, and Australia could also help build the capabilities of other allies and partners. By prioritizing joint research and development for commonly shared defense interests—such as unmanned systems, artificial intelligence, and directed energy capabilities—there is a significant opportunity to enhance interoperability and integration while sharing costs. New mechanisms and policies would need to be established, and industrial security practices would need to be significantly strengthened. Yet the potential for shared gain in this area is significant and should be considered.

Due to their own advanced indigenous defense industries, India, Japan, Australia, and South Korea all have a unique opportunity to empower other allies and friends and contribute to the long-term success of the liberal order. Indeed, these allies and partners may in some ways be better positioned than the United States to build the capabilities of other Asian allies and partners. This is because their defense industries produce high-quality, yet affordable, military capabilities that are better suited to the limited requirements and resources of many of those in South and Southeast Asia. South Korea exported $3.19 billion in weapons in 2017, a 25 percent increase from 2016. This included the sale of eight Korea Aerospace Industries Golden Eagle advanced jet trainer aircraft to Thailand.[114] The appeal of Korean military hardware has been attributed to quality, reasonable costs, and the lack of "negative geopolitical strings" compared with countries like Russia and China.[115] Japan lifted its ban on defense exports in 2014 and began to offer financial aid to buyers, making purchases by developing countries more affordable.[116] India is also playing a larger role in providing military capabilities to like-minded nations—for example, by establishing a far more robust defense relationship with Vietnam.[117] Australia also seeks to become a top ten defense exporter by 2030.[118]

The United States, India, Japan, South Korea, and Australia should therefore establish a security assistance coordination mechanism, with the defense establishments of each side ensuring that their national policies toward security assistance in the Indo-Pacific work toward shared geopolitical ends and enhance the interoperability of US military forces with their Indo-Pacific counterparts. This would not mean that their defense industries would not compete with one another; rather, it would ensure that the four allies are not working at cross-purposes.

However, coordinating between allies and partners will require more than establishing mechanisms in areas of mutual interest. Unfortunately, many US allies and partners across the Indo-Pacific have rather poor relations with one another. This is most obvious in the relationship between Japan and South Korea, where memories of horrible abuses under Japanese colonial rule continue to inflame anti-Japanese sentiments in many members of the South Korean public. In polling by the Pew Research Center, only 31 percent of the South Korean public reported a favorable view of Japan in 2017. Although this was an improvement over the 25 percent who reported the same in 2015, this share is still lower than those reported in other countries in the Indo-Pacific, ranging from 42 percent in India to 88 percent in Australia.[119]

South Korean president Park Geun-hye and Japanese prime minister Shinzo Abe demonstrated tremendous vision and political bravery in December 2015, when they announced a landmark agreement to resolve their dispute over Korean women who were forced to serve as sex slaves for Japan's Imperial Army. Japan issued an apology and promised $8.3 million in payments for the care of the women, and the two sides stated the agreement to be a "final and irreversible resolution" of the issue. Of course, such political agreements do not immediately dissipate the anger and suspicion that have built up for decades, and true reconciliation will take time.

Although the credit for such an agreement should go to the South Korean and Japanese leaders, the role of the United States in this situation should not be ignored. President Obama invested a great deal of his own political capital in advancing efforts toward reconciliation, which helped both sides overcome domestic political barriers.

Efforts to improve relations bore significant fruit during the Obama administration. Because of the political efforts on all sides, the United States, Japan, and South Korea were also able to make unprecedented progress in enhancing trilateral security cooperation in response to the common threat they faced from North

Korea. Most significantly, in November 2016, South Korean and Japanese officials signed the General Security of Military Information Agreement, enhancing trilateral cooperation by enabling the sharing of sensitive information on North Korean nuclear and missile development.[120]

Developments during the Trump administration have presented more challenges for the three countries. In October 2017, as part of negotiations with China over THAAD, South Korean foreign minister Kang Kyung-wha stated that it would not join any United States–led regional missile-defense system, accept any more THAAD batteries, or join in a trilateral military alliance with Japan and the United States.[121] In November, South Korea rejected Japanese involvement in joint military drills with the United States.[122] Bilateral tensions over historical issues reemerged, as President Moon Jae-in appointed a Special Task Force to reexamine Park and Abe's 2015 agreement to compensate Korean women forced into sexual slavery, which then publicly announced that the agreement was flawed.[123] This spurred protests from the Japanese government and reports that Prime Minister Abe might not attend the 2018 Winter Olympics.[124] Ultimately, however, Abe attended the opening ceremony in February, and the trilateral talks continued, including a meeting on the sidelines of the Foreign Ministers' Meeting on Security and Stability on the Korean Peninsula in January 2018.[125]

Yet since that time, relations between Japan and South Korea have deteriorated significantly. A series of incidents and government decisions have driven a wedge between Seoul and Tokyo, and precipitated a decision by Seoul to dissolve the General Security of Military Information Agreement. This is to be somewhat expected, as domestic politics in South Korea and Japan tend to repel one another. For decades, the two nations have been able to manage their differences because of two external forces: shared perceptions of a mutual external security threat and sustained, high-level encouragement from the United States. Yet both factors diminished beginning in 2017, with the Moon government deciding to engage rather than confront North Korea and the Trump administration refraining from playing a significant or sustained role in helping Seoul and Tokyo manage these issues.

Although the tension between South Korea and Japan is the most obvious example of animosity and suspicion between allies and partners, it is certainly not the only case. Rivalry and suspicion among Southeast Asian nations, for example, have a long history of complicating US efforts to build ASEAN cohesion and help the region act with coordination toward shared interests.[126] Additionally, tensions between Indonesia and Australia occasionally flare up over Canberra's policy toward migrant flows and other geopolitical issues.

The United States is the only power with the political capital and the strategic vision to drive reconciliation among its allies and partners and better unite them in a common cause—although in some instances the role for the United States may be limited. Washington should therefore continue to focus diplomatic and political efforts toward pressing its allies and partners in Asia to constructively address their differences or, failing that, to put such differences aside in order to cooperate on issues of much greater national interest.

MANAGING UNINTENDED CONSEQUENCES

Of course, there is an inherent danger in a strategy that builds the capabilities of allies and partners that, at times, have significant disputes with one another. Recall that the United States first established its alliances in East Asia in order to restrain, not empower. There is also the possibility that allies and partners could use their newfound capabilities to assert their own claims and undermine the liberal order, or to provoke a conflict that would entrap the United States in a conflagration it would prefer to avoid. Although diplomacy can certainly address such concerns, it would be incumbent on the United States to ensure that its efforts to build up the capabilities of its allies and partners are implemented responsibly.

A great deal can be done by limiting the capabilities provided by the United States to ensure they are primarily defensive in nature and of limited utility in an offensive campaign. Accomplishing this would be fairly simple in the realm of regional cooperation arrangements, which could be dissolved if concerns grew that they were being used for nefarious purposes. Other capabilities, such as missile defense systems and radar installations, are not threatening and should not worry other allies and partners.

The primary concern regarding enhancing the capabilities of allies and partners is the potential for recipients of US military assistance to combine such capabilities with offensive strike capabilities acquired from other sources. Such a "Frankenstein approach," though technically complicated, is certainly possible. Yet it is not created by the US effort to assist its allies and partners, but rather by a theoretical party offering to provide offensive systems. Such capabilities will be available regardless of US assistance, but close cooperation with allies and partners in the security sphere would provide the United States with greater access and influence over the actions of its allies and partners. In other words, enhancing cooperation with allies and partners will not solve the problem of conventional offensive weapons proliferation, but it could provide Washington with stronger tools to manage and address the threat.

The second potential unintended consequence of a strategy of ally empowerment is geopolitical: that such a strategy could be interpreted by US friends and adversaries alike as a cover for US decline and withdrawal. In this way, it would echo the Nixon Doctrine (in which the United States reiterated its commitment to provide extended nuclear deterrence to its allies but otherwise ceded primary responsibility for conventional defense to its allies, while promising military and economic assistance) and the disastrous reaction it generated across Asia. This is a valid concern, and US policymakers should be aware of these dynamics.

This potential problem would not apply to the strategy proposed here because, unlike with "Vietnamization," this strategy is not conceived as a rationalization for a general reduction in US military presence and engagement in the Indo-Pacific. On the contrary, this book recommends efforts to enhance the capabilities of US allies and partners while also strengthening US engagement and presence in the region in order to better account for the region's changing balance of power and its effects on the region's liberal order. Implementing a strategy of ally empowerment and US empowerment will send a strong signal to the region that the United States is doubling down in the region and is bringing its friends along.

EXPANDING ECONOMIC INTERCONNECTIVITY

As the Indo-Pacific has grown into the world's leading global engine for economic growth, trade and investment in the region have taken on increasingly critical geopolitical significance. Not only does economic connectivity between nations bring their people into more frequent contact with one another, it also facilitates the transfer of ideas and values and more deeply intertwines the fates of the countries involved. It would not be an overstatement to say that economic connectivity is as important to Asia in the twenty-first century as the military balance of power was in Europe during the Cold War.

Yet though the United States had previously enjoyed economic dominance in the Indo-Pacific, Asia's rise has gradually diminished the economic role of the United States in Asia. Overall, the Indo-Pacific region has a positive outlook and remains the leader of global growth. The Organization for Economic Cooperation and Development predicts that China's economic output and growth will continue to grow stronger in the coming years: growth in China was projected at 6.7 percent in 2017, 7.0 percent in 2018, and 6.4 percent in 2019; in comparison, growth in the United States was only projected at 2.2 percent in 2017, 2.5 in 2018, and 2.1 percent in 2019.[127] The economic outlook for ASEAN is particularly promising, with an expected growth average of 6.3 percent between 2018 and 2022.[128] In addition to the strong rate of economic growth, infrastructure projects, especially in ASEAN, could be a source of continued economic growth and dynamism throughout the region.

The United States has been slow to react to the changing geopolitical realities of the Indo-Pacific. Although it has concluded several high-quality free trade agreements with South Korea and other nations, it has failed to follow through on building multilateral economic initiatives that would increase its regional economic influence and tie it more closely to the region. Indeed, the Obama administration's inability to have the TPP ratified by Congress was its most significant geopolitical failure in the region, and the Trump administration's decision to abandon the agreement altogether greatly diminished the ability of the United States to engage the region in its most geopolitically critical arena.

This stands in sharp contrast to China. The Belt and Road Initiative (BRI) has become the central foreign policy concept of Chinese president Xi Jinping, and it seeks to incorporate networked infrastructure linking Europe, Africa, and Asia. BRI encompasses more than an economic corridor; instead, it seeks to utilize both people-to-people exchanges and monetary connectivity.[129] The Asian Infrastructure Investment Bank (AIIB), launched by China in January 2016, serves as a multilateral intergovernmental bank. The AIIB has been utilized by China to finance large-scale infrastructure development throughout Asia, often supporting projects central to Xi's BRI vision across the region. Fifty-seven participating nations were represented at the signing of the AIIB, which showcased Beijing's influence and vision to shape the economic and political order.

STRENGTHENING ECONOMIC INTEGRATION UNDER US LEADERSHIP

If the United States seeks to preserve a regional liberal order and successfully compete with a rising China, it will need to dramatically up its game in economic and trade policy toward the Indo-Pacific. Although reversing course and acceding to the TPP is the most obvious option available to the Trump administration, such a dramatic and significant reversal would, in itself, be insufficient. To truly enhance the ability of the United States to effectively engage the Indo-Pacific, Washington will need to get more creative and more ambitious in its economic and trade policies toward the region.

This would be especially true for US allies and partners, many of which are among the region's largest and most advanced economies. Most egregiously, the United States does not have a free trade agreement with India, Japan, or Taiwan. This is a tremendous strategic error, so significant political pressure should be brought to bear to jump-start negotiations and break long-standing hurdles to completing these agreements.

BUILDING PHYSICAL AND DIGITAL INFRASTRUCTURE

If economics is the lifeblood of the Indo-Pacific, infrastructure is its veins and arteries. Infrastructure facilitates trade and investment, empowers countries to trade more efficiently and effectively, and shapes the contours of regional economic integration. Moreover, demand for infrastructure in the Indo-Pacific has been expanding dramatically along with its economic development. For example, the Asian Development Bank estimates that infrastructure investment in ASEAN from 2016 through 2030 will be about $2.8 trillion. Yet an outside analysis found that the countries in ASEAN only have about 50 percent of the public-sector capital needed to finance all the required projects.[130] This represents not only a major challenge for the ASEAN member states but also a significant opportunity for the United States and its allies and other partners. By playing a larger role in shaping the infrastructure landscape of the Indo-Pacific, Washington has an opportunity to both enhance its ability to influence regional economic flows and to strengthen economic ties between the United States and the region (figure 3.5).

In this, the United States has a major strategic advantage: its allies and partners are already focused on building infrastructure around the region. For example, Tokyo and New Delhi have become major players in building infrastructure across the region in a way that both facilitates open trade while also competing with Beijing's ambitions for a more China-centric regional economic order. In countries like Burma and Thailand, India has contributed to efforts

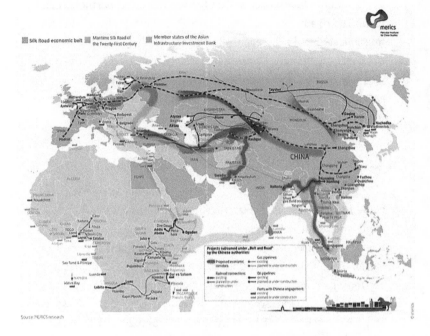

FIGURE 3.5 China's infrastructure projects for its Belt and Road Initiative

Note: The map shows projects planned and completed as of March 2017.

SOURCE: MERCATOR INSTITUTE FOR CHINESE STUDIES. USED BY PERMISSION.

to build infrastructure that facilitates greater East–West integration in Southeast Asia—in direct competition to China's efforts to foster North–South integration. Japan has also expanded its role in building East–West connectivity in Southeast Asia, and it has been investing heavily in infrastructure across the region to compete with China. For example, in January 2017, Prime Minister Shinzo Abe began a two-day trip to the Philippines by announcing an aid package worth $8.66 billion. The aid package comprised both public- and private-sector financing for a variety of development projects, specifically targeting projects supporting infrastructure development. Currently, Japan is backing a project that will bring the Makati-Pasay-Taguig Mass Transit System to metro Manila; the project is valued at $8 billion. In Indonesia, Japan is funding the Train III Project, Tangguh LNG [liquefied natural gas] Facility, and in Vietnam, Japanese investment is funding the Long Thanh International Airport project—all multi-billion-dollar endeavors.[131] Thus far, Japan has outspent China, $230 billion to $155 billion, in building Southeast Asian infrastructure.

However, China is quickly gaining ground on Japan as it increasingly competes to extend its influence. To combat China's growing footprint in the region, the United States, Japan, and India have launched several initiatives aimed at promoting alternatives to Chinese infrastructure development projects throughout the Indo-Pacific.[132] The US-based Overseas Private Investment Corporation (OPIC), the Japanese-based Nippon Export and Investment Insurance, and the Japan Bank for International Cooperation have provided grants and loans to help companies in South and Southeast Asia develop various infrastructure and development projects.[133] OPIC has also recently signed memoranda of understanding with Australia's Department of Foreign Affairs and Trade and the Association of Bilateral European Development Finance Institutions to establish greater cooperation on investments and development in emerging markets—clear signals that US allies and partners are already playing a greater role in economic statecraft.

Considering their geographic locations, Canberra, Tokyo, and Delhi (the so-called Quad) make natural partners for the United States in this endeavor, especially considering the tremendous demand for infrastructure construction in the region. Cooperation between India and Japan has been institutionalized in the so-called Asia–Africa Growth Corridor, which is a concept endorsed by prime ministers Abe and Modi in November 2016. It seeks to drive investment, construction, development assistance, and diplomatic engagements by both India and Japan across Asia and Africa—a clear, if implicit, challenge to China's Belt and Road Initiative.[134] Japan has also formed a partnership with India in the India-Japan Coordination Forum for Development of North East, in which Japanese firms are building infrastructure in India's Northeast—an area under increased geopolitical pressure from a rising China.

These developments are very much in the interests of the United States. They promote greater connectivity and cohesion under the principles of the rule of law and economic liberalism. The United States should support these efforts with the injection of capital, expertise, and cooperation from the US private sector. The Asia–Africa Growth Corridor represents an especially compelling avenue for US engagement across the region as part of the US Indo-Pacific strategy. Most critical, however, would be high-level encouragement from Washington to build and sustain momentum between Tokyo, New Delhi, Canberra; other key partners across the region; and potentially even Europe.

The United States should also broaden the aperture of its infrastructure engagement with the region by investing heavily in areas upon which the future economy will depend, notably digital infrastructure. As described by former deputy assistant secretary of state Nirav Patel, the United States will be best positioned to compete with China by advancing more ambitious technology in the region.[135] By establishing a fund—the Asia-Pacific Technology Fund (TAP-TF)—the United States would enable a diverse range of companies, private investors, and international financial institutions to create digital highways and develop technological infrastructure that enable greater economic connectivity between the United States and the rest of the Indo-Pacific. By working with other regional partners—such as the governments of Singapore, Japan, South Korea, and India, as well as the Asian Development Bank—Patel argues that the TAP-TF could focus on large-scale, national technology projects that support market goals for US companies that would otherwise have a difficult time competing against subsidized Chinese offerings. TAP-TF would also enable US companies and their partners to more effectively bid on large-scale projects that require government financing to offset risk, demonstrate a contemporary and forward-looking American economic strategy, ensure the promulgation of secure and safe technologies, and further advance regional connectivity and transparency. Secretary Pompeo's announcement about new investments in the digital economy,[136] and similar efforts by US allies and partners to enhance their funding of similar ventures—such as Taiwan's Digital Nation and Innovative Economic Development Plan (known as "DIGI+")—suggest that the framework for such an initiative may already be coalescing.

DEEPENING DIPLOMATIC COORDINATION

Alliances and partnerships should be conceived as relationships that go beyond military cooperation. Rather, these relationships should be thought of as platforms for diplomatic coordination across a range of issues of geopolitical significance. In the Indo-Pacific, this diplomatic coordination should cut across a wide variety of issues related to security, trade, environmental policy, and human rights. Yet, despite the multiplicity of issues involved, the purpose of these engagements would remain consistent: advancing the national interests of the United States and its allies and partners, strengthening the regional liberal order, and promoting economic and political liberalism.

Security issues are about far more than military maneuvers and calculations. Indeed, adroit diplomacy is the most important aspect of any security policy—both as a tool to advance interests and as a means to avoid and defuse tension before disagreements explode into conflict. The United States could benefit from closer diplomatic coordination with its allies and partners across a wide range of issues, including on maritime security, in space, and in promoting liberal values in the digital domain.

With respect to maritime security, in 2016, an international tribunal dramatically criticized China for its actions in the South China Sea, including its construction of artificial islands, and found that its expansive claim to sovereignty over the waters had no legal basis.[137] Although this should have been a stunning rebuke to Beijing's ambitions, it was not. This was because the United States decided not to emphasize the decision, primarily in hopes of alienating the newly elected president of the Philippines, Rodrigo Duterte. Yet while Duterte has leaned closer to Beijing anyway, Washington has to date refrained from emphasizing this ruling in its diplomatic approach to the South China Sea. The ruling of the international tribunal on the South China Sea represents an untapped opportunity for the United States. This ruling could be used as a basis not only for a legal offensive by the United States but also as a foundation for a diplomatic offensive by its allies and partners in the South China Sea and beyond. By emphasizing the decision as the legal rationale for a range of actions, the United States could both strengthen its influence in the region while also enhancing the relevance and power of international law in peacefully addressing disputes.

Regarding space, considering its significance for the global economy, they have remained relatively free of international laws. Indeed, the last (and only) major international law governing the general use of space was the Outer Space Treaty, which entered into force in 1967.[138] Yet the number of states that have the ability to use space has expanded dramatically since then, and the technologies available in space have grown astronomically more sophisticated. Indeed, space is becoming increasingly congested and contested, even as it has become more essential to the global economy.[139] These issues have particular salience in Asia as a result of the significance of this domain for the regional economy, and because the region's major powers are also increasingly major space powers. Although only three countries have the capability to support human space flight—the United States, China, and Russia—many Indo-Pacific countries rely on the capacity of major powers' space programs to host satellite communications that support space assets, intelligence gathering, domain awareness, and other important communication functions. China is increasingly developing advanced capabilities to operate in space and hamper adversaries' free and open use of space in crisis or conflict scenarios, signaling a need to adopt a multilateral approach with cooperative agreements governing the use of space. Considering the importance of space for the

Indo-Pacific, the United States has an opportunity to lead its allies and partners in diplomatic initiatives that seek to ensure the stability and reliability of space and cyberspace and advance liberal values within them. This may be an especially fruitful area of engagement because of shared concerns across the region that China's capabilities in these domains are increasingly troubling,[140] and because the lack of historical or territorial disputes in these domains may enable a greater degree of coordination and competition than in other, more traditional, arenas.

Similarly, the United States will need to pursue a coordinated diplomatic effort to coordinate its policies and those of its allies and partners on issues related to emerging technologies, such as 5G, artificial intelligence, and the Internet of Things. Though the specifics of these technologies will differ widely, the United States should identify common principles to guide its diplomacy: protecting and promoting freedom and openness in the face of China's technology-enabled illiberalism. And though the Trump administration has sought to pursue a coordinated diplomatic approach on some of these issues, its approach has been hampered by a lack of compelling alternatives that allies and partners can choose. Demanding that countries ban Chinese technologies from their networks is in itself insufficient—the United States must have a positive alternative vision that others can choose.

Increasing diplomatic coordination with allies and partners in Asia also means listening more and valuing US allies and partners in the region beyond their regional context. This will primarily mean considering the views of US allies and partners in Asia when considering foreign policy issues outside the region. For example, American policies vis-à-vis in the Middle East carry particular weight in US diplomatic engagements with Muslim-majority nations in Southeast Asia, such as Malaysia and Indonesia. If the United States has ambitions to expand its cooperation and coordination with these countries, it will need to recognize that its actions in the Middle East have an impact on its ability to engage in Southeast Asia.

NETWORKING ALLIANCES AND PARTNERSHIPS

Traditionally, the United States has approached its alliances and partners in Asia through the prism of a hub-and-spokes framework, in which the United States sits at the center and the other nations, while working closely with Washington, do little to engage one another. In the face of a more critical and competitive Indo-Pacific, the United States should break away from its old conceptions and focus on a more networked approach that sees allies in closer cooperation and coordination with one another.

This approach would simply reflect the increasingly interconnected nature of the Indo-Pacific. In addition to political and economic connections, the region's militaries are coming together in new ways to uphold the security and stability that are critical for their respective national interests. These connections should be harnessed and built by the United States to enable the US military to better plan, exercise, train, and operate with its Indo-Pacific counterparts more effectively.

The objective of the United States, as described by then secretary of defense Ash Carter in 2016, should be to weave bilateral, trilateral, and multilateral relationships together in a way that enables each nation to do more, over greater distances, with greater economy of effort.[141] It should include a wide variety of different areas, from humanitarian crises and confronting terrorism to ensuring the security of and equal access to the global commons. It would involve identifying and strengthening areas of specialization, developing mechanisms to facilitate greater planning and cooperation, and establishing habits of cooperation to address issues of common interest and concern.

Although the bulk of this book focuses on building the United States' bilateral relationships in the Indo-Pacific, other arrangements that do not involve the United States should also be encouraged and allowed to flourish, as long as they broadly enhance regional stability and support a regional liberal order. For example,

Vietnam and India have established a robust (in underappreciated) defense relationship—based on a shared heritage utilizing Russian equipment and mutual concerns about China's growing power—that promises to greatly enhance Vietnam's maritime capabilities.[142] Japan has also built robust relationships with Vietnam and the Philippines, among other nations, and has sought to enhance maritime cooperation by establishing bilateral exercises and building their capabilities. Indonesia has also proposed trilateral joint maritime patrols with Malaysia and the Philippines.

The United States should also seek to build the capabilities of the region's trilateral and multilateral arrangements. Although the United States–Japan–South Korea partnership will be critical to coordinating responses and policies toward North Korea, other trilateral arrangements will be critical as well. Forming partnerships with Japan and Australia, and with Japan and India, will also be important to building US strategic connectivity across the region. And though the agendas of the various meetings will depend on the interests and concerns of the participating nations, each has tremendous potential to strengthen the liberal regional order and respond to common challenges. In fact, the United States should see the trilateral relationship with Japan and Australia as the emerging core of its Indo-Pacific relations.

One mechanism that has taken on added focus under the Trump administration has been the Quad established between the United States, Japan, Australia, and India—a seeming melding of two of the trilateral relationships discussed above. This initiative, which reflects Japanese prime minister Abe's 2012 proposal for a Democratic Security Diamond, suggests a new alignment based on shared principles and values, a common embrace of political and economic liberalism, mutual concerns about the rise of China and its implications for the region, and a joint determination to do something about it.[143] Although still in its infancy as of this writing, hopes are high regarding the potential for Quad cooperation and engagement.

Sustaining and building on this promise will require deft diplomatic skill from each participant, but especially from Washington and New Delhi. To keep the group together, Washington will need to thread the needle between demonstrating relevance and creating a purpose for the Quad, and moving out too aggressively in a way that would raise concerns in New Delhi that India is being used as a pawn in the great game of US–China competition. Thus, the United States should allow other participants—especially New Delhi and Canberra—to be in the Quad's driver's seat. They can best navigate the complexities of their own domestic political sensitivities, and the United States should mostly seek to play the role of active supporter.

Opportunities for cooperation within the Quad are broad. Prospects for diplomatic coordination to sustain international rules of the road in the global commons and to address Chinese assertiveness in the East China Sea and South China Sea and the Indian Ocean are manifest. Moreover, multilateral military exercises to build interoperability and strengthen military-to-military relationships should be considered. Indeed, one might imagine an annual quadrilateral exercise that would shift each year to the waters near each participant—the Western Pacific, hosted by the United States; the East China Sea, hosted by Japan; the Timor Sea or the South China Sea, hosted by Australia; and the Indian Ocean, hosted by India. Such an approach, which could also rotate the purpose of each exercise depending on the interests of each military, would demonstrate the flexibility and breadth of the Quad while gradually building its depth. At times, other democratic allies—such as the Philippines, Taiwan, and South Korea—should be considered for an invitation to observe or participate as well.

Finally, the United States should recommit to creating a multilateral regional security architecture through the ASEAN Defence Ministers' Meeting–Plus. By reinforcing ASEAN's centrality and actively advocating for an action-oriented agenda, the United States has an opportunity to establish the ASEAN Defence Ministers' Meeting–Plus as the foundation for a networked Indo-Pacific security architecture that strengthens the regional liberal order and maintains regional stability and prosperity.

4

COUNTRY STUDIES

My fellow citizens of the world: ask not what America will do for you, but what together we can do for the freedom of man.

—PRESIDENT JOHN F. KENNEDY

Even though the United States may see the Indo-Pacific from a regional perspective, it must recognize that any strategy to enhance the capabilities of its allies and partners cannot be one size fits all; each country brings its own history, interests, concerns, politics, and ambitions. For the United States to succeed, it must find a way to adapt its regional strategy to be compatible with those of its allies and partners.

This chapter consists of a series of country-by-country analyses of several critical US Indo-Pacific allies and partners, and how the United States could work with each one to enable their more effective contributions to the long-term survival of the liberal regional order. These analyses draw heavily from three edited volumes in the *Strategic Asia* series of books, a trilogy I originally designed along with Ashley Tellis to describe how major powers in the region build, assess, and utilize power.[1] This is not an exhaustive review of all US allies and partners in the Indo-Pacific, but rather is representative of some of the United States' key relationships in the region and beyond.

THE ASSOCIATION OF SOUTHEAST ASIAN NATIONS

The ten nations that belong to the Association of Southeast Asian Nations (ASEAN)—Indonesia, Malaysia, the Philippines, Singapore, Thailand, Brunei, Laos, Myanmar, Cambodia, and Vietnam—have a critical role to play in the future geopolitics of the Indo-Pacific. Each confronts the complexities described in this book: a rising and potentially problematic China, and a powerful yet uncertain United States. Although two ASEAN members—the Philippines and Vietnam—are discussed in detail later in this chapter, the United States also must engage ASEAN as a whole if it is to succeed in strengthening a regional liberal order.

If ASEAN were a single country, it would have the world's seventh-largest economy ($2.4 trillion, between the United Kingdom and Brazil), a population of more than 600 million people (greater than the European Union or North America), and the world's third-largest labor force (behind China and India).[2] Taken as a whole, ASEAN is the United States' third-largest Asian trading partner and the largest Asian destination for US investment.[3] At current growth rates, by 2030 ASEAN is poised to become the world's fourth-largest market after the EU, the United States, and China.[4]

Yet ASEAN's cohesion and integration are far behind those of the EU, and therefore it should not be engaged as a unified bloc. It includes Singapore—one of the world's wealthiest and most advanced countries—and Cambodia, with a per capita income of $1,500.[5] It includes democracies like Indonesia and the Philippines, single-party communist states like Laos and Vietnam, and monarchies like Brunei and Thailand. These broad disparities and differences, combined with numerous lingering historic animosities and strategic suspicions, mean that unity remains a distant goal. Yet despite these difficulties, ASEAN's members remain loyal and committed to the institution to a degree that surprises newcomers.

Also surprising to newcomers is the so-called ASEAN Way, which emphasizes consensus and nonintervention. It makes a priority of dialogue and process over practical accomplishments, preferring to avoid situations that call differences and turbulence to the fore. As a result, the organization's accomplishments often fall short of its ambitions. Yet its accomplishments promoting regional engagement and cooperation are undeniable.

As is often true with smaller and middle powers, several ASEAN members (though certainly not all) are deeply committed to the importance of international norms and laws—especially those that promote stability and prosperity while also restraining the actions of larger powers. Considering ASEAN's geographic location ($5.3 trillion in global trade passes through its waters each year) and the deep concerns that many of its members have about China, it represents a critical opportunity for the United States to expand its influence in the Indo-Pacific and strengthen a liberal regional order.[6]

BUILDING REGIONAL ORDER

ASEAN's member states have long sought to position the institution as a driver of Asian regionalism, and they are deeply suspicious of foreign powers seeking to dominate the agenda. More recently, they have grown increasingly concerned about the implications of strategic competition between China and the United States for the region's smaller states.[7] As a result, Southeast Asian nations have in recent years grown more focused on developing and asserting their own vision for the future development of the Indo-Pacific.

In June 2019, ASEAN made significant progress toward these ends by publishing the "ASEAN Outlook on the Indo-Pacific." In this document, the ASEAN states noted the region's shifting geopolitical dynamics and noted that while economic growth represents a significant opportunity to alleviate poverty and elevate living standards, the rise of major economic and military powers "requires avoiding the deepening of mistrust, miscalculation, and patterns of behavior based on a zero-sum game."[8]

ASEAN envisions itself as the center of the region's geopolitical order, and it seeks to promote ASEAN-centric mechanisms and institutions—such as the East Asia Summit—as the critical driver of regional engagement and cooperation. It seeks to deepen regional integration and engagement by pursuing four objectives:

1. Offering an outlook to guide cooperation in the region;
2. Helping to promote an enabling environment for peace, stability, and prosperity in the region in addressing common challenges; upholding the rules-based regional architecture; promoting closer economic cooperation; and thus strengthening confidence and trust;
3. Enhancing ASEAN's community-building process and further strengthening the existing ASEAN-led mechanisms, such as the East Asia Summit; and
4. Implementing existing and exploring other ASEAN priority areas of cooperation, including maritime cooperation, connectivity, the Sustainable Development Goals, and economic and other possible areas of cooperation.[9]

The principles and policies identified in the "ASEAN Outlook on the Indo-Pacific" are deeply compatible with the principles and policy lines described in chapter 3 of this book. ASEAN highlights the need to peacefully resolve disputes and base regional dynamics on international law, and calls for greater economic interconnectivity and economic development. Therefore, instead of repeating the principles and policies already described, this section instead focuses on actions the United States could take specifically vis-à-vis ASEAN.

ENDORSING ASEAN CENTRALITY

Even considering its flaws and complications, a robust and active ASEAN is firmly within the interests of the United States. Its mechanisms are important drivers of regional engagement and help manage the historical and political disputes that could otherwise threaten to tear Southeast Asia apart. Moreover, ASEAN gives the Southeast Asian nations added geopolitical weight that they could not hope to accrue individually. Although its consensus-based traditions certainly limit ASEAN's ability to galvanize actions and take politically difficult stances, ASEAN nevertheless has ultimately demonstrated itself to be a positive force for stability and peaceful engagement.

Because ASEAN is across the Indo-Pacific, a key feature of any ASEAN-related diplomacy is simply showing up. This is especially important for the United States, considering its great distance from continental Asia. The United States' absences from any of the region's key forums, or even a downgrading of its representation, signals to the region that it is not a top priority for Washington. As a baseline, the United States should sustain regular, high-level engagements with ASEAN's key mechanisms, such as the East Asia Summit, the ASEAN Defence Ministers' Meeting–Plus, and the ASEAN Regional Forum.

Additionally, the United States has a critical role to play in encouraging ASEAN to overcome its internal fractures and tensions. Beijing seeks to exploit these differences in order to prevent ASEAN from acting counter to China's interests—a phenomenon that can be clearly seen whenever ASEAN discusses (or fails to discuss) disputes in the South China Sea.[10] Beijing would prefer to handle the disputes bilaterally, because multilateral engagement would strengthen the hand of China's neighbors. The same logic applies to the United States: an ASEAN whose members can work together is an ASEAN that can more effectively push back against Beijing's revisionist ambitions. A good example of this dynamic was witnessed at the 2015 ASEAN Defence Ministers' Meeting–Plus. The meeting failed to produce a joint statement, and this failure was reported to be the result of efforts by the United States and its allies and partners to mention disputes in the South China Sea and by China to block it.[11] Without the United States, the region would have not had any option but to yield to the pressure from Beijing and ignore the realities of China's actions in the South China Sea.

BUILDING NORMS

ASEAN has a critical role to play in building norms for the rest of the region. The United States has an opportunity, therefore, to engage ASEAN and work with it to ensure that the laws and norms it supports are fundamentally liberal. This will require Washington to engage ASEAN directly, both as an institution as well as its individual members, to discuss how the principles of political and economic liberalism are in their interests.

Specifically, the United States should engage ASEAN to strengthen norms surrounding the peaceful resolution of disputes, transparency and good governance, cybersecurity, economic development, and international trade based on high-quality trade agreements that protect the interests of people as well as governments and corporations. These are all areas where ASEAN has significant interests that would generally align with those of the United States.

Ultimately, American interests are advanced with an ASEAN that is effective, empowered, and focused on the region's critical issues. This will require sustained engagement from Washington, and commitment to engaging in processes that may be seen by some American policymakers as overly slow, cumbersome, and unproductive. Despite these challenges, ASEAN has a critical role to play in the Indo-Pacific, and it is a role the United States should encourage.

AUSTRALIA

Though Australia has long been a close and reliable ally of the United States, in recent years Australia's community of foreign policy scholars has entered a period of self-reflection and reconsideration in the face of a rising China and burgeoning concerns about the sustainability and reliability of American power. And though the core of Australian strategic thinking—especially within its government—has remained committed to sustaining an alliance with the United States that has served Australia well for decades, changing geopolitical dynamics across the region have had a significant effect on the alliance and on how Australia views its role in the world. This represents not only a challenge for the United States to sustain this key alliance, but also an opportunity to encourage and enable Australia to take on a more active and constructive role in the Indo-Pacific.

The modern era of United States–Australia relations truly began in 1908, when the Great White Fleet visited Sydney, Melbourne, and Albany during its circumnavigation of the world. It was the first time a non–Royal Navy fleet had visited Australian waters, and marked the beginning of Canberra's gradual strategic shift in orientation from London to Washington. Australian and American forces cooperated closely during World War I, but it was World War II that laid the foundation for the United States–Australia alliance. The supreme commander of Allied Forces in the Southwest Pacific Area, General Douglas MacArthur, included many Australian troops under his command. Indeed, Australia played a critical role in supporting the Allied push to retake the Pacific from Imperial Japan, serving as the location for MacArthur's headquarters until 1944 and as the jumping-off point for allied troops advancing in the South Pacific. Australian and American troops fought together in several key World War II battles, including Coral Sea, Midway, and Guadalcanal.

The alliance was formalized in 1951. Since that time, Australia has been involved in most major American military actions, including the wars in Korea, Vietnam, the Persian Gulf, Afghanistan, and Iraq. In 2004, the Australia–United States Free Trade Agreement was fast-tracked as a result of Australia's strong support for the war on terrorism. Today, the United States is an important economic partner for Australia—the United States ranks as Australia's fourth-largest export market and its second-largest source of imports. Foreign direct investment is also a critical aspect of the economic relationship; the United States is Australia's largest foreign investor, while Australia is the fifth-largest foreign source of investment in the United States.

At the same time, however, Australia's economy has grown increasingly dependent on China. Unlike virtually every other economy in the Indo-Pacific, Australia has enjoyed twenty-five years of sustained annual economic growth, including during the Great Recession of 2008–10. This was primarily driven by incredible demand from China for minerals and other resources. Australia is the world's fourth-largest coal producer and second-largest exporter of liquefied natural gas, both of which are in high demand to fuel China's rising economy. Australia's Department of Industry, Innovation, and Science projects that Australia will surpass Qatar in 2020 to become the world's largest exporter of liquefied natural gas.[12]

This bifurcation—strategic alignment with the United States and a deepening economic dependence on China—is not unique in the Indo-Pacific. What is unique about Australia, however, is how publicly the implications of this bifurcation have played out. At the vanguard of this debate (but certainly not its only participant) has been Hugh White, a professor of strategic studies at the Strategic and Defence Studies Centre of the Australian National University in Canberra. He has argued that a concert of powers is needed in Asia (similar to Europe's in the nineteenth century), that Australia will one day be forced to "choose" between China and the United States, and that Australia should significantly expand its investments in maritime military capabilities in order to play a larger, more independent role in the region.[13] Most starkly, White has called for Australia to prepare for a future in which "America will lose. China will win."[14] Although many in Australia have disagreed with White on various points,[15] White's argument speaks to a broader geopolitical trend with which US allies and friends have been wrestling: how to manage a rising China that is a critical economic partner and a potential geopolitical threat, and how to manage a United States that seems increasingly unreliable and distracted.

Emerging from this debate has been a rough consensus in Canberra that maintaining a close relationship with the United States remains in Australia's strategic interest, even if it comes at a degree of economic and political expense from China. Speaking at a major defense conference in Singapore in 2017, Australia's then prime minister Malcom Turnbull issued a strong rebuke to Chinese assertiveness and a recommitment to the United States–Australia alliance. He warned that "a coercive China would find its neighbors resenting demands they cede their autonomy and strategic space and look to counterweight Beijing's power by bolstering alliances and partnerships between themselves and especially with the United States."[16]

Turnbull's government subsequently released a foreign policy white paper, which expressed deep concerns about China's assertive actions and included a strong endorsement for the continued relevance of Australia's alliance with the United States. "The alliance is a choice we make about how best to pursue our security interests," states the white paper. "[The Alliance] is central to our shared objective of shaping the regional order. It delivers a capability edge to our armed forces and intelligence agencies, giving Australia added weight and regional influence."[17]

This conclusion has been reinforced politically by revelations of Chinese efforts to interfere in Australian politics, media, and academia.[18] The Australian public was shocked by revelations that Chinese entities had sought to influence Australian government policies, including going so far as to detain an Australian academic. Australia's domestic spy chief Duncan Lewis warned that, if left unchecked, foreign interference in Australia has "the potential to cause serious harm to the nation's sovereignty, the integrity of our political system, our national security capabilities, our economy and other interests."[19]

Deepening anxiety about a rising China, and a tested commitment to the alliance, represent good opportunities for Washington and Canberra to work together to enhance Australia's role in the Indo-Pacific. Although Australia will remain highly sensitive to indications of American distraction or a slackening commitment from Washington, persistent anxieties about the United States may have the ironic role of driving Australian ambitions in a way that would be largely compatible with American interests.

Given the considerations discussed above, the United States and Australia have a shared interest in sustaining a free and open Indo-Pacific in the face of greater Chinese illiberal expansionism. This will require an active campaign by Canberra, with Washington's assistance and support, to compete with Beijing politically, economically, and militarily.

COMPETING WITH CHINA POLITICALLY

Australia has been on the frontline of confronting the realities of Chinese interference in its domestic politics and intellectual life. Most notably, former Australian Labor Party senator Sam Dastyari became embroiled in a campaign finance scandal that highlighted Australia's lax political finance laws and ultimately ended his promising political career. Reports emerged that Dastyari had accepted political donations from Chinese billionaire Huang Xiangmo around the same time that Dastyari's public stance began to soften toward China—toward positions contrary to the Liberal Party government and the Labor Party.[20] The Australian Security Intelligence Organisation recently stated that foreign governments have been acting within ethnic civic societies and religious organizations that were "designed to diminish their criticism of foreign government." It went on to further state, in its annual report, that "these activities . . . represent a threat to our sovereignty, the integrity of our national institutions and the exercise of our citizens' rights.[21] Additionally, Canberra and Washington have been concerned by Beijing's deepening influence with the Pacific island nations, primarily achieved through infrastructure building and the promise of loans.[22] Australia has become weary of Beijing's encroaching interests in the South Pacific, specifically the proposed Chinese military outpost in Vanuatu.[23]

Washington and Canberra should identify opportunities to share information and coordinate policies designed to understand and mitigate Beijing's efforts to influence their respective domestic politics. They should consider establishing an active and robust intelligence exchange working group dedicated to monitoring, assessing, and producing recommendations to mitigate the activities of the United Front Work Department of the Chinese Communist Party and other organizations that seek to influence the domestic politics of Australia and the United States. This working group would develop recommendations for legislators and policymakers in Washington and Canberra, and would produce an annual public report detailing its findings and recommendations.

Additionally, the United States and Australia should work to closely coordinate diplomatic and policy initiatives that would assist in a broader geopolitical competition with China across the Indo-Pacific, primarily by sustaining openness and liberalism across the region. From the United Nations and other international forums, common values and interests should enable cooperation and coordination on a wide variety of diplomatic issues, including continuing efforts to isolate and maximize pressure on North Korea, defending norms related to freedom of navigation and the peaceful resolution of disputes, and consolidating democratization across the Indo-Pacific.

COMPETING WITH CHINA MILITARILY

Since 2016, the Australian government has identified its three strategic defense interests as a resilient Australia, with secure northern approaches and proximate sea lines of communication; a secure near region, encompassing maritime Southeast Asia and the South Pacific; and a stable Indo-Pacific region and rules-based global order.[24] Australia's defense budget is slated to increase by over 80 percent between 2016 and 2026, from roughly $25 billion to roughly $45 billion. Investments will focus on command, control, communications, computers, intelligence, surveillance, and reconnaissance capabilities; a new class of submarines; a short-range air defense system; and equipment for electronic warfare. Taken together, these represent an opportunity for robust defense cooperation between Australia and the United States across the Indo-Pacific.

US–Australia military cooperation should focus on four major lines of effort:

- *Extending Australia's military presence.* In November 2018, Vice President Mike Pence announced plans to work with Australia and Papua New Guinea to develop the Lombrum Naval Base on Manus Island. Lombrum was an important base for the US Navy during World War II, and is positioned along critical trade routes in the West Pacific. This is a very important initiative, and could be a model for additional efforts to empower the Australian military to operate for extended periods of time at greater distances from Australian shores. Australia's strategic geography—especially its islands close to Indonesia's strategic waterways, as well as its close proximity to the Indian Ocean—should be seen as an opportunity to enable Australian forces to become a regular presence in the South China Sea and the Indian Ocean, with frequent sojourns to the East China Sea and the Western Pacific. This would allow Australia's forces to boost its national presence and influence across the region, and would clearly demonstrate Australia's commitment to its interests and values.
- *Promoting a rules-based order.* By working with the United States and other allies to demonstrate the continued viability of international laws and norms, the Australian military—especially its air and naval forces—would become a major force in pushing back against efforts to circumscribe freedom of navigation. Unilateral and multilateral operations in international waters, such as freedom-of-navigation operations and military exercises, would send a strong signal about Australian values and determination.
- *Building defense capacity across the Indo-Pacific.* In coordination with Japan, South Korea, and other advanced allies and partners, Australia and the United States should coordinate efforts to build the capacity

and defense capabilities of their other, less-developed partners across the region. With this initiative, Australia's defense industries can identify niche markets to provide less-developed partners that share a commitment to a rules-based order and a free and open Indo-Pacific with capabilities appropriate to their level of sophistication and the level of resources they can devote to defense. Moreover, Australian forces can work to build capacity, train the militaries and coast guards of their Indo-Pacific partners, and conduct joint exercises in order to enhance their ability to operate freely and effectively in the face of Chinese pressure.

- *Enabling a more robust US military presence.* Since 2012, after an announcement by US president Barack Obama and Australian prime minister Julie Gillard, US military forces have been operating out of Darwin in Northern Australia.[25] Although this has initially supported a relatively small rotational presence of US Marines and advanced fighter aircraft, Washington and Canberra should identify opportunities to build a joint military presence in that area that could support other types of military operations. Geographically, Darwin could play host to advanced radar installations and other equipment that would be helpful for missile defense, space operations, and naval operations. Moreover, the allies should examine opportunities along Australia's West Coast to support additional air and naval forces that could help establish a more regular presence in the Indian Ocean and support other activities in Southeast Asia.

For years, there has been an active debate in Australian foreign policy circles about whether to take part in freedom-of-navigation operations. Although some have claimed doing so would be a strong signal of alliance cohesion and defiance against Chinese assertiveness, others in Canberra argue that doing so would accomplish little while aggravating relations with Beijing. Such a debate unfortunately detracts from other, more significant issues at play between Washington and Canberra. The United States should not weigh in on the subject, but instead should defend Australia's right to operate wherever international law allows.

COMPETING WITH CHINA ECONOMICALLY

The US–Australia alliance should also be seen as a platform to advance and consolidate economic liberalism across the Indo-Pacific. Although the United States' decision to pull out of the Trans-Pacific Partnership (TPP) was a major setback for such an agenda, bilateral cooperation can still make significant progress.

Historically, liberalism and democracy have had the best opportunity to flourish when people see the tangible benefits of these systems. China's illiberal efforts at development and economic engagement—which often include exploitative terms—would be undercut by a robust, well-resourced development initiative that not only demonstrates commitment by the United States and Australia but also embodies the best practices that are fundamental to Western socioeconomic development.[26] A development initiative of several hundred million dollars—a large number for international development, but a relatively small sum when compared with the defense investments made by both nations—would have a tremendous geopolitical impact across Asia, would do much to revitalize perceptions of commitment to the region by the United States and Australia, and would help stem the tide of China's illiberal expansionism.

Canberra deserves significant credit for its ability to link economic and development initiatives, such as it has done with ASEAN. Canberra recognizes that development supports economic initiatives, and that free and open trade arrangements facilitate development.[27] Similarly, Australia was able to use aid funds to outbid the Chinese corporation Huawei for a telecommunication cable that will connect Papua New Guinea, the Solomon Islands, and Australia—another demonstration of how development funds can be used to address both development and geopolitical objectives.[28]

Additionally, the United States and Australia should cooperate in strengthening liberal economic institutions across the Indo-Pacific. Supporting organizations such as the Asian Development Bank, the

World Bank, the International Monetary Fund, and the Friends of the Lower Mekong Initiative—organizations devoted to transparency and accountability—would be a bulwark for economic liberalism in the region. Similarly, Australia and the United States should engage Chinese-led institutions, such as the Asian Infrastructure Investment Bank, to ensure that they also meet established high standards.

EUROPE

Writing in the *Financial Times* in October 2019, foreign affairs columnist Gideon Rachman argued that the European Union should move beyond ambitions for a global law-based system and instead get with the power politics being employed by Xi Jinping's China and Trump's America.[29] Although he does not delve deeply into the purpose of such European power politics, one can imagine some of Europe's larger powers seeing the strengthening of a liberal order as both a normative goal for its Union but also an aspect of power politics itself. And though this would likely be an important aspect of any strategy in Russia, it would also be a potentially useful approach by Europe toward the Indo-Pacific.

Unlike the United States, European powers do not have alliances or a permanent military presence in Asia, though a few maintain sovereignty over some small islands in the Indian Ocean in the South Pacific. Rather, Europe has—especially since the end of the Cold War—seen Asia primarily as a region of tremendous economic opportunity, with potential regional conflicts in which it has few national interests, and little else. Yet as the Indo-Pacific grows in importance for the world's geopolitics, it is only natural for Europe—like the United States—to engage the region anew. This represents a unique opportunity for Washington to engage its allies in Europe vis-à-vis Asia, and to enlist their support for a broader effort to preserve and strengthen a liberal order in the Indo-Pacific.

DRIVERS OF EUROPEAN ENGAGEMENT IN THE INDO-PACIFIC

In recent years, governments in London, Paris, Berlin, and at NATO headquarters in Brussels have begun to see the Indo-Pacific in a broader context that includes both economic opportunities as well as geopolitical challenges that are impossible to ignore. Although this reflects the region's importance as a whole, Europe's resurgent focus on Asia through a geopolitical lens is primarily due to deepening concerns about the broad strategic implications of China's rise for Europe and for the international liberal order, as well as by a broader recognition across Europe that what happens in the Indo-Pacific will have extensive implications for the international liberal order generally, and in particular for critical European unity and its interests in stability, trade, and the promotion of human rights and democratic values.

Though this trend has largely flown under the radar in the United States, China has in recent years become an important player in the geopolitics of Europe. A visit to Italy, Monaco, and France by Xi Jinping in March 2019 highlighted this growing role, and was notable for Italy's announcement that it would become the first major European economy to join China's Belt and Road Initiative. This highlighted growing tensions within Europe over China, as some in Southern and Eastern Europe thirsted over the opportunities of Chinese investment while the larger countries of Western Europe have grown more skeptical. Beijing has exacerbated these divisions by intensifying its engagement with potentially friendly countries, including with the establishment of the 16+1 format, also called the China–CEEC (Central and Eastern European Countries) summit. It was established in 2012, with the intention of enhancing engagement between China a group of eleven EU member states and five Balkan countries (Albania, Bosnia and Herzegovina, Bulgaria, Croatia, the Czech Republic, Estonia, Hungary, Latvia, Lithuania, Macedonia, Montenegro, Poland, Romania, Serbia, Slovakia, and Slovenia) in a way that ignored established groupings of European nations and unsurprisingly did not include the larger, more developed European nations. Outside analysts have found that "China has contributed around $15.4 billion toward infrastructure and other investment in the 16+1 countries since 2012 in areas such as energy, transport, information and communication technology, . . . manufacturing, real estate, and mergers and acquisitions." They further noted that since 2012, "70 percent of announced deals have been in non-EU member states even though they make up only 5 of the 16 participants and only 6 percent of the group's collective GDP [gross domestic product]."[30] This is driving concerns in some parts of Europe that Beijing's strategy is to undermine Europe's fledging ability to act collectively.

As a result, many in Europe no longer see China as a distant theoretical challenge but rather as a nearby, resident actor within Europe itself. This is why the European Commission issued a paper in March 2019 that describes China thusly: "China is, simultaneously, in different policy areas, a cooperation partner with whom the EU has closely aligned objectives, a negotiating partner with whom the EU needs to find a balance of interests, an economic competitor in the pursuit of technological leadership, and a systemic rival promoting alternative models of governance."[31]

In addition, the sheer geopolitical weight of the Indo-Pacific as a whole has awakened Europe to its challenges and opportunities. The EU-Japan Economic Partnership Agreement, for example, was the largest in the world when it was signed in February 2019—covering nearly one-third of global GDP and 635 million people. Overall, merchandise trade between Asia and Europe stands at $1.5 trillion annually, overtaking each continent's trade with the United States.[32] These dynamics, and their implications for global geopolitics, make the Indo-Pacific a region Europe can no longer ignore. France, for instance, released an Indo-Pacific strategy in June 2019 that identifies five main priorities for Paris in the region:

1. Protecting France's sovereign interests, nationals, territories, and exclusive economic zones;

2. Contributing to regional stability through military and security cooperation;

3. Preserving free and open access to maritime lines of communication;

4. Contributing to strategic stability through multilateral action; and

5. Anticipating and mitigating risks to the environment in the region from the effects of climate events.[33]

Similarly, in May 2019 the United Kingdom's House of Commons Foreign Affairs Committee released a report focused on China and the United Kingdom's approach to the Indo-Pacific.[34] The report raised concerns that the rise of China threatened key priorities identified by London's Foreign and Commonwealth Office, including raising the cost of malicious cyberactivity and defending a free, open, peaceful, and secure cyberspace; strengthening the rules-based international system; and championing democracy, human rights, and the rule of law.[35]

Germany has also sought to enhance its engagement in the region, although its approach has to date been more circumspect than what has come from Paris and London.[36] Chancellor Angela Merkel has called for European political and business leaders to work more closely together to address the economic challenge posed by Asia's rising and dynamic economies, and she has pushed for a European investment agreement with Beijing. Although this approach is an understandable reflection of the importance of the Chinese market for German exports—China was Germany's largest single trading partner in 2018—it has had the effect of keeping broader discussions in Germany about the Indo-Pacific largely relegated to backrooms.[37]

Moreover, NATO has also come to see China not only as a challenge to the existing international order in the Indo-Pacific but also as a direct and resident challenge to NATO members themselves. NATO secretary-general Jen Stolenberg has been particularly outspoken on this view, noting that China's increasing assertiveness raises concerns about Beijing's intentions. "This is not about moving NATO into the Pacific," he said, "but this is about responding to the fact that China is coming closer to us."[38] Under Stolenberg's leadership, NATO has sought to engage like-minded partners in the Indo-Pacific such as Australia, Japan, and South Korea—although such efforts have been limited and are in early phases.

Taken as a whole, this greater focus on the Indo-Pacific by Europe's major powers represents an opportunity for engagement from the United States. It is in the interest of the United States for its European allies—in different ways—to play a more significant role in the Indo-Pacific. They share a commitment to political and economic liberalism, have concerns about the implications of China's rise, and have a profound interest in sustaining a liberal international order.

As a foundation for this effort, the United States and Europe should establish a regular dialogue to discuss the geopolitical trends of the Indo-Pacific and coordinate policies and strategies. This dialogue—which would necessarily encompass diplomatic, security, economic, and other issue areas—would serve as the primary mechanism through which the United States could encourage Europe to play a more significant role in the Indo-Pacific and, as appropriate, to coordinate their approaches. Although many of the issues described earlier in the book would apply to such a dialogue, the next subsections give specific areas of cooperation that would be especially fruitful for discussions between Europe and the United States.

COOPERATION BEYOND GEOGRAPHY

The primary impediment to Europe playing a more significant role in the Indo-Pacific is geography. It would be unrealistic to expect Europe to take on a role and scale of responsibilities in the Indo-Pacific that even closely approximates that of the United States. Yet that should not be an impediment to greater cooperation between Europe and the United States on the Indo-Pacific, especially when the issues involved transcend considerations of geography. Specifically, Europe and the United States should deepen economic and diplomatic cooperation on a wide range of issues, united in the promotion of common principles and in a shared commitment to strengthening the liberal international order. Progress in this direction has already begun—the EU has signed free trade agreements with Japan, Singapore, South Korea, and Vietnam. It is also negotiating additional agreements with Australia, New Zealand, India, and ASEAN, although the latter two have been stalled for years.

Yet the United States and Europe can do far more. Encouraging European investment in Indo-Pacific infrastructure projects—especially in Southeast Asia and the South Pacific—would greatly augment ongoing efforts by the United States, Japan, Australia, and India. But more ambitiously, the EU should pursue additional high-quality free trade agreements with other major powers in the Indo-Pacific—especially South Korea, India, Australia, and ASEAN. If the United States is able to conclude free trade agreements along the lines of what was proposed by the TPP and Transatlantic Trade and Investment Partnership, the resulting economic bloc—based on liberal economic principles—would be an unstoppable economic force with which Beijing could not hope to compete. Other issues—such as supporting good governance, development assistance, and technology—make the United States and Europe natural Indo-Pacific partners.

Though certainly ambitious—especially considering sentiments against free trade that have gained political traction in Europe and the United States as well as deepening fissures within the EU—such ambitions are achievable over the long term, and would be a tremendous geopolitical asset in the Indo-Pacific. All that is required is for both sides to recognize one another's value and common interests, overcome mistrust, and establish regular dialogues to coordinate policies on Indo-Pacific issues.[39]

A RESIDENT MILITARY POWER

The United States should work with France and England to deepen their presence in the Indo-Pacific. This is a relatively low bar for France, which retains territorial sovereignty on islands in the Indian Ocean and South Pacific. Yet both France and England lack sufficient resources, assets, or facilities in the region to sustain a permanent military presence on their own. Although, in recent years, both have deployed naval vessels to the region, these operations have been sporadic.

Deepening cooperation between the United States and its allies and partners in the Indo-Pacific can directly enable a greater presence for European navies in the Indo-Pacific, eventually making them resident powers in the region. To this end, the United States and its Indo-Pacific allies—especially Australia and Japan—should pursue agreements that would enable a rotational presence for European navies in the region. Royal Australian Air Force Base Darwin— located in Northern Australia—is already the site of a rotational presence for US Marines and represents an especially promising potential location for a more sustained European military presence in the region. British defense officials have also reportedly mentioned Singapore and Brunei as possible locations for a Far East base for the UK military, though London currently lacks the resources to fully realize such ambitions.[40]

Even as such facilities are under consideration, the militaries and defense institutions of the United States and its European allies should be discussing options for cooperation in the Indo-Pacific. Combined military operations and coordinated messaging are each prime areas for practical cooperation, and dialogue can ensure that such operations serve broader geopolitical objectives.

Ultimately, such operations and facilities would necessarily support broader geopolitical interests shared by the United States, its European allies, and like-minded partners in the Indo-Pacific to promote freedom of navigation and multilateral military cooperation. Such operations are a necessary aspect of any declarative policy, giving a physical manifestation to long-standing policy and sending a strong message to allies, partners, and adversaries alike about Europe's commitment and engagement on these issues in the Indo-Pacific.

A critical mechanism for such cooperation could be establishing Individual Partnership and Cooperation Programme agreements, which NATO has already signed with South Korea and Japan. This mechanism allows for deeper cooperation on a wide variety of issues, including cyberdefense; maritime security; humanitarian assistance and disaster relief; nuclear nonproliferation; defense science and technology; and women, peace, and security.[41] Both Korea and Japan also participate in the Partnership Interoperability Initiative (PII), though they emphasize different aspects of what kind of cooperation they emphasize with NATO. Several other Indo-Pacific allies and partners are part of the PII, including Australia and New Zealand.

The United States should serve as a conduit for enhanced cooperation between its allies in Europe and its allies and partners in NATO. Countries like Singapore, the Philippines, and India represent good candidates for prospective Individual Partnership and Cooperation Programme and PII participants. Such an arrangement may be difficult for some Indo-pacific partners to embrace at first, fearing that doing so would overly align them with the United States and the West. However, slow and patient engagement with NATO has the potential to gradually convince these same countries of the benefits that greater engagement with NATO could provide to advance their own interests and defend their own security.

Most important, the United States and Europe have a direct interest in the geopolitical dynamics of the Indo-Pacific. From economics and politics to security dynamics, Europe can no longer afford to see the Indo-Pacific as peripheral. It is central, and thus it should become an essential component of diplomacy between Europe and the United States.

INDIA

There is tremendous opportunity for India to play an increasingly critical role in the Indo-Pacific in the coming years. Under the leadership of Prime Minister Narendra Modi and his Act East policy, India has been more engaged and active in the geopolitics of East Asia. Yet persistent issues related to history, geography, domestic politics, and ideology will likely limit India's ability to focus on issues beyond its immediate periphery. Ultimately, the key uncertainties surrounding India's future role in the Indo-Pacific involve questions about Modi's ability to shift India's traditional geopolitical orientation and how long such adjustments may survive after he leaves the prime minister's office.

Given this opportunity, the time has come for India and the United States to expand their relationship and establish a comprehensive strategic partnership founded on shared values and common interests, and dedicated to enhancing India's geopolitical role in the region and in promoting liberal principles. Establishing this partnership will require patience and vision, but will ultimately be in the strategic interests of both nations.

Critical to the success of this strategy will be a shared, high-level vision for the relationship that addresses the needs and concerns of both Delhi and Washington. For India, this will mean a relationship that buttresses its leadership role in the Indo-Pacific, enables more effective competition with China in South Asia and the Indian Ocean, and preserves Indian independence and sovereignty. The United States, for its part, would seek assurances that an empowered and more capable India would be an effective competitor with China, and a reliable partner in strengthening a liberal regional order.

Building a successful partnership will also require setting aside differences in favor of pursuing broader ambitions for the India–United States relationship. For example, India's traditionally strong relationships with Russia and Iran, which have often been a sticking point in its relationship with the United States, should not be significant impediments to forming a comprehensive partnership. Although both sides should certainly seek a common understanding on their differences, disagreements over these issues should not undermine momentum in building this partnership. Certainly, if the United States can disagree with key allies in Europe and Asia on other issues of foreign policy (e.g., Europe's opposition in 2017 to shifting the US Embassy in Israel to Jerusalem, or Japan's efforts in

2016 to engage Russia despite US objections), Washington and New Delhi should be able to overcome such disagreements.

The most critical element in building a successful partnership between India and the United States, therefore, will be vision and commitment from top leaderships in New Delhi and Washington. Without this, negotiators on both sides will be incapable of making the concessions necessary to achieve the broader objective of enhanced bilateral coordination and cooperation. As such, a new joint vision statement—building on the 2015 statement—should be pursued in order to set an ambitious vision to build a comprehensive strategic partnership between India and the United States.

Since achieving independence in 1947, India has played an important international role. Originally courted by both the Soviet Union and the United States, New Delhi sought to pursue a non-aligned approach (although often leaning toward Moscow) while seeking to play the role of leader for other developing nations. Non-alignment continues to have significant sway across India's foreign policy establishment and strategic culture today, even as its leaders and leading thinkers seek to update its strategic orientation.

With a large population and abundant natural resources, India has enjoyed regular, and fairly rapid, economic growth. Indeed, India's GDP grew in 2016 by 7.1 percent—faster than that of China (6.7 percent) and the United States (1.6 percent). India's economy was estimated by the International Monetary Fund to be $9.4 trillion, the third-largest in the world behind China ($23 trillion) and the United States ($19 trillion).[42]

India is set to spend $250 billion to modernize the Indian Armed Forces by 2025. These plans are geared toward enabling India to address significant challenges from both China and Pakistan, which have very different military capabilities. India is also investing heavily in the development of a modern, multiship aircraft carrier force and is in the process of constructing six nuclear-powered attack submarines. To support these efforts, India is engaging the United States (through a carrier working group[43]) and Russia (which is assisting in the design of India's submarines[44]).

Since achieving independence in 1947, and especially since the early 1960s, Indian strategists have been forced to contend with two very different strategic challenges—Pakistan to the west, and China to the north. China's invasion of India in 1962 brought the Chinese threat to the fore, and strategic competition with China has since persisted. Indeed, India's subsequent alignment with the Soviet Union should be best understood as an effort to check Chinese power as much as it was motivated by allergies to alignment with the West.

As the Cold War came to a close in 1991, India's strategy to balance against Chinese power evolved into what became known as the Look East policy. Prime Minister P. V. Narasimha Rao advocated for more active economic and strategic engagement with Southeast Asia to build a counterweight to China and as a path to develop India's own regional power. Rao's successors—Atal Bihari Vajpayee and Manmohan Singh—sustained this approach and maintained regular engagements across Southeast Asia.

Nevertheless, many in India felt that the Look East policy was lacking in ambition and execution, and that China's rising power and influence in Asia demanded a more vigorous Indian approach. As a result, Prime Minister Modi announced Act East as a way to signal his intent to engage the region with greater energy and determination. Speaking at a summit with ASEAN leaders in November 2014, Modi declared that "a new era of economic development, industrialization and trade has begun in India. Externally, India's 'Look East Policy' has become 'Act East Policy.'" He announced the establishment of a tailored vehicle for project financing, building information highways, and inviting ASEAN member countries to participate in India's ongoing economic transformation. Modi also touched on the South China Sea, reiterating the importance for all actors in "following international law and norms on maritime issues."[45]

Another critical aspect of the evolution of India's foreign policy under Prime Minister Modi has been a greater willingness to confront China directly. Although Modi had previously reached out to China when it announced the Asian Infrastructure Investment Bank and other regional initiatives, suggestions that this indicated a general realignment toward Beijing were premature. During a 2017 standoff between India and China at Doklam, for instance, India deployed 270 troops to stop China from constructing a road that, Indian leaders argued, would threaten Indian interests and the sovereignty of India's ally, Bhutan. Modi's notable tolerance for risk and friction with China sent a clear message to Beijing that New Delhi's foreign policy had entered a new phase.

Modi's willingness to confront and openly compete with China was paired with a greater tolerance for closer engagement with the United States. Cooperation between Delhi and Washington has increased dramatically in recent years, especially in the diplomatic and security spheres. Since the United States lifted sanctions against India in 2001, bilateral defense relations have seen significant improvements and cooperation.

Under the Obama administration, the relationship was further advanced with the commitment to the Joint Strategic Vision for the Indo-Pacific and Indian Ocean region, which helped lay the groundwork for enhanced cooperation and deepening strategic ties across diplomatic and security fronts.[46] In 2016, India was classified as a "major defense partner" by the United States, which heightened the level of cooperation and underscored the importance Washington placed on its relationship with New Delhi, propelling the relationship forward.[47] The Malabar exercises have served as the premier annual bilateral maritime exercises. In alternating years, Malabar has been open to multilateral participation, which in the past has included the navies of Japan, Australia, and Singapore. These exercises serve as a valuable tool to foster professional and friendly relationships between navies and build familiarity to better integrate operations.[48] On the diplomatic front, the US–Indian Strategic and Commercial Dialogue, launched in 2015, is the signature mechanism to advance the two nations' shared priorities and provides opportunities to enhance partnerships in areas including energy, climate change, trade, education, and counterterrorism.[49]

Taken together, it would seem that the stars are aligning for India to emerge as a critical player in the Indo-Pacific and an attractive new partner for the United States that can greatly contribute to a liberal regional order. Yet Western ambitions regarding India's emergence should be tempered with a realistic understanding of the constraints India still faces.

Many outside analysts have pointed out that India's power potential remains largely unrealized, due to administrative inefficiency and political dysfunction.[50] Rajesh Rajagopalan, for instance, argues that "unless [India's] bureaucratic apparatus becomes more efficient or less dominant—or both—the country's capacity to generate power will continue to suffer." The fragmentation of India's political systems often leads to gridlock and inaction, and this lack of cohesion among the political elite serves as a major stumbling block to India's power realization. Despite India's democratic political culture, economic performance, large military potential, and youthful demographic, John Gill also laments India's unrealized potential, hampered by its reticent national security strategy and internal and external security challenges.[51]

A further challenge to pursuing enhanced US–India cooperation will be overcoming the deeply held convictions of some in India's strategic community about aligning too closely with the West. Traditional Indian strategic thought—forged during British colonial rule and deepened during the Cold War—has infused many Indian elites with a strong preference for strategic independence and autonomy and an allergy to perceptions of geopolitical alignment with or against the world's great powers.[52] As such, explicit efforts to gain Indian cooperation in supporting a liberal order may ultimately backfire. Rather, it would be more productive to engage India on specific issue areas of mutual interest, and to allow such cooperation to gradually widen the aperture for cooperation on additional, more difficult issues.

BUILDING ECONOMIC INTEGRATION

As noted in the previous chapter, India has long played an important role in international development and economic integration across Southeast Asia. New Delhi and Tokyo make natural partners in expanding economic integration throughout the region, which should be very much in the interests of the United States. Both India and Japan promote greater connectivity and cohesion under the principles of the rule of law and economic liberalism. The United States could support these efforts with the injection of capital, expertise, and cooperation from the US private sector. The Asia–Africa Growth Corridor represents an especially compelling avenue for US engagement across the region as part of the US Indo-Pacific strategy. Most critical, however, would be high-level encouragement from Washington to build and sustain momentum between Tokyo, New Delhi, and other key partners across the region.

Yet a great deal of work must also be done on the bilateral economic relationship. Clearly, it is in the strategic interests of both sides for India and the United States to have stronger economic relations. Indeed, in the first line of his first speech as ambassador to India, Ken Juster called for a US–India free trade agreement (FTA) on the basis that President Trump's "America First" philosophy is compatible with Prime Minister Modi's "Make in India" initiative.[53] However, despite the incredible size and potential of India's economy and a shared commitment to the rule of law and economic liberalism, the framework undergirding economic relations between India and the United States is remarkably threadbare. Indeed, the idea of a US–India FTA at this time is a very distant hope.

New Delhi and Washington should therefore prioritize a more realistic objective—the conclusion of a high-quality bilateral investment treaty (BIT). Such an agreement will be necessary to create a more predictable investment environment and increase bilateral investment flows. However, negotiations have stalled over core foreign investment protection standards,[54] even though the two sides agreed to negotiate a high-level BIT in the 2015 joint vision statement.[55] At its core, these negotiations are moribund not because of technical disagreements but due to a lack of political leadership, commitment, and vision. Washington and New Delhi should make the finalization of a BIT a top strategic priority, and empower their negotiators to make the necessary concessions in order to rapidly conclude an agreement.

MILITARY COOPERATION

For several years, the United States and India have been gradually expanding the scope and depth of their bilateral military cooperation. Former US secretary of defense Ash Carter referred to this as reflecting a "strategic handshake" between the two countries as the US policy of rebalance to the Asia-Pacific converged with Indian prime minister Modi's Act East policy.[56] This "handshake" should continue, and even grow, with the Trump administration, which has already signaled its interest in expanding cooperation with India through the announcement of its strategy to secure a free and open Indo-Pacific.

In 2012, the United States and India launched the Defense Technology and Trade Initiative, composed of seven joint working groups exploring collaborative projects and programs, and they signed two science and technology government-to-government project agreements: the Next Generation Protective Ensembles and Mobile Hybrid Power Sources.

Cooperation between the two nations' defense industries has also expanded. In 2012, Tata Advanced Systems Limited and Lockheed Martin established a joint venture to produce C-130J Super Hercules airframe components. Tata Advanced Systems Limited also has a joint venture with Sikorsky to coproduce S-92 helicopter cabins, and with Boeing to manufacture components for Apache helicopters and collaborate on integrated systems development opportunities in India.[57]

After nearly a decade of discussions, in August 2016 India and the United States signed a landmark defense agreement that substantially increased bilateral military cooperation. This Logistics Exchange Memorandum of Agreement is highly technical and seems somewhat pedestrian on the surface. It primarily deals with logistical support and makes it clear that India has no obligation to carry out any joint activity or host bases or basing arrangements—belying the agreement's strategic significance.[58] Yet the significance of logistical support and cooperation is very important as a foundation for further military cooperation.

First on the agenda should be the rapid conclusion of two agreements that have been under negotiation for several years, but have stalled due to Indian hesitation. The two agreements—the Communications Compatibility and Security Agreement and the Basic Exchange and Cooperation Agreement for Geospatial Intelligence—are seen in Washington as fairly mundane. The United States has signed these types of agreements with dozens of other countries—including both allies and partners of varying degrees of alignment—but Indian officials have expressed concerns. Specifically, India fears that the agreements may undermine its strategic autonomy and pave the way for the United States to establish bases on Indian territory. It also fears that the agreements may give Pakistan access to sensitive information about the Indian Armed Forces, due to the US military relationship with Pakistan. Yet these concerns are unfounded. The United States maintains similar agreements with other countries that do not want US bases on their territory, and it can ensure that sensitive information is not conveyed to other countries.[59] Concluding these agreements will enable deeper cooperation between the two militaries. India's political leadership should make the case to skeptics that their concerns are unwarranted, and that these agreements are a necessary part of improving military cooperation between India and the United States.

With the agreements in place, the United States and India will be able to greatly expand the breadth of their defense cooperation. The primary objective of this cooperation should be to enhance India's ability to contribute to security in Asia and ensure that India has the capacity to compete and prevail against China in the Indian Ocean and beyond.[60] This will primarily involve building India's air and naval capabilities—namely, enhancing the quality of Indian military hardware, improving India's ability to operate effectively in contested environments, and strengthening interoperability between the Indian armed forces and those of the United States and its allies and partners.

As in other areas, this will require both sides to make concessions in the pursuit of a broader, more important objective. For the United States, it would need to reconsider its opposition to assisting India in the acquisition of naval nuclear power technologies, which are critical to advanced aircraft carriers and submarines. Similarly, India would need to assure the United States of its commitment to employ its newfound military capabilities in a way that is stabilizing and supports a free and open Indo-Pacific on the principles of a liberal order.

Yet competition with China in the Indian Ocean and beyond is about more than hardware. Regular operations in the Indian Ocean, the South China Sea, and even into the East China Sea and the Western Pacific will all be essential for effective competition. Presence—demonstrating to the rest of the region that the Indian Navy is active and reliable—will be critical to establishing India's naval power in the region. So too will be India's positive and constructive use of these capabilities—through humanitarian assistance and disaster relief operations, military diplomacy, and multilateral exercises.

JAPAN

Japan is poised to emerge as a critically important leader in the Indo-Pacific. In the face of a rising China and an increasingly threatening North Korea, Japan's leadership has already set it on a path to significantly increase its economic, political, and security role in the region. Moreover, often lingering beneath the surface of these efforts by Tokyo are burgeoning concerns among Japan's policy elite about the reliability of American power and long-term US leadership in the region. These concerns act as an additional motivation for Tokyo's expanding regional ambitions. If properly managed, such dynamics can be leveraged to significantly enhance the strength of the regional liberal order and foster regional stability and prosperity.

Japan is vital to American interests in the Indo-Pacific. It is the third-largest economy in the world by nominal GDP and the fourth-largest by purchasing power parity.[61] It is also the United States' fourth-largest trading partner, with $195 billion in total trade in goods and $75.3 billion trade in services in 2016.[62] Japan is home to over 50,000 US American service members and 42,000 of their dependents. Additionally, Japan plays a highly constructive role in the Indo-Pacific. Japan has encouraged economic integration throughout the Indo-Pacific, especially Southeast Asia, through its overseas investments, economic partnership agreements, efforts to support infrastructure development, and leadership role in the Asian Development Bank.[63]

Recent years have seen a marked expansion in Japan's ability to play a more significant role in the US–Japan alliance and in the Indo-Pacific. Under the leadership of President Obama and Prime Minister Abe, the US–Japan alliance grew and deepened with the 2015 update of the Guidelines for Japan–US Defense Cooperation, the foundational document defining the parameters of the alliance. This update was grounded in a July 2014 decision by Abe's cabinet to officially reinterpret the Constitution to conditionally permit collective self-defense.[64] The guidelines now take into account the greater interoperability resulting from this decision, as well as developments in military technology such as ballistic missile defense and the defensive use of space.[65] They also seek to address peacetime crises and "gray zone" contingencies, including the use of nonmilitary agents by China in maritime disputes, by establishing an alliance coordination mechanism that would allow for coordination between all relevant agencies in both governments.[66]

Yet Japan is also concerned about whether Washington will continue to play its leadership role in the region—a role that Tokyo has long seen as essential to its security and prosperity. The decision by President Donald Trump to withdraw the United States from the TPP has not only altered the landscape of regional and global trade, it has also undermined prospects for multilateralism in the Indo-Pacific region and beyond, and called into question the sustainability of American power and influence in the region. Although the US Indo-Pacific strategy indicates an ongoing recognition of the Indo-Pacific's strategic significance to the United States, the Trump administration's rejection of economic multilateralism has fundamentally hindered its ability to elucidate a compelling vision for the region's economic destiny.[67] The result has been a geo-economic vacuum in Asia.

Japan has sought to fill this vacuum. Although still hoping that the United States will eventually return to supporting multilateral trade agreements, Tokyo has not stood still waiting for America to come to its senses. Rather, Japan has begun actively asserting its interests by promoting its own vision for the region's economic future. Japan's leadership was critical to the rapid development of the Comprehensive and Progressive Agreement for Trans-Pacific Partnership, which appears to be specifically designed to ensure that the Indo-Pacific's economic architecture continues to embrace multilateralism without being forced to accede to Chinese geopolitical leadership. Tokyo has also partnered with New Delhi in the creation of the Asia–Africa Growth Corridor Initiative—a potential answer to China's Belt and Road Initiative.[68]

Prime Minister Abe Shinzo and other senior Japanese officials have consistently voiced their support for a liberal order. In an address before the United Nations General Assembly on September 20, 2017, Abe stated, "What Japan wants to safeguard in every respect is the free, liberal, open liberal order and multilateral frameworks."[69] He has also vocally supported the international economic order, attributing Japan's success to "the postwar economic system that the United States had fostered by opening up its own market and calling for a liberal world economy," in a speech before a 2015 joint session of the US Congress.[70] This makes Japan a critical partner for the United States in any strategy to promote the liberal order across the Indo-Pacific.

ENHANCED SECURITY COOPERATION

The aforementioned April 2015 update to the Guidelines for Japan–US Defense Cooperation primarily sought to deepen alliance coordination and integration, widen the aperture of the alliance to include a greater variety of missions and capabilities, and expand Japan's role in the alliance.[71] Although Japan is still formally restrained by its pacifist Constitution, the true constraint on the alliance is more cultural. The guidelines themselves did not automatically expand alliance cooperation in the desired areas; they merely opened the door for the two sides to move ahead at a later time. Yet Japan's political leaders and bureaucrats prefer to move cautiously and deliberately, in order to avoid a public backlash. Fully implementing the guidelines, therefore, should be a priority for the alliance.

One primary area on which the alliance should focus is the development of Japan's ability to conduct offensive strike operations. Although Japanese forces have traditionally been restricted to defense, the Abe government has sought to permit the Japan Self-Defense Forces to play offense. This would be helpful primarily in the context of Japanese preemption against a North Korean (or, implicitly, a Chinese) attack.

Those in Japan who have advocated for Japan to develop a strike capability have argued that it would enhance Japan's contribution to stability in the Indo-Pacific. They argue that such a capability would operate within the bounds of the alliance, which seeks to allay concerns in the United States (and in some circles in Japan) that a strike capability could lead to a rebirth of Japanese militarism. Although some in Washington may suspect that such a capability could be an implicit way for Japan to hedge against possible abandonment by the United States, such a capability should ultimately be supported and encouraged by the United States.

A Japanese strike capability would diversify alliance military options, and thus complicate North Korean (and Chinese) military planning and decisionmaking. Further, an indigenous Japanese strike capability could give the alliance greater flexibility in dealing with an imminent North Korean threat. For example, a limited preemptive Japanese strike on a North Korean medium-range ballistic missile capable of reaching Japan would demonstrate resolve while avoiding the greater escalation inherent in a US preemptive strike on the same North Korean threat.

Beyond strike capabilities, the US and Japanese militaries should enhance the already robust cooperation they have established in areas such as missile defense, security assistance, island defense, and maritime security:

- *Missile defense.* US–Japan missile defense cooperation is already quite robust and is on a positive trajectory. Japan hosts significant US missile defense assets and has made significant investments in both land- and sea-based missile defense capabilities. Moreover, Tokyo is considering the acquisition of Aegis Ashore, which would further enhance Japan's ability to defend itself from missile attacks. Yet more should be done across the Indo-Pacific to improve missile defense cooperation and capacity. By strengthening multilateral missile defense cooperation with Australia and South Korea in particular, Japan and the United States would enhance their ability to defend themselves while also buttressing multilateral cooperation against a shared security threat.

- *Security assistance.* The United States and Japan should enhance coordination to build the defensive capabilities of mutual partners across the Indo-Pacific. Japan's defense industry, though highly capable, is new to the business of defense exports. Although US defense companies tend to manufacture systems that are too expensive and overly advanced for the less developed militaries of US partners in Southeast Asia, Japan's industries can find their niche by providing high-quality, affordable systems that are better suited to the needs of Southeast Asian militaries. Yet just as important, Japan has tremendous expertise in training the militaries of less-developed partners to sustain the abilities they acquire with top-notch maintenance practices.

- *Island defense.* Japan's claims in the East China Sea are under increasing pressure from Chinese maritime forces. According to the Japan Coast Guard, after the purchase of three of the Senkaku Islands by the government of Japan, the number of Chinese vessels entering Japanese territorial waters drastically increased, expanding from 2 in 2011 to 73 in 2012.[72] In 2017, this number reached 108.[73] In response, the Japan Coast Guard has established a 600-person unit to patrol the Senkaku Islands, and Japan has built up missiles, facilities, and ground troops on the three government-owned islands.[74] Although the United States has repeatedly stated its position that Japan's claimed islands in the East China Sea fall under its commitments in the US–Japan Mutual Defense Treaty, it should do more to enhance Japan's ability to defend these claims. As such, the US military and Japan Self-Defense Forces should establish an island defense working group that develops exercises and force acquisition plans to enhance Japan's island defense capabilities and identify ways in which the United States could come to Japan's assistance during a time of crisis. Although actually emplacing such capabilities would be highly provocative for Beijing, they would also demonstrate seriousness and resolve by the alliance.

- *Maritime security.* As a maritime nation, security in sea lanes is an overriding security concern for Tokyo. Yet these concerns have taken on additional significance in recent years due to the parallels Japanese analysts often see between the South China Sea and East China Sea.[75] They fear that Chinese success at changing the status quo and establishing a military position in the South China Sea could set a precedent and embolden Chinese adventurism in the East China Sea. Tokyo, therefore, has taken a keen interest in countering Chinese assertiveness in the South China Sea, and in maritime security issues more generally. Enhancing US–Japan cooperation in maritime security—both in the East China Sea and South China Sea, and even into the Indian Ocean—would significantly enhance the alliance's ability to counter Chinese assertiveness while also enhancing Japan's efforts to strengthen its relationships across South and Southeast Asia.

STRENGTHENING ECONOMIC INTEGRATION

For decades, Japan has been a critical driver of economic integration across the Indo-Pacific. Although Japan's strategy was fundamentally undermined by the US withdrawal from the Trans-Pacific Partnership, several opportunities remain for the United States and Japan to work together to enhance economic integration and consolidate economic liberalism across the region.

Most important would be the conclusion of a bilateral free trade agreement. Although Japan has to date refused to agree to US demands for the concessions Japan was ready to make for the TPP, both sides should recognize that a bilateral FTA—even if not as substantial as TPP would have been—is in the strategic interests of both countries. Strengthening bilateral economic bonds would help both nations diversify their economic relationships and create significant opportunities for corporations on both sides. Moreover, it could serve as an entry point for the United States into the economic arrangements that Japan has established with other countries across the Indo-Pacific.

Beyond bilateral trade, the United States and Japan should work together to enhance economic integration across the region by cooperating in a major initiative to build infrastructure and enhance intraregional connectivity. Japan has already established itself as a major player in building infrastructure across the region. It won a $15 billion contract to build and manage India's first high-speed rail link, and it is building a high-speed link in northern Thailand. Indeed, in 2015 Japan responded to China's creation of the Asian Infrastructure Investment Bank by announcing $110 billion in aid for infrastructure development in Asia through 2020.

Yet though Japan has already been a major force for infrastructure development in Southeast Asia and has established its own infrastructure development bank, cooperation with the United States would bolster the scope and force of this initiative. Combining American and Japanese capital, and enhancing cooperation between American and Japanese firms, would turn this effort into a major initiative with significant geopolitical implications.

Another promising proposal to enhance regional economic integration is to establish "a fund that allows a diverse range of companies, private investors and international financial institutions the ability to lead the creation of digital highways, which will facilitate the development of technological infrastructure and enable the success of markets worldwide." This Indo-Pacific Technology Fund, as proposed, would support market goals for US companies and help them compete with subsidized Chinese companies, while allowing private companies to bid on large-scale projects that require government support to offset risk.[76] Politically, such a fund would demonstrate that the United States has a proactive, inclusive economic strategy that both benefits other countries and further ties the United States to the region. Japan would play a crucial role in this endeavor, as the Asian Development Bank would likely be a key partner for the United States in capitalizing such an initiative.

THE PHILIPPINES

The US–Philippines Alliance has endured significant turbulence in recent years, from one that was primarily focused on internal security issues to an alliance that, through 2016, emphasized enhancing the Philippines' external security in the face of an increasingly assertive China. Yet the alliance was thrown into uncertainty with the election of Rodrigo Duterte, who sought to embrace China and distance the Philippines from the United States. Today, the alliance—and the future of the Philippines itself—is at a crossroads.

Like most Southeast Asian countries, the Philippines has traditionally been broadly supportive of international laws and norms that regulate the behavior of larger powers. Although it is a US ally, Manila is also highly suspicious of Washington and fears efforts by the United States to dominate its politics or dictate its policies.

Yet much of this is up in the air today under President Duterte, and an alliance that has weathered significant changes in its recent past seems poised for more uncertainty.

A TURBULENT ALLIANCE

After the terrorist attacks of September 11, 2001, the US–Philippines Alliance intensified its focus on countering international terrorism and fighting a somewhat related insurgency challenge in the Mindanao region under Operation Enduring Freedom–Philippines. Mohammed Jamal Khalifa, Osama bin Laden's brother-in-law, had begun to establish al-Qaeda affiliates in the Philippines in the late 1980s, and in Manila in 1995, al-Qaeda leaders Ramzi Yousef and Khalid Sheikh Mohammed had planned to carry out "the Bojinka plot," which would have involved the bombing of eleven airliners in flight from Asia to the United States.

Operation Enduring Freedom–Philippines involved support by US military forces of the Philippine military, which regularly fought with terrorist groups and Moro insurgencies—many of which had loose affiliations with one another. The alliance made steady progress in these operations, and the Comprehensive Agreement on the Bangsamoro between the government of the Philippines and the primary insurgent organization—the Moro Islamic Liberation Front—was signed in 2014. Yet the insurgency and concerns about terrorism have persisted, though not at the intensity of the post-9/11 period.

As the alliance made progress in countering terrorism and insurgencies in the Philippines, Manila began to focus its attention externally. China had begun to act more assertively against Philippine claims in the South China Sea, which Beijing claimed as its own. The Philippines and China found themselves in 2012 in a standoff over the Scarborough Shoal.[77] Chinese fishing vessels were discovered by the Philippine Navy to have been operating in what Manila claimed to be its waters. Attempts by the Philippines to arrest the fishermen were blocked by Chinese maritime surveillance ships. After several weeks of tension, the United States mediated an agreement that both sides would withdraw their forces from the shoal until a deal over its ownership could be reached. Although the Philippines complied and withdrew, China did not.[78] China has since militarized its position in the Scarborough Shoal and has erected a barrier at the shoal's entrance. China has maintained a steady presence at the shoal ever since, and it routinely turns away Filipino vessels that sail into the area.

This incident galvanized the Philippines. President Benigno S. Aquino III later compared China's behavior and the West's failure to adequately respond with Nazi Germany's annexation of Czechoslovakia.[79] The next year, in 2013, Manila brought an arbitration case against China under the UN Convention on the Law of the Sea concerning China's claims in the South China Sea. Although China refused to participate in the arbitration, the tribunal ruled in July 2016 in favor of the Philippines. And though the tribunal found that it would not rule on questions of sovereignty, it rejected China's claim of having "historical rights" in the South China Sea and clarified the status of many of the features in the South China Sea.[80]

The Obama administration made significant progress in diversifying its regional military posture vis-à-vis the Philippines in 2014 by signing the Enhanced Defense Cooperation Agreement (EDCA), which sought to modernize the alliance by enhancing its ability to address Chinese assertiveness in the South China Sea and respond to natural disasters in the Philippines. Yet the pace and scope of this agreement have been greatly diminished, primarily due to the election of Rodrigo Duterte as president of the Philippines in June 2016. Dutere sought to reverse his predecessor's more confrontational approach to China, and instead embraced Beijing while severely criticizing the United States and publicly questioning the utility of the US–Philippines Alliance.[81] Yet it remains unclear how much of Duterte's pronouncements will translate into tangible shifts in policy or strategic orientation. Despite his threats to do so, Duterte has not walked away from the EDCA, agreeing to allow it to continue with reduced ambitions.[82]

Duterte's options are somewhat limited. China has not backed off of its claims, and the Philippine Constitution constrains Duterte's flexibility in this area because it defines the Philippines' national territory as "the Philippine archipelago, with all the islands and waters embraced therein, and all other territories over which the Philippines has sovereignty or jurisdiction, consisting of its terrestrial, fluvial and aerial domains, including its territorial sea, the seabed, the subsoil, the insular shelves, and other submarine areas. The waters around, between, and connecting the islands of the archipelago, regardless of their breadth and dimensions, form part of the internal waters of the Philippines."[83] Compromising on these issues with China may actually be an impeachable offense for Duterte; at the least, it would be difficult to defend politically.

One persistent sore spot in the US–Philippines Alliance has been questions about Washington's commitment to come to Manila's aid if China were to attack. This goes beyond normal alliance anxieties about abandonment, largely because of the ambiguities of the US–Philippines Mutual Defense Treaty. Articles IV and V commit the United States to defending a broad and somewhat ambiguous set of Filipino assets, including its territories, armed forces, and public ships and aircraft operating in the Pacific area.[84] This is far more expansive than the treaty the United States has with Japan, for instance, which confines itself to the "territories under the administration of Japan."[85]

Recently, Manila's attitude toward its alliance with the United States appears to have vacillated wildly between anxiety over US abandonment and anxiety about getting entrapped in a conflict between China and the United States. In late 2018, Defense Minister Delfin Lorenzana called for a review of the US–Philippines Mutual Defense Treaty to determine whether it should be maintained, strengthened, or scrapped altogether. A legislator from Manila went further in explaining the underlying anxieties for this review, stating that previous statements by the United States regarding its commitment to defend the Philippines have been "vague" and "noncommittal," and that "the US [has] opted to assume a seemingly hands-off attitude."[86]

Washington responded to these anxieties by clarifying, at a high level, its commitment. Vice President Mike Pence flew to Manila and declared "as the South China Sea is part of the Pacific, any armed attack on Philippine forces, aircraft, or public vessels in the South China Sea will trigger mutual defense obligations under Article 4 of our Mutual Defense Treaty."[87] Yet this reassurance only triggered anxiety about potential entrapment in a conflict between China and the United States.[88] Ultimately, these vicissitudes suggest that Manila is struggling with the same strategic complexities that the region's middle powers confront: how to navigate between Chinese assertiveness and power and American uncertainties.

NEXT STEPS

Given current strategic realities, it would make sense to keep defense cooperation under the US–Philippine Alliance relatively quiet. Although it is unfortunate that the pace and ambition of alliance defense cooperation has slowed, positive progress can and should be sustained. Assuming that implementation of the EDCA continues to move apace, the alliance should focus on four areas.

First, it needs to focus on enhancing the Philippines' maritime capabilities. The Philippines' maritime forces are quite limited in size, budget, and sophistication. This constrains Manila's ability to police its own waters, let alone its ability to confront Chinese assertiveness. Moreover, the Philippines' naval force is heavily weighted toward the military—maritime law enforcement and surveillance capabilities are fairly humble. In fact, some believe that the reason Manila's initial response to Chinese pressure at Scarborough Shoal was military in nature was because its Coast Guard did not have the ability to reach the scene quickly. As such, Washington—especially in cooperation with other allies like Tokyo and Canberra—should work with Manila on a major initiative designed to enhance the Philippines' maritime capabilities. This could involve the provisioning of used ships and aircraft for low cost, as well as the sale of maritime surveillance assets and including the Philippines in regional maritime information-sharing mechanisms. Finally, the United States and its other allies should work with the Philippines on its maritime forces to enhance its ability to sustain and maintain the assets it has.

Second, it needs to prepare for contingencies at Ayungin and Scarborough. Manila and Washington should work together to plan for future tensions surrounding the Filipino ship the *Sierra Madre*—which is grounded 105 nautical miles from the Philippines' mainland on a feature Manila calls Ayungin in the Spratley Islands—and at Scarborough Shoal.[89] Efforts to keep the small contingent of Filipino Marines stationed on the *Sierra Madre* supplied is a major potential flashpoint, as would be Chinese efforts to reclaim and build permanent military facilities at Scarborough Shoal. Washington and Manila should quietly consult with one another on how they would respond to various coercive contingencies from Beijing, both to ensure a coordinated allied response and to address concerns that both sides may have about the reliability of the other.

Third, it needs to stay the course. With President Duterte rapidly compiling a reputation for wanton violations of human rights, there may come a time when the United States considers diminishing alliance cooperation. Though some adjustments may be in order depending on what may occur, completely isolating Manila would be a strategic mistake, as it would be more likely to drive Manila toward Beijing while not actually helping those who may be victimized. Instead, steady and open engagement with the government of the Philippines, especially its military, would be critical to both maintaining communication with Manila while at the same time not harming broader US interests in the Indo-Pacific. Although this does not mean the United States should ignore human rights concerns, it does mean that engagement—not isolation—may be a more effective and strategically beneficial option.

And fourth, it needs to deepen economic development and connectivity. Although the United States and the Philippines enjoy a relatively robust economic relationship, much more could be done.

Improving infrastructure, especially outside Manila, is one area that would greatly benefit the Filipino people while at the same time strengthen the foundation of the Philippines' ties with the United States, Japan, and India. Indeed, engaging other US allies and partners from Asia and Europe may be an essential aspect of US regional strategy in the future—both as a check against China and also as a conduit for greater competition in Asia among the world's major powers.

SOUTH KOREA

Korea is unique among US allies and partners in Asia, primarily because of the ever-present existential threat posed by North Korea but also because of its history and geography. This poses distinctive challenges for the United States, as it must account for Seoul's singular perspective and strategic environment when crafting its alliance policy. Yet Washington must also develop mechanisms through which Seoul can expand its strategic aperture and contribute not only to its own defense but also to the liberal order upon which it depends.

South Korea faces an existential threat from North Korea. Although the Korean People's Army has posed an existential conventional threat to South Korea for decades, North Korea's development of weapons of mass destruction and its ability to strike US forces in Japan and Guam have significantly changed the security dynamics on the Korean Peninsula. Moreover, North Korea's rapid progress in developing the ability to strike the United States itself with nuclear weapons threatens to add another, more dangerous dynamic to the peninsula.

A North Korea armed with nuclear weapons—and the means to use them against South Korea, Japan, and the United States—poses a different and more dangerous kind of existential threat than it has posed in the past. Although North Korea has conducted small-scale attacks against Seoul and its interests for decades, Pyongyang may feel emboldened to act with even more impunity if it feels the power of having a credible nuclear deterrent. In a dynamic that political scientists call the *stability/instability paradox*, North Korea may believe that its nuclear deterrent would prevent a massive retaliation if it were to attack its neighbors, thus potentially inspiring an even greater degree of North Korean belligerence. Moreover, North Korea may attempt to employ nuclear coercion to extract concessions from its neighbors and the international community. In fact, Kim Jong-un's statement that "these weapons will be used only if our security is threatened" could be understood as allowing for a very broad use of nuclear weapons, considering past North Korean rhetoric referring to international sanctions and US military exercises as declarations of war.[90]

EMPOWERING THE MILITARY

This emerging threat will require a new strategy from the United States and South Korea—which is beyond the scope of this study. Yet it speaks to the role that South Korea could play in its own defense, and how the United States could enable South Korea to defend itself. Although the two sides have been gradually making progress toward empowering South Korea militarily—in a process to eventually transfer wartime operational control (OPCON) of its forces from the United States to South Korea—significant progress will need to be made if the South Korean military is to be ready to accept OPCON.

In 2016, the United States and South Korea signed the Conditions-Based Operational Control (OPCON) Transition Plan, which will guide the alliance toward South Korea's assumption of wartime operational control of its forces.[91] It set aside past agreements that had tied the OPCON transition to an arbitrary date, and instead focused the two sides on achieving specific conditions that would enable the OPCON transfer. A major part of these conditions involves the South Korean military acquiring or developing a range of necessary capabilities and capacities, which in turn requires the significant allocation of resources. Making progress toward acquiring these capabilities is a necessary step toward South Korea doing more to defend itself.

A major aspect of enhancing South Korea's ability to defend itself is in the realm of its own missile capabilities. Although the United States recently agreed to do away with past limitations on the size of warheads that South Korea could use on its own ballistic missiles,[92] significant additional progress in this area is necessary. South Korea has developed several unilateral doctrines, such as the so-called Kill Chain and Korea Massive Punishment and Retaliation plans, which would involve a range of capabilities that would be launched by Seoul to kill or incapacitate North Korea in the opening minutes of a conflict.[93] Such a doctrine would pose significant challenges for the US–South Korea alliance, as many of these attacks would require significant US support. Moreover, it raises the possibility that Seoul could initiate a conflict without prior approval by Washington. A situation that is especially problematic, and the answer to this challenge, lies in the fact that South Korea's ballistic missile forces lie outside the combined command structure and are commanded by only the South Korean military commanders. By ensuring that these missiles cannot be fired without US approval, and by making such an arrangement a requirement for US support for such a strike, the two challenges posed by these plans and capabilities can be resolved.

Another aspect of US–South Korea military cooperation that deserves more attention is maritime cooperation. Although South Korea is geographically located on a peninsula, cooperation between the US and South Korean navies has long lagged behind cooperation between their respective air and ground forces. This should change. South Korea has significant naval capabilities, and enhanced cooperation between the two navies could enhance alliance capabilities in areas that would be critical in defending against North Korean provocations. North Korea poses a significant naval threat, with a range of minisubmarines that it can use for the clandestine insertion of special operations forces. Moreover, North Korea has been gradually developing a larger submarine that may, one day, have the ability to fire nuclear-capable ballistic missiles.[94]

Enhancing alliance naval cooperation could involve regular exercises on a range of operations, including missile defense and strategies to identify and counter the insertion of special forces. The United States and South Korea should therefore consider the rotational presence of US naval forces on the Korean Peninsula, with the distant possibility of forward-stationing some forces in South Korea on a permanent basis. Additionally, the US and South Korean navies should explore opportunities to cooperate with one another beyond the peninsula to both assert the importance of freedom of navigation and to stress Seoul's security interests beyond the peninsula.

South Korea's deep technological base also provides significant opportunities for deeper alliance cooperation in space and cyberspace. This is especially critical considering the significant threat that North Korea poses in cyberspace, as well as the reliance that both the United States' and South Korea's economies have on open and stable space and cyber domains. The United States and South Korea have begun biannual working-level talks, and the US–ROK Cyber Cooperation Working Group has resulted in further joint cyber defense training.[95] However, they have yet to establish a combined cyberthreat response system, which is needed to respond to North Korean cyberthreats in a unified, strategic manner.[96]

BEYOND THE PENINSULA

Despite the profound focus that Seoul must maintain on the existential threat from the North, South Korea has significant interests beyond the Korean Peninsula. Like Japan, South Korea depends on open and stable maritime supply lines for access to overseas markets and resources. Considering the Korean economy's profound dependence on free and open trade, the preservation of political and economic liberalism across Asia is very much in Seoul's interests.

Yet Seoul must also balance these interests, and any concerns it may have about Beijing's assertiveness, against the tremendously important role China plays on the Korean Peninsula.

Any government in Seoul, regardless of its political orientation, will be reluctant to antagonize Beijing over issues like freedom of navigation or assertiveness in the South China Sea. Washington should be comfortable with this situation, and thus should attempt to avoid putting Seoul in a difficult position in which it may feel it must choose the United States over China with respect to an issue of tertiary importance for South Korea.

South Korea has built up a tremendous amount of soft power by investing and conducting development assistance across the Indo-Pacific. In fact, Seoul's soft power allows it to often punch above its weight in international forums. Although it was an aid recipient fewer than twenty years ago, it provided $1.9 billion in net overseas development assistance in 2015, 0.14 percent of its gross national income.[97] It has implemented most of its bilateral assistance through government-to-government agreements, rather than non-governmental organizations, giving the government an explicit role in generating goodwill overseas.[98] Its foreign assistance program has centered on loans and technical consulting, based on its own experience as an aid recipient.[99]

South Korea is a living example of the benefits of economic and political liberalism, and it has been an incredible advocate for these values across the region. As the United States engages its allies and partners in securing a free and open Indo-Pacific—building infrastructure, advocating for economic liberalism, consolidating democracy, and driving economic integration—it should be sure to involve South Korea.

The challenge for the United States is that, to a greater degree than with other countries, South Korea will be especially sensitive to accusations that it is helping to contain China. As in the security sphere, Washington should be sensitive to such concerns. One way to alleviate this dynamic would be for Seoul to invest in mechanisms and initiatives led by Beijing as well as those led by Washington, Tokyo, or New Delhi. This would help Seoul alleviate any strategic pressure it may be under from Beijing, while also further diversifying its relationships. Moreover, Seoul could bring its commitment to economic and political liberalism into Beijing's initiatives and advocate for these values within Beijing's tent.

Yet Seoul must also make a strategic choice about the role it will play in the region. Take, for instance, the "Quad" mechanism involving Japan, the United States, India, and Australia. These countries represent a broad set of perspectives on regional order and on China specifically, yet they have still found a way to work with one another on areas of mutual interest. South Korean strategists should view the Quad as indications of an impending geopolitical sidelining of South Korea—why is the Quad not a "Quint"?

As the region grows more competitive and middle powers in the region navigate its complexities, South Korea will need to make uncomfortable strategic choices. If lingering animosities with Japan and concerns about angering China—no matter how genuine—are able to frame its geopolitical ambition, South Korea may find its options increasingly narrowed.

NEW ZEALAND

For decades, New Zealand has occupied a unique spot among US allies and partners in the Indo-Pacific. Although formally an ally as a result of the 1951 Australia, New Zealand, United States Security Treaty (ANZUS Treaty), Washington suspended its treaty obligations in 1985 to New Zealand over a dispute over the location of US nuclear weapons. The United States downgraded New Zealand from "ally" to "friend," and diminished its military and intelligence cooperation.

Yet despite this dispute, relations between Washington and Wellington have remained largely constructive and have warmed considerably in the first decade of the new millennium. New Zealand contributed to US-led operations in Afghanistan beginning in late 2001 and to an engineering unit to assist postwar reconstruction and humanitarian aid efforts in Iraq. As a result of these initiatives, the George W. Bush administration sought to move the relationship beyond the nuclear issue in a way that, in the words of then secretary of state Condoleezza Rice, was no longer "harnessed to or constrained by the past."[100]

In recent years, China has emerged as a major strategic conundrum for New Zealand. China is New Zealand's most important trading partner, but Wellington has grown increasingly concerned about its vulnerabilities to coercion and influence from Beijing. New Zealand's largest telecommunications provider announced in November 2018 that it would block the use of Huawei equipment in its 5G infrastructure, citing advice from New Zealand intelligence agencies that to do so would present "significant national security risks." This prompted Huawei to run ads in New Zealand's two largest newspapers, declaring that 5G without Huawei was "like rugby without New Zealand."[101]

Such concerns in Wellington were informed by previous reported efforts by Beijing to interfere in New Zealand's domestic politics. National Party leader Simon Bridges had been accused of disguising a donation of roughly $67,000 in campaign donations orchestrated by a businessman with links to the Chinese government—an allegation that Bridges denied.[102] In 2017, a prominent Chinese-born member of New Zealand's Parliament, Jian Yang, was reported to have lied to the authorities about his educational background on his citizenship application for New Zealand. Specifically, he was accused of having worked for fifteen years in China's military intelligence community and having obtained a master's degree at the People's Liberation Army University of Foreign Languages, one of China's best-known military intelligence schools. Later, at the same institute, he reportedly taught English to students who were studying how to intercept and decipher English-language communications on behalf of Chinese military intelligence. Yang has admitted that he was a member of the Chinese Communist Party but has insisted that he was not an active member after leaving China in 1994.[103]

New Zealand therefore finds itself in a position similar to that of so many other countries in the Indo-Pacific: tied to China economically, but concerned about the implications of China's rise for its interests and sovereignty. These developments suggest an opportunity for the United States and New Zealand to inaugurate a new era of cooperative relations.

ECONOMIC AND DEVELOPMENT COOPERATION

The United States is an important economic partner for New Zealand. The United States is New Zealand's fourth-largest trading partner—behind China, Australia, and the European Union—with two-way trade amounting to $591 million in 2018–19.[104] Similarly, foreign direct investment from the United States is also third ($390 million), behind that from Australia and Hong Kong.[105]

Yet despite these economic ties, a free trade agreement has been long been a goal seemingly out of reach for Washington and Wellington. New Zealand was a party to the TPP and joined its successor—the Comprehensive and Progressive Agreement for Trans-Pacific Partnership—so it seems that the major impediment to such an agreement seems to come more from the United States than from New Zealand. It is clear that an FTA between the two countries would likely need to come through a broader multilateral agreement—a challenge that goes far beyond any issues that may exist in the bilateral relationship.

More can be done, however, in expanding cooperation between the two countries on encouraging greater economic development and infrastructure connectivity across other parts of the Indo-Pacific. New Zealand has a deep history of engagement in the South Pacific. In fact, New Zealand's Pacific neighbors receive almost 60 percent of its official development assistance funding, and Wellington has allocated NZ$1.13 billion to official development assistance in the Pacific between 2018 and 2021.[106]

Considering Wellington's history of engaging the islands in the South Pacific, and Beijing's efforts to deepen its relations and influence these islands, enhanced cooperation between Wellington and the United States in these areas has a clear strategic logic. Indeed, Wellington has increased its economic engagement with the

Pacific islands in part to directly compete with Beijing's efforts to build influence in the region.[107] According to Winston Peters, New Zealand's deputy prime minister, the South Pacific has become an "increasingly contested strategy space."[108]

Given that New Zealand's relations with these countries are often deeper and longer-lasting than those of the United States, at times it may be wise for New Zealand to not only coordinate its actions with the United States but also to be a conduit for American resources and assistance. As such, the United States should work to include New Zealand in discussions about regional infrastructure construction strategies and other efforts related to development and governance assistance that may occur with other US allies and partners. The critical variable for the United States in this instance would be for it to support liberal principles—and less that the United States remains out in front of such efforts.

SECURITY COOPERATION

Despite challenges in the broader security relationship, cooperation between the United States and New Zealand has proven remarkably durable. Troops from New Zealand have fought alongside American troops in Korea, in Vietnam, during the Gulf War, and in Afghanistan. More than three hundred personnel from the Royal New Zealand Navy participated in the 2018 Rim of the Pacific Exercise in Hawaii, conducting activities ranging from diving and salvage operations to maritime security operations and complex war fighting.[109] And in November 2016, the USS *Sampson* became the first US Navy ship to visit New Zealand in three decades.[110] The expansion of the relationship was made possible by a declaration signed in June 2012 in the Pentagon by Defense Minister Jonathan Coleman and Secretary of Defense Leon Panetta. The agreement, though it was not binding and though it did not renew the ANZUS Treaty obligations, paved the way for increased defense cooperation.

Washington and Wellington should establish the renewal of the ANZUS Treaty as a long-term objective for both sides. The unique and critical role that New Zealand can play in the Indo-Pacific, combined with the challenges posed by China to the region and to New Zealand in particular, make clear the geopolitical role that a renewed ANZUS Treaty could play. Such an agreement would reflect the greater geopolitical demands that both nations will face in the Indo-Pacific, and would serve as the foundation for greater cooperation between Washington and Wellington that the Indo-Pacific's new era will require.

More immediately, Washington and Wellington should gradually expand the breadth and accelerate the pace of their security cooperation. Building on the 2016 ship visit, additional visits should continue in order to make them a normal and regular feature of regional security dynamics. Other security cooperation initiatives, including joint naval patrols and New Zealand's participation in important regional multilateral exercises—such as Cobra Gold—would further enhance Wellington's regional security role in a way that is both politically sustainable and strategically sound.

Ultimately, New Zealand has an important role to play in sustaining a regional liberal order. Wellington plays a critical role in the South Pacific, and its values and interests make it a natural partner for Washington in pursuing their shared broader regional objectives. Doing so would require significant vision and commitment from both sides, but the forward-looking nature of the relationship—growing out of enhanced cooperation against international terrorism—serves as a critical foundation for a stronger, more strategically effective alliance.

TAIWAN

In her inaugural address as the president of Taiwan, Tsai Ing-wen spoke about how Taiwan must participate proactively in regional affairs, remain the "staunch guardian of peace" in cross–Taiwan

Strait relations, and fulfill its duties as a citizen of the world.[111] This role for Taiwan would also be in the interests of the United States, given that Taiwan has long played an important role in contributing to peace and prosperity around the world. Taiwan is a model for the world, showing how a former autocracy can transition into a robust democracy and act responsibly on the world stage.

Taiwan already plays an important part in contributing to global stability. In the wake of the 2014 Ebola outbreak in West Africa, Taiwan donated 100,000 sets of personal protective equipment and $1 million to help those most urgently affected. Taiwan has also helped people who have had to flee their homes in Iraq and Syria. These types of international assistance are a testament to the important role that Taiwan has to play in the world—a role I would note that in no way comes at the expense of mainland China.

Despite these important accomplishments, Taiwan's strategic environment remains one of the world's most challenging. China was the conduit for 41 percent of Taiwan's international trade in 2017, and for about 45 percent of its investment in 2016;[112] China also has the ability to determine the scope and breadth of Taiwan's international space, and at the same time represents an existential military threat that is just 90 miles away. Moreover, Taiwan sits at one of the most geographically and climatologically vulnerable locations on the planet, and thus it regularly experiences devastating earthquakes, typhoons, and tsunamis. As such, Taiwan's leading authorities must confront tremendous challenges.

Despite the unofficial relationship that has existed between Taiwan and the United States since 1979, when Washington officially recognized the People's Republic of China and downgraded its diplomatic relations with Taipei, the two sides have established a robust and highly effective dynamic. Trade between Taiwan in the United States used to be much more important to Taiwan than it is today: In 1985, trade with the United States accounted for 48 percent of Taiwan's total exports. Thirty years later, it accounted for only 12 percent. Yet Taiwan is still the ninth-largest goods trading partner for the United States with $63.74 billion in total commodity trading in 2015, with an additional $20 billion in two-way trade in services. According to the US Department of Commerce, trade with Taiwan in 2014 supported an estimated 217,000 jobs.[113] Taiwan is one of the biggest customers of the US defense industry. Both Taiwan and the United States have agreed to $10.75 billion in arms sales since 2004.[114]

The Taiwan Relations Act commits the United States to "provide Taiwan with arms of a defensive character and shall maintain the capacity of the United States to resist any resort to force or other forms of coercion that would jeopardize the security, or social or economic system, of the people of Taiwan."[115] Yet as China's military has continued to modernize and expand at a rapid pace, questions about Taiwan's ability to defend itself, and the ability of the United States to resist Chinese aggression, have intensified.

Both sides of this relationship have to up their game. If Washington truly seeks to preserve Taipei's security and its social or economic system, a situation in which Taipei's economic and political future can be increasingly dictated by Beijing, and the cross-strait military balance continues to slide in Beijing's favor, is unsustainable over the long term. Although this study is not calling for the United States' overall approach to change—indeed, Taipei's future status should be peacefully determined by the people of both sides— both Washington and Taipei should undertake policies to enhance Taipei's ability to determine its own future and defend itself from aggression or coercion.

DIVERSIFYING ECONOMIC RELATIONS

Taiwan's economic destiny is tightly wrapped around that of the mainland. Taiwan relies on exports for economic growth, and its reliance on the Chinese market has increased significantly since 2000. As shown by figure 4.1, since 2005, Taiwan exports about 40 percent of its goods and services to China (including Hong Kong). Notably, in 2000, China's market share of Taiwan's total exports, excluding Hong Kong, was only 2.84 percent. This figure grew to 28.04 percent by 2017.[116]

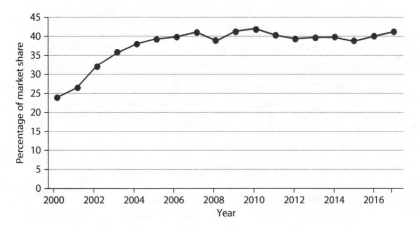

FIGURE 4.1 Chinese market share of Taiwan's total exports, 2000–2017

SOURCE: DA-NIEN LIU, "THE TRADING RELATIONSHIP BETWEEN TAIWAN AND THE
UNITED STATES: CURRENT TRENDS AND THE OUTLOOK FOR THE FUTURE,"
BROOKINGS INSTITUTION, NOVEMBER 2016, HTTPS://WWW.BROOKINGS.EDU
/OPINIONS/THE-TRADING-RELATIONSHIP-BETWEEN-TAIWAN-AND-THE-UNITED
-STATES-CURRENT-TRENDS-AND-THE-OUTLOOK-FOR-THE-FUTURE/.

This dynamic has been driven by two interrelated factors. The first is purely a difference of scale—mainland China's economy was 23.5 times larger than that of Taiwan in 2017, which gives Beijing a significant geopolitical advantage.[117] The second is that the mainland's economy has likewise grown at a faster rate than that of Taiwan. In 2017 the People's Republic of China's real GDP growth was 6.8 percent, while Taiwan's was 2 percent.[118] The result is that mainland China's economy is both larger and more attractive for international and cross-strait investors and entrepreneurs, with 407,000 people from Taiwan living and working in China. This number accounts for 55.9 percent of the Taiwanese working overseas.[119]

This dynamic became a major issue in Taiwan's 2016 election, in which future president Tsai Ing-wen criticized the opposition for building closer economic ties with the mainland at the expense of Taiwan's own economy and innovation. Tsai argued that Taiwan had not protected domestic enterprises from state-sponsored Chinese competition. "Taiwan's environment for innovation and entrepreneurship is getting worse and worse," she said. "Workers are going overseas, and a huge number are being poached by Chinese enterprises. Many of our young people abroad can't find a way home."[120]

These dynamics also have potentially significant geopolitical implications. Such close, but asymmetric, economic ties provide Beijing with significant options to exert leverage over Taipei and influence its political dynamics. China can choose where capital may flow and who may get favorable economic treatment in the mainland—decisions that could potentially change politics in Taiwan. Indeed, Beijing has in its portfolio the ability to assign winners and losers in Taipei based on their political positions, which is not a recipe for the long-term survival of Taipei's social and economic system.

The clear answer to this challenge is to diversify Taipei's economic relationships and thus dilute Beijing's economic power in Taipei. Taipei signed nominal free trade agreements with Singapore and Wellington in 2013, which were largely seen as the opening moves of Taipei's ambition to join the Trans-Pacific Partnership. Upon her election, President Tsai announced the New Southbound initiative, which seeks to expedite trade, investment, and cultural interactions between Taiwan and the nations of South and Southeast Asia. Since President Trump's announcement that the United States would be withdrawing from TPP negotiations, some Taiwan-focused scholars have called for Taiwan to join the reconstituted TPP (known as TPP-11).[121] Although these are certainly worthwhile ambitions for Taiwan, the United States should not sit by and hope that South Asian and Southeast Asian nations and a reconstituted TPP can, on their own, help Taiwan diversify its economic relationships. Rather, US leadership is sorely needed.

The United States and Taiwan should rapidly seek to negotiate and conclude an agreement that would functionally serve as a bilateral FTA. Such an agreement has been considered for over a decade, but little progress has been made. Although the challenges preventing the signing of an agreement have nominally been the issues that affect most trade relationships—in this case, Taiwan wants better access to US markets, and the United States seeks improved policies on electronic commerce, intellectual property, food safety, and agricultural goods—the real roadblock has been a lack of political prioritization on both sides. Taipei knows that such an agreement would force it to implement sorely needed, but politically toxic, domestic economic reforms, while Washington knows that such an agreement would trigger a strong negative reaction from Beijing, while not bringing comparatively significant benefits for American corporations.

Yet the geopolitical realities of Taiwan's strategic environment, combined with the significant interests the United States has in diversifying Taiwan's economic relationships, demands action from both sides. Political leaders in Washington and Taipei should direct their trade negotiators to rapidly develop an appropriate economic agreement that would serve to benefit the economies of both sides.

The geopolitical benefits of a US–Taiwan FTA would be significant. It would send a strong signal to the entire region that the United States remains committed to maintaining its unofficial relationship with Taiwan, and it would provide some political cover for other Indo-Pacific nations to include Taiwan in TPP-11. This agreement would also send a strong deterrent signal to Beijing—a far stronger deterrent signal than would be derived from normal defense exchanges and occasional arms sales.

EXPANDING TAIWAN'S INTERNATIONAL SPACE

Although Taiwan's international space has gradually receded since it lost its seat at the United Nations in 1971, the pace of this regression has accelerated since the inauguration of Tsai Ing-wen as president in 2016. This was entirely due to an apparent decision by Beijing to call an end to the "diplomatic truce" that had begun under Tsai's predecessor, Ma Ying-jeou. In September of that year, the International Civil Aviation Organization did not invite Taiwan to participate in its annual conference, which many saw as an element of Beijing's broader campaign to exclude Taiwan from international forums. This was quickly followed by an announcement by São Tomé and Príncipe that it would be shifting diplomatic recognition from Taipei to Beijing—a decision widely thought to be driven by financial considerations.[122] The next May, Taiwan was not invited to the World Health Assembly's annual meeting for the first time since 2009. Similarly, in June 2017, Taiwan was not allowed to participate in the International Labor Organization's conference. In 2017 and 2018, Panama, the Dominican Republic, and Burkina Faso all announced a switch of diplomatic recognition from Taipei to Beijing, leaving Taipei with eighteen so-called diplomatic allies.

It would be hypocritical for Washington to criticize or pressure those capitals that have switched diplomatic relations to Beijing; as noted above, Washington did the same thing in 1979. Yet the United States also has an interest in ensuring that the people of Taiwan are appropriately represented in the international community. This will require a concerted effort by the United States to advocate for Taiwan's participation in appropriate international forums, where status as a nation is not required for membership (e.g., Asia-Pacific Economic Cooperation), and to encourage its other allies and partners to do the same. These should include Taiwan's "diplomatic allies," which could use the support of the United States when making such decisions in the likely face of pressure from China.

The United States should also endeavor to ensure that Taiwan's interests are represented when Taiwan is not able to participate in international meetings. This would primarily mean that the United States should undertake a whole-of-government effort to ensure that Taiwan remains engaged in international dialogue. When Taiwan is not able to attend, the United States should pre-brief and back-brief Taiwan officials to ensure that Taiwan remains engaged. For example, the US Centers for Disease Control and Prevention should engage with its Taiwanese counterparts both before and after World Health Assembly and World Health Organization meetings to ensure that Taiwan's health infrastructure remains capable of effectively engaging the international community in the event of a global or regional health event. After all, disease does not care about Taiwan's international status, but leaders around the world should care about Taiwan's ability to manage health crises. Similar efforts could be made for a host of other issues, from addressing the refugee crisis to cooperating on climate change and energy.

STRENGTHENING CROSS-STRAIT DETERRENCE

For several decades, and at an accelerating pace, Taiwan's security situation has deteriorated significantly. Whereas American strategists once worried about restraining Taiwan from attacking the mainland, today most military strategists wonder how long Taiwan may be able to hold out before the United States intervenes.[123] The reality is that mainland China now poses an existential threat to Taiwan, primarily because of issues of scale and focus. Beijing has more resources than Taipei, and it has devoted more energy attention to changing the cross–Taiwan Strait military balance than has Taiwan.

The military balance in the Taiwan Strait is tilting in China's favor. In an invasion scenario, it is increasingly likely that China would seize air and sea control. In the air, the People's Liberation Army Air Force's (PLAAF) fifth-generation fighter J-20 is now combat ready,[124] while at the same time the PLAAF also enjoys quantitative advantages over Taiwan's 384 fourth-generation aircraft. The PLAAF's operations against Taiwan in the air would be further aided by the 1,000 to 1,200 short-range ballistic missiles and the new S-400 air defense batteries from Russia.[125] On the sea, China is modernizing its navies in addition to increasing its quantitative advantages. Coupled with the People's Liberation Army Navy's long history of antiship cruise missiles investment, the new Type 055 missile-guided destroyers would be critical to China's antiaccess/area denial strategy.[126]

Even though Taiwan has invested in its capable Tuo River class (沱江艦) corvette and Hsiung Feng III (雄風三型) antiship cruise missiles in recent years, an engagement on the sea still appears to be in China's favor, given the PLAAF's advantages in the air.

Despite the increasingly unbalanced military power in the Taiwan Strait, there remains doubt over Taiwan's commitment to its self-defense. Since 2012, defense spending as a share of Taiwanese GDP has dropped below 2 percent.[127] This figure is far below 3 percent, a baseline that all three recent administrations in Taiwan promised to maintain. On a positive note, Taiwan's defense spending as a share of its national budget has remained rather stable for the past seventeen years (figure 4.2).[128]

It is also worth questioning the feasibility of Taiwan's all-volunteer force policy. This year, it is expected that Taiwan will be short 2,000 military personnel from meeting its "effective combat capabilities [有效戰力]." The definition of effective combat capabilities, according to Taiwan's Defense Ministry, is to maintain at least 90 percent

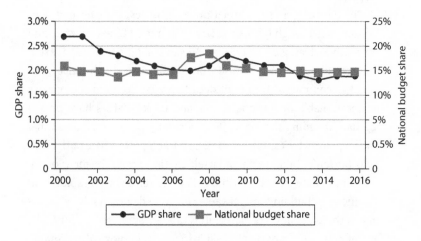

FIGURE 4.2 Taiwan's defense spending, 2000–2016

SOURCE: SIPRI MILITARY EXPENDITURE DATABASE.

of the overall authorized complement, which is 196,000 soldiers. In addition, the shortage of 2,000 personnel is true even after including about 11,000 "last-generation" conscripts in the estimate.[129]

This is not to say that an all-volunteer force does not come with some advantages. In the beginning of a Chinese invasion scenario, Taiwan would need an experienced and technology-savvy volunteer force from its Navy and Air Force to carry out not only combat but also logistics operations. Conscripts can only contribute to the Army, but a Chinese amphibious invasion is likely to take place after bombing and blockade operations. This would have a negative impact on the psychology of the Taiwan Army if both the Navy and Air Force were to fail to show a minimum degree of resistance, even given the former's strong antilanding capabilities.[130]

Yet the situation is not unsolvable. There is still the prospect that Taiwan could make itself virtually impossible to invade. But this would require significant investments in capabilities that take advantage of Taiwan's natural advantages, exploit mainland China's military deficiencies, and enable the United States to effectively respond in the case of Chinese aggression or coercion.

The US–Taiwan defense relationship is in desperate need of revitalization. Although both sides have committed to asymmetric and innovative strategies to ensure Taiwan's ability to defend itself, political discourse has focused on symbolism or substance. Taiwan has committed to a multidecade project to build submarines of questionable operational value, and US legislators have passed legislation calling for higher-level visits by US military personnel and ship visits by Taiwan naval vessels to US ports. Little of this will help Taiwan's ability to defend itself anytime soon. The focus of the US–Taiwan defense relationship should therefore be on rapidly and significantly building up Taiwan's ability to defend itself by focusing on the acquisition of capabilities that are survivable, affordable, and effective. Considering Taiwan's robust technological and industrial capacities, its defense industry should be an able partner in the development of such capabilities.

VIETNAM

Vietnam has successfully emerged from the shadow of decades of war against the West and is today a major geopolitical player in Southeast Asia. It was able to reform and open itself domestically, in large part because of the relatively stable regional environment provided—somewhat ironically—by the United States. This has been especially true since the end of the Cold War, because Hanoi has no longer needed to navigate between Moscow and Washington and has been freer to pursue its own interests.

However, in recent years the rise of China has proven to be a special cause of concern for Vietnam's leaders, and Hanoi finds itself again trying to find a balance between competing major foreign powers. Long-simmering disputes with China over the status of various features in the South China Sea have emerged as a major potential source of instability for Vietnam—disputes that have rekindled Hanoi's traditional animosity toward Beijing. Indeed, in interviews conducted with Vietnamese officials and academics, each made the same point—that Vietnam had been invaded by China twenty times in two hundred years, with one senior Vietnamese official telling me that "anyone from Vietnam who liked China left generations ago."

Many in Vietnam see the United States—as well as India—as natural checks against an increasingly assertive and powerful China. As a result, Hanoi has sought to diversify its foreign relationships and to enlist Washington and New Delhi in its efforts to balance against China.

Still, there is a ceiling to how far and how fast Vietnam is willing to go with its foreign partners, and especially with the United States. Hanoi does not seek formal alliances and will never put itself in a position to be dominated, dictated to, or dependent upon a foreign power—no matter how much their geopolitical interests may converge. Rather, as a cold geopolitical calculation, Vietnam's leaders

seek to engage the United States in order to balance against potential Chinese aggression. Yet lingering hostility in some Vietnamese
circles over history, ideology, and fears of American domination are
not likely to dissipate any time soon. Moreover, Vietnam's undemocratic political system and its continued human rights abuses will
likely limit the pace and scope of US engagement.

One of Vietnam's most significant geopolitical relationships is
also one that is underrecognized by most American observers: its
relationship with India. In 2017, India and Vietnam signed twelve
agreements to facilitate bilateral cooperation on a swath of security and economic issues, and New Delhi extended Hanoi a $500
million line of credit to facilitate deeper defense cooperation.[131]
India's state-run energy company, ONGC, and PetroVietnam Exploration Production Corporation have repeatedly worked together to
explore the South China Sea for oil in areas also claimed by China.
Vietnam has acquired significant military capabilities from India,
and Indian military officers train their Vietnamese counterparts on
a regular basis.

The United States has also taken several important steps that
were necessary to enhance cooperation with Vietnam. In 2016, the
United States finally lifted its arms embargo against Vietnam—
permitting the transfer of lethal weapons.[132] Yet Vietnam's interest
in such capabilities is fairly limited—they are often too expensive
for Hanoi's limited defense budget, and are often far more capable
that what it can handle. To date, the most significant acquisitions
from Vietnam of American capabilities have been the 2016 transfer of a Hamilton-class cutter from the US Coast Guard, the sale of
Boeing-Insitu ScanEagle drones for maritime surveillance, and the
transfer of six new Metal Shark boats. The significance of this burgeoning military relationship became apparent in January 2018,
when the US aircraft carrier *Carl Vinson* visited Vietnam—the first
such visit since the end of the Vietnam War.

Economically, US–Vietnam relations have increased steadily
since a bilateral trade agreement came into force in 2001. Trade in
goods has burgeoned, from $451 million in 1995 to more than $54

billion in 2017.[133] Yet Vietnam stood to benefit the most from the TPP being concluded with the United States. Although Vietnam has remained with the TPP since the United States withdrew, this represents both a significant blow to Vietnam's ability to trade internationally and a sedative for those in Vietnam who sought to use the TPP to force through additional economic reforms.

HANOI'S VIEWS ON REGIONAL ORDER AND REGIONAL POWER

Vietnam's fundamental objective is to sustain a stable regional environment in order to facilitate its continued domestic development and reform. Even though Vietnam does not agree with how the United States interprets or enforces all aspects of international law, Hanoi nonetheless sees a US-led regional order as conducive to stability. According to the Vietnamese scholar Tran Viet Thai, who is affiliated with the Ministry of Foreign Affairs, Hanoi sees four elements that have been essential to sustaining regional order:

1. The relatively stable balance of power and the dynamic relationship between the major powers, with the United States as the unchallenged hegemon;
2. The established regional institutional arrangements that serve as vehicles for all the regional actors to interact with each other for the sake of dialogue and trust building;
3. Common rules and norms; and
4. The role of ASEAN as a unique and important group of small and medium-sized countries in mediating between major powers.[134]

With this in mind, one can see how the rise of an aggressive China and intensifying questions about the reliability of American power would be of great concern in Hanoi. The most significant security issue that Vietnam must confront is its persistent disputes with China over which nation can rightfully claim sovereignty over dozens of features in the South China Sea, especially the Paracel and

Spratley Islands. China and Vietnam fought two brief naval battles in these areas—in 1974 and 1988, respectively—and this issue has been the source of significant tension in recent years, especially as Beijing has sought to assert its claims over much of the entire South China Sea. Indeed, in July 2017, Beijing reportedly threatened Hanoi with war if it were to proceed with oil drilling in a disputed area.[135] Vietnam backed down.

Of course, Vietnam is not alone in its concerns about China's ambitions in the South China Sea. In fact, Hanoi was very supportive of Manila filing a grievance under the UN Convention on the Law of the Sea, and was generally willing to cheer on the Philippines in its confrontations with Beijing. However, with the election of Rodrigo Duterte as president of the Philippines and his subsequent decision to improve relations with Beijing, Hanoi found itself in the uncomfortable position of being out in front of regional efforts to confront Beijing. As described by the RAND Corporation scholar Derek Grossman, Duterte left Vietnam holding the proverbial bag when he abruptly decided to shelve Manila's July 2016 victory in the Permanent Court of Arbitration to dispute China's expansive territorial claims in the region.[136] Vietnam's attempts to take the lead on hashing out a legally binding code of conduct with China and other claimants have proven futile. Vietnam has since suppressed its more vitriolic rhetoric, likely both in order to sustain contrastive relations with Beijing and out of concern that the United States would not support them if a confrontation with China grew into a crisis.

OPPORTUNITIES FOR US ENGAGEMENT AND EMPOWERMENT

Vietnam has the potential to be a critical player in sustaining crucial aspects of a regional liberal order. It is supportive of key principles—such as freedom of navigation and the peaceful resolution of disputes—and it is also committed to robust, open, and rules-based institutions. Strategically, Vietnam also seeks to geopolitically balance against China with a mixture of external and internal balancing—both of which the United States can encourage and support.

The United States can empower Vietnam by supporting Hanoi in any diplomatic initiatives it may take to push back against Chinese encroachments in the South China Sea—this will be especially critical when Vietnam holds the ASEAN chairmanship in 2020. The UN Convention on the Law of the Sea tribunal's ruling on the South China Sea may present a unique opportunity for similar diplomatic initiatives, and it could also provide a basis for further US–Vietnam diplomatic engagements based on international laws and norms. Additionally, Washington can actively support Hanoi's efforts to diversify its international relationships, especially with Europe. Representing both an economic and diplomatic opportunity for Hanoi, Europe (with the exception of France) does not carry the same kind of historic baggage as the United States among some in Vietnam.

Militarily, the United States has an opportunity to enhance Vietnam's ability to defend itself against Chinese coercion and aggression. Enhanced maritime surveillance capabilities—including both hardware and bilateral and multilateral information sharing arrangements—would significantly help Vietnam's ability to monitor its maritime claims. Additionally, coastal defense capabilities—many of which can be provided at low cost—would significantly boost Vietnam's defensive capabilities. Finally, the United States can work with its most technologically advanced allies—especially Japan—to coordinate security assistance programs to maximize efficiency and ensure interoperability.

A key element to all this cooperation would be stronger military-to-military cooperation, which for reasons of domestic politics in Vietnam has underperformed in recent years. This can be addressed with careful and patient engagements, additional regular and reciprocal visits by American and Vietnamese military personnel, more exchanges for professional military education at American universities and training centers, and joint military exercises that gradually grow in sophistication and ambition.

The United States should also be realistic about the scope and pace at which cooperation with Vietnam will proceed. Vietnamese officials often point to their "three no's" of foreign engagements: no military alliances, no foreign troops stationed on Vietnamese soil, and no partnerships with a foreign power to combat another.[137] Even though the United States likely would not seek any of these three items, American policymakers should listen carefully to the underlying message of wariness—wariness about being taken advantage of, about foreign exploitation, and about foreign dominance. These are not insurmountable obstacles, but they are very real and should be understood and taken into account.

Vietnam is not interested in being a pawn in the broader effort by the United States to compete with China. Yet US interests generally converge on several critical issues, and patient engagement and deft diplomacy can ensure that the United States and Vietnam continue to make progress toward building a robust and mutually beneficial partnership.

CONCLUSION

Toward an Allied Strategy in the Indo-Pacific

We must mobilize allies and partners to take collective action. We have to broaden our tools to include diplomacy and development; sanctions and isolation; appeals to international law; and, if just, necessary and effective, multilateral military action. In such circumstances, we have to work with others because collective action in these circumstances is more likely to succeed, more likely to be sustained, less likely to lead to costly mistakes.

—PRESIDENT BARACK OBAMA, MAY 2014

A lliances and partners are fundamental geopolitical assets and a critical strategic advantage for the United States. This is especially true in the Indo-Pacific, where major geopolitical shifts have both highlighted the benefits of a liberal order while simultaneously risking its collapse. It is a fundamental interest of the United States to preserve key liberal principles in the Indo-Pacific, and it cannot do so without robust engagement from Washington and a strategy that empowers its allies and partners.

For over a century, American strategy toward the Indo-Pacific has shifted between a focus on continental Asia and a focus on maritime

Asia—a debate more currently replicated by those that advocate for a strategy focused on China, and a strategy focused on America's allies and partners.[1] Some may interpret this book as a call for the latter—that the United States should base its strategy toward the Indo-Pacific on its allies and partners.

The reality, however, is that the duality in American strategy toward the Indo-Pacific is shifting. This is because the Indo-Pacific is no longer a peripheral theater to a broader strategic drama; the region today is at the center stage of international geopolitics. For the United States to succeed, it cannot afford to get China wrong, and it cannot afford to get its approach to its allies and partners wrong. In fact, this book argues that the United States' approach to China *cannot* be successful without a focus on its allies and partners, and its approach to its allies and partners *cannot* be successful without a realistic and visionary strategy for China. No longer dichotomies, these aspects of strategy toward the Indo-Pacific are now inextricably interwoven.

Preserving and strengthening a liberal order in the Indo-Pacific will be critical to US interests, and US allies and partners have a critical role to play in contributing to this order's health and success. Collective action among allies and partners will become increasingly necessary for success, even as such action will likely be piecemeal, episodic, and haphazard at the outset.

Setting objectives and ideal states is needed for leadership, but so too is flexibility. For example, a highly significant indication of successful empowerment of US allies and partners would be the occasional establishment of a peacetime combined multinational carrier group operating in the Indo-Pacific's international waters. Given enough time, such a group could involve Japanese carriers, American submarines, South Korean and Indian surface vessels, and ground-based aerial support from Indonesia, Australia, and Singapore.

Yet the success of any strategy in the Indo-Pacific will hinge on Washington's ability to work with its allies and partners to develop a compelling liberal alternative to the well-funded but illiberal vision being promoted by Beijing. Too often, Washington's competitive strategies—especially outside the military sphere—have been to simply oppose Beijing at every turn. From the Asian Infrastructure Investment Bank and the Belt and Road Initiative to Huawei, it seems that Washington's strategy too often boils down to "just say no." Unfortunately, that will not cut it in an increasingly competitive and consequential Indo-Pacific. The United States needs a compelling liberal alternative for other countries to choose, and to promote a transparent, rules-based environment that allows for open and honest competition between these visions. Ultimately, Washington must have confidence in its own vision and that countries in the middle will align with it more often than not because liberalism is, fundamentally, a better deal than illiberalism.

If the United States fails to preserve a liberal order in the Indo-Pacific, and allows its alliances and partnerships to continue to wither, strategic disaster awaits. If we do not act to define the geopolitics of the twenty-first century, China will be free to remake the system according to its own interests and values.

Yet for all the talk of China's rise and American decline, the United States remains particularly well suited to lead the Indo-Pacific toward a brighter future. The United States has never been a nation to sit on its laurels or drift in splendid isolation. Rather, the United States is a country that is forever aspirational, ever vigorous, and consistently optimistic that it can be a force for good in the world. In this, American policymakers seeking to strengthen the region's liberal order can embrace the ideals of the US Constitution, which envisioned "a more perfect union" as a clarion call for a project that is an aspiring, optimistic, never finished, and forever just beyond our reach.

NOTES

PREFACE

1. For example, at his press conference in Singapore on June 12, 2018, after a summit with North Korean leader Kim Jong Un, President Trump said "But on NATO, we're paying 4.2%; she's paying 1% of a much smaller GDP than we have. We're paying 4.2% on a much larger—we're paying for—I mean, anyone can say—from 60 to 90% of NATO. And we're protecting countries of Europe. And then on top of it, they kill us on trade. So we just can't have it that way. It's unfair to our taxpayers and to our people. But no, I have a good relationship with Justin. And I have a, I think, a very good relationship with Chairman Kim right now. I really do." Donald J. Trump, "Press Conference by President Trump," White House. June 12, 2018, https://www.whitehouse.gov/briefings-statements/press-conference -president-trump/.

INTRODUCTION: CHALLENGED FRIENDSHIPS IN CHALLENGING TIMES

Henry Kissinger, "Kissinger On the Controversy Over the Shah," *Washington Post*, November 29, 1979, https://www.washingtonpost.com/archive/politics /1979/11/29/kissinger-on-the-controversy-over-the-shah/a3153d91 -02be-40d5-958b-8784c4991941/?utm_term=.aa6cdcbc088a.

1. George Washington, "Washington's Farewell Address," 1796, Avalon Project, http://avalon.law.yale.edu/18th_century/washing.asp. For an exceptional summary of America's historical approach to alliances and partnerships, see Ashley J. Tellis, "The Long Road to Confederationism in US Grand Strategy," in *US Alliances and Partnerships at the Center of Global Power*, edited by Ashley J. Tellis, Abraham M. Denmark, and Greg Chaffin (Seattle: National Bureau of Asian Research, 2014), 2–32.

2. See US Department of Defense, *Indo-Pacific Strategy Report: Preparedness, Partnerships, and Promoting a Networked Region*, June 1, 2019, 2, https://media.defense.gov/2019/Jul/01/2002152311/-1/-1/1/department-of-defense-indo-pacific-strategy-report-2019.pdf.

3. Victor D. Cha, *Powerplay: The Origins of the American Alliance System in Asia* (Princeton, NJ: Princeton University Press, 2018), 4.

4. For more on the linkage between the hedging strategies on Asian middle powers and heterarchy, see Van Jackson, "Power, Trust, and Network Complexity: Three Logics of Hedging in Asian Security," *International Relations of the Asia-Pacific* 14, no. 3 (2014): 331–56, https://doi.org/10.1093/irap/lcu005.

1. ORDER AND POWER IN THE INDO-PACIFIC

Hans J. Morgenthau, *Politics Among Nations* (New York: Alfred A. Knopf, 1973), 29.

1. Henry Kissinger, *World Order* (New York: Penguin Books, 2015), 173.

2. The division of human history into discrete eras necessarily involves simplification, but also has the potential to illuminate what a deluge of details would obscure.

3. To say that law is "binding" is a descriptive rather than normative statement. See, e.g., John Gardner, "Legal Positivism: 51/2 Myths," *American Journal of Jurisprudence* 46, no. 1 (2001): 199–227, https://doi.org/10.1093/ajj/46.1.199.

4. In *The Anarchical Society*, Hedley Bull draws an important contrast between a "world order," providing universal justice, and an "international order," which only entails that states have settled expectations. Bull argues that the latter, unlike the former, can exist in the absence of world government. Hedley Bull, *The Anarchical Society: A Study of Order in World Politics* (New York: Columbia University Press, 1977). See also Patrick Porter, "Sorry, Folks: There Is No Rules-Based World Order," *The National Interest*, August 29, 2016, https://nationalinterest.org/blog/the-skeptics/sorry-folks-there-no-rules-based-world-order-17497.

5. *Bellum omnium contra omnes*, a Latin phrase meaning "the war of all against all," is the description that Thomas Hobbes gives to human existence in the state-of-nature thought experiment that he conducts in *De Cive* (1642) and *Leviathan* (1651).

6. Robert O. Keohane, *After Hegemony: Cooperation and Discord in the World Political Economy* (Princeton, NJ: Princeton University Press, 2005).

7. See, e.g., G. John Ikenberry, *Liberal Leviathan: The Origins, Crisis, and Transformation of the American World Order* (Princeton, NJ: Princeton University Press, 2011), 47.

8. Michael J. Mazarr, Miranda Priebe, Andrew Radin, and Astrid Stuth Cevallos, *Understanding the Current International Order* (Santa Monica, CA: RAND Corporation, 2016), 7.

9. Mazarr et al., 10–12.

10. Kenneth Neal Waltz, *Theory of International Politics* (Long Grove, IL: Waveland Press, 2010); John J. Mearsheimer, *The Tragedy of Great Power Politics* (New York: W. W. Norton, 2002).

11. G. John Ikenberry, "Why the Liberal World Order Will Survive," *Ethics & International Affairs* 32, no. 1 (2018): 17–29, https://doi.org/10.1017/S0892679418000072.

12. Ikenberry, 27.

13. For a more complete analysis of how nations build power, see *Strategic Asia 2015-16: Foundations of National Power in the Asia-Pacific*, ed. Michael Wills, Ashley J. Tellis, and Alison Szalwinski (Seattle: National Bureau of Asian Research, 2015), and especially the overview chapter by Tellis.

14. Historians disagree about how to divide the history of Asia' regional order, and this review does not seek to contribute to that discussion. Rather, it seeks to establish the historical link between the regional balance of power and the regional order across several iterations.

15. David C. Kang, *East Asia Before the West: Five Centuries of Trade and Tribute* (New York: Columbia University Press, 2012).

16. John King Fairbank, *The Chinese World Order: Traditional China's Foreign Relation* (Cambridge, MA: Harvard University Press, 1974), 2.

17. Kang, *East Asia Before the West*.

18. Orville Schell and John Delury, *Wealth and Power: China's Long March to the Twenty-First Century* (London: Abacus, 2016).

19. See Howard W. French, Ian Johnson, Jeremiah Jenne, Pamela Kyle Crossley, Robert A. Kapp, and Tobie Meyer-Fong, "How China's History Shapes, and Warps, Its Policies Today," *Foreign Policy*, March 22, 2017, https://foreignpolicy.com/2017/03/22/how-chinas-history-shapes-its-foreign-policy-empire-humiliation/.

20. This includes the Korean War (1950–53) and the Vietnam War (1955–75).

21. Daniel Deudney and G. John Ikenberry, "Liberal World," *Foreign Affairs*, July–August 2018.

22. Mazarr et al., *Understanding*, 1; NSC-68, 34.

23. The elements of the US-led order are derived from Ikenberry, *Liberal Leviathan*, 169–93.

24. It should be noted that allied and partner views of a liberal order were not entirely aligned with the United States. Japan, e.g., sought to pursue protectionist policies that supported its expanding postwar economy but were contrary to the rules of the established liberal order and became a major challenge in the US–Japan relationship in the 1970s and 1980s.

25. Stuart R. Schram, "Mao Tse-Tung and the Theory of the Permanent Revolution, 1958–69," *China Quarterly* 46 (1971): 221–44. https://doi.org/10.1017/s0305741000010675.

26. Richard M. Nixon, "Asia after Viet Nam," *Foreign Affairs* 46, no. 1 (1967): 111, https://doi.org/10.2307/20039285. The US play for East Asia would have significant consequences for South Asia. When, in 1971, East Pakistan sought independence under the name of Bangladesh, Washington provided material support to Pakistan, a close friend of China, while the Soviet Union aided Bangladesh and its Indian allies.

27. John J. Mearsheimer, "Bound to Fail: The Rise and Fall of the Liberal International Order," *International Security* 43, no. 4 (2019): 7–50, https://doi.org/10.1162/ISEC_a_00342.

28. G. John Ikenberry, *After Victory: Institutions, Strategic Restraint, and the Rebuilding of Order After Major Wars* (Princeton, NJ: Princeton University Press, 2000), 20.

29. Simon Fraser University, *Human Security Report 2013* (Vancouver: Human Security Press), 2014, https://reliefweb.int/sites/reliefweb.int/files/resources/HSRP_Report_2013_140226_Web.pdf.

30. Steven Pinker, *The Better Angels of Our Nature: Why Violence Has Declined* (New York: Penguin Books, 2011), 249–51.

31. Hegre Havard, "Predicting Armed Conflict, 2010–2050," University of Oslo, November 21, 2011, http://folk.uio.no/hahegre/Papers/PredictionISQ_Final.pdf.

32. Joshua S. Goldstein, *Winning the War on War: The Decline of Armed Conflict Worldwide* (New York: Plume/Penguin, 2012), 4, as quoted in the *Human Security Report 2013*, 25. Explanations regarding the decreasing frequency and scale of war have come under question, with some arguing that improvements in medical medicine can account for the reduction in battlefield deaths overall. See Tanisha M. Fazal, "Dead Wrong?," *International Security* 39, no. 1 (2014): 95–125, doi:10.1162/ISEC_a_00166. Ultimately, the question of battlefield deaths against overall casualties is beyond the focus of this book. The

key point—that the frequency and scale of major power conflict decreasing significantly since the end of World War II—is not disputed.

33. Simon Fraser University, *Human Security Report 2013*, 87.
34. Simon Fraser University, 93.
35. Mearsheimer, "Bound to Fail."

2. A REGION IN FLUX

Zbigniew Brzezinski, Twitter post, May 4, 2017, https://twitter.com/zbig/status/860177803194630144?lang=en.

1. E.g., as described by Henry Kissinger, the ability of any country to dominate "Eurasia's two principal spheres . . . remains a good definition of strategic danger for America." Henry Kissinger, *Diplomacy* (New York: Simon & Schuster, 1994), 813.

2. International Monetary Fund, World Economic Outlook Database, April 2019. The Asia-Pacific countries include Australia, Bangladesh, Brunei Darussalam, Cambodia, the People's Republic of China, Fiji, India, Indonesia, Japan, South Korea, Laos, Malaysia, Mongolia, Myanmar, Nepal, New Zealand, Papua New Guinea, the Philippines, Singapore, Sri Lanka, Taiwan, Thailand, Timor-Leste, and Vietnam.

3. Stockholm International Peace Research Institute (SIPRI), Military Expenditure Database, http://sipri.org/. The percentage change is calculated in constant (2017) US dollars.

4. Jiang Zemin, "Build a Well-Off Society in an All-Round Way and Create a New Situation in Building Socialism with Chinese Characteristics," report at 16th National Congress of the Communist Party of China, November 8, 2002. As quoted by Evan Medeiros, *China's International Behavior: Activism, Opportunism, and Diversification* (Santa Monica, CA: RAND Corporation, 2009), 23.

5. Xi Jinping, "Secure a Decisive Victory in Building a Moderately Prosperous Society in All Respects and Strive for the Great Success of Socialism with Chinese Characteristics for a New Era," Xinhuanet, October 18, 2017, http://www.xinhuanet.com/english/download/Xi_Jinping's_report_at_19th_CPC_National_Congress.pdf.

6. Portions of this section were originally presented in the author's lecture "Beyond Nationalism: Considering a Chinese World Order," to the Princeton-Harvard China and the World Program. April 18, 2018, at Princeton University.

7. C. W. Freeman Jr., "The United States and China: Game of Superpowers," remarks to the National War College, February 8, 2018, https://chasfreeman.net/the-united-states-and-china-game-of-superpowers/.

8. Richard M. Nixon, "Asia after Viet Nam," *Foreign Affairs* 46, no. 1 (1967): 111. https://doi.org/10.2307/20039285.

9. Nixon, 111.

10. Robert B. Zoellick, "Whither China: From Membership to Responsibility?," *NBR Analysis* 16, no. 4 (2005): 5.

11. This is based on my discussions with Chinese scholars in 2009 and 2010. Perceptions of America's weakness were informed by its continuing military operations in Iraq and Afghanistan, and especially the financial crisis and resulting Great Recession.

12. James Mann, "America's Dangerous 'China Fantasy,'" *New York Times*, October 27, 2016, https://www.nytimes.com/2016/10/28/opinion/americas -dangerous-china-fantasy.html.

13. World Bank, "Data for East Asia & Pacific, China," https://data.worldbank .org/?locations=Z4-CN.

14. Parag Khanna, "Opinion: Asia Is Building Its Own World Order," CNN, August 8, 2017, https://www.cnn.com/2017/08/08/opinions/china-and -the-asian-world-order-parag-khanna-opinion/index.html.

15. SIPRI, Military Expenditure Database.

16. Zachary Keck, "China's J-20 Stealth Fighter Is Now Training for War," *The National Interest*, January 20, 2018. https://nationalinterest.org/blog /the-buzz/chinas-j-20-stealth-fighter-now-training-war-24147.

17. Department of Defense, "Military and Security Developments Involving the People's Republic of China 2017," https://www.defense.gov/Portals/1 /Documents/pubs/2017_China_Military_Power_Report.pdf.

18. Oriana Skylar Mastro, "Ideas, Perceptions, and Power: An Examination of China's Military Strategy," in *Strategic Asia, 2017–2018: Power, Ideas, and Military Strategy in the Asia-Pacific*, ed. Ashley J. Tellis, Alison Szalwinski, and Michael Wills, 19–44.

19. John J. Mearsheimer, *The Tragedy of Great Power Politics* (New York: Norton, 2002).

20. Graham Allison, *Destined for War: Can America and China Escape Thucydides's Trap?* (Boston: Houghton Mifflin Harcourt, 2017).

21. Some of these points are derived from the author's testimony before the US Congress. See Abraham M. Denmark, "The Department of Defense's Role in Long-Term Major State Competition," Testimony before the House Committee on Armed Services, February 11, 2020, https://docs.house .gov/meetings/AS/AS00/20200211/110518/HHRG-116-AS00-Wstate -DenmarkA-20200211.pdf; Abraham M. Denmark, "The China Challenge: Military and Security Developments," Testimony before the Senate Foreign Relations Subcommittee on East Asia, the Pacific, and International

Security Policy, September 5, 2018, https://www.foreign.senate.gov/imo
/media/doc/090518_Denmark_Testimony.pdf; and Abraham M. Denmark,
"Across the Other Pond: US Opportunities and Challenges in the Asia-Pacific,"
Testimony before the House Committee on Foreign Affairs Subcommittee
on Asia and the Pacific, February 26, 2015. https://docs.house.gov/meetings
/FA/FA05/20150226/103064/HHRG-114-FA05-Wstate-DenmarkA-20150226
.pdf.

22. Carl Thayer, "Alarming Escalation in the South China Sea: China Threatens
Force If Vietnam Continues Oil Exploration in Spratlys," *The Diplomat*,
July 25, 2017, https://thediplomat.com/2017/07/alarming-escalation-in
-the-south-china-sea-china-threatens-force-if-vietnam-continues-oil
-exploration-in-spratlys/.

23. "Making China Stronger in the New Era," China.org.cn. 京ICP证,
December 27, 2017, http://www.china.org.cn/business/2017-12/27/content
_50168555.htm.

24. Tanner Greer, "Xi Jinping in Translation: China's Guiding Ideology,"
Palladium Magazine, May 31, 2019, https://palladiummag.com/2019/05/31
/xi-jinping-in-translation-chinas-guiding-ideology/.

25. Quoted by Greer.

26. M. Taylor Fravel, J. Stapleton Roy, Michael D. Swaine, Susan A. Thornton, and
Ezra Vogel, "China Is Not an Enemy," *Washington Post*, July 3, 2019, https://
www.washingtonpost.com/opinions/making-china-a-us-enemy-is-count
erproductive/2019/07/02/647d49d0-9bfa-11e9-b27f-ed2942f73d70_story
.html?noredirect=on.

27. Greg Ip, "Has America's China Backlash Gone Too Far?," *Wall Street Journal*,
August 28, 2019, https://www.wsj.com/articles/has-americas-china
-backlash-gone-too-far-11566990232.

28. Ministry of Foreign Affairs of the People's Republic of China, "China–US
Joint Statement," November 17, 2009, Beijing, http://www.fmprc.gov.cn
/eng/wjb/zzjg/bmdyzs/xwlb/t629497.htm.

29. Council on Foreign Relations, "A Conversation with US Secretary of
State Hillary Rodham Clinton," July 15, 2009, https://www.cfr.org/event
/conversation-us-secretary-state-hillary-rodham-clinton-1.

30. Abraham M. Denmark and Nirav Patel, "China's Arrival: A Strategic
Framework for a Global Relationship," Center for a New American Security,
September 22, 2009, https://www.cnas.org/publications/reports/chinas
-arrival-a-strategic-framework-for-a-global-relationship.

31. James B. Steinberg, "Keynote Address at the Center for a New American
Security," September 24, 2017, https://2009-2017.state.gov/s/d/former
/steinberg/remarks/2009/169332.htm.

32. Kurt M. Campbell and Ely Ratner, "The China Reckoning," *Foreign Affairs*, March–April 2018, https://www.foreignaffairs.com/articles/china/2018-02-13/china-reckoning.

33. Allison, *Destined for War*; Walter Russell Mead, "In the Footsteps of the Kaiser: China Boosts US Power in Asia," *The American Interest*, September 26, 2010; Aaron Friedberg, "Will Europe's Past Be Asia's Future?," *Survival* 42, no. 3 (2010): 147–60, https://doi.org/10.1093/survival/42.3.147.

34. See Cameron G. Thies and Mark David Nieman, *Rising Powers and Foreign Policy Revisionism: Understanding BRICS Identity and Behavior Through Time* (Ann Arbor: University of Michigan Press, 2017).

35. Jacob Mardell, "The 'Community of Common Destiny' in Xi Jinping's New Era," *The Diplomat*, October 25, 2017, https://thediplomat.com/2017/10/the-community-of-common-destiny-in-xi-jinpings-new-era/.

36. Liza Tobin, "Xi's Vision for Transforming Global Governance: A Strategic Challenge for Washington and Its Allies," *Texas National Security Review* 2, no. 1 (2018), http://dx.doi.org/10.26153/tsw/863.

37. Xi Jinping, remarks delivered at 19th National Congress of Communist Party of China, "Secure a Decisive Victory in Building a Moderately Prosperous Society in All Respects and Strive for the Great Success of Socialism with Chinese Characteristics for a New Era," October 18, 2017, 9–10, http://www.xinhuanet.com/english/download/Xi_Jinping's_report_at_19th_CPC_National_Congress.pdf.

38. Xi Jinping, 24–25.

39. Xi Jinping, 25.

40. See Howard W. French, *Everything Under the Heavens: How the Past Helps Shape China's Push for Global Power* (New York: Vintage Books, 2017).

41. Kenneth Rapoza, "China's Mostly Closed, Communist Party–Run Economy Touts Free Markets," *Forbes*, July 18, 2017, https://www.forbes.com/sites/kenrapoza/2017/07/18/chinas-mostly-closed-communist-party-run-economy-touts-free-markets/#5c1b0fae731c.

42. Bill Hayton, Twitter post, April 12, 2018, https://twitter.com/bill_hayton/status/984416871184257024.

43. Nicholas R. Lardy, "Zhu Rongji's Promise," Brookings Institution, October 28, 2002, https://www.brookings.edu/opinions/zhu-rongjis-promise.

44. Abraham Lincoln, "Annual Message to Congress—Concluding Remarks," December 1, 1862.

45. 刘珊珊, "President Xi Addresses CICA Summit," *China Daily*, May 21, 2014, https://www.chinadaily.com.cn/world/2014-05/21/content_17529363_3.htm.

46. Peter Mattis provides a more specific definition of united front work: "Mao Zedong described the purpose of this work as mobilizing the party's friends

to strike at the party's enemies. In a more specific definition from a paper in the 1950s, the Central Intelligence Agency defined united front work as 'a technique for controlling, mobilizing, and utilizing non-communist masses.' Put another way, united front policy addresses the party's relationship with and guidance of any social group outside the party. The most important point here is that what needs to be shaped is not just the Chinese people or world outside the People's Republic of China, but rather those outside the party." Peter Mattis, "China's Digital Authoritarianism: Surveillance, Influence, and Political Control," Testimony Before the House Permanent Select Committee on Intelligence, May 16, 2019, https://docs .house.gov/meetings/IG/IG00/20190516/109462/HHRG-116-IG00-Wstate -MattisP-20190516.pdf.

47. "Zhuan she tongzhan gongzuo lingdao xiaozu zhongyang 'da tongzhan' siwei shengji" [United Front Leading Small Group: More Emphasis on CCP Politburo's "Big United Front"], *Renminwang*, July 31, 2015, http://cpc .people.com.cn/xuexi/n/2015/0731/c385474-27391395.html; as quoted by Anne-Marie Brady, *Magic Weapons: China's Political Influence Activities under Xi Jinping* (Washington: Woodrow Wilson International Center for Scholars, 2017), 7, https://www.wilsoncenter.org/sites/default/files/for_website _magicweaponsanne-mariesbradyseptember2017.pdf.

48. Brady, *Magic Weapons*, 7.

49. Hoover Institution, "Appendix 2: Chinese Influence Activities in Select Countries," https://www.hoover.org/sites/default/files/research/docs/13 _diamond-schell_app2_web.pdf.

50. Larry Diamond and Orville Schell, "China's Influence & American Interests: Promoting Constructive Vigilance," November 29, 2018, https://www .hoover.org/research/chinas-influence-american-interests-promoting -constructive-vigilance; Ryan Hass, "Democracy, the China Challenge, and the 2020 Elections in Taiwan," *Taipei Times*, March 18, 2019, http://www .taipeitimes.com/News/editorials/archives/2019/03/18/2003711694.

51. See Randall L. Schweller and Xiaoyu Pu, "After Unipolarity: China's Visions of International Order in an Era of US Decline," *International Security* 36, no. 1 (2011): 41–72.

52. World Bank, DataBank, http://databank.worldbank.org/data/reports. aspx?source=2&country=CHN; for more information on various "traps" threatening China's rise, see "The Four Traps China May Fall Into," blog post by Yanzhong Huang, Council on Foreign Relations, https://www.cfr .org/blog/four-traps-china-may-fall.

53. World Bank, DataBank; Chong-En Bai and Qiong Zhang, "Is the People's Republic of China's Current Slowdown a Cyclical Downturn or a Long-Term

Trend? A Productivity-Based Analysis," *Journal of the Asia Pacific Economy* 22, no. 1 (2017): 29–46.

54. David Shambaugh, *China's Future* (Cambridge: Polity Press, 2016), 3. See also David Shambaugh, "The Coming Chinese Crack Up," *Wall Street Journal*, March 6, 2015, https://www.wsj.com/articles/the-coming-chinese-crack -up-1425659198; and David Shambaugh, "Writing China: David Shambaugh, *China's Future*, interview by Andrew Browne," *Wall Street Journal*, March 14, 2016, https://blogs.wsj.com/chinarealtime/2016/03/14/writing-china-david -shambaugh-chinas-future.

55. Nadège Rolland, "China's National Power: A Colossus with Iron or Clay Feet," *Strategic Asia* 16 (2015): 23–54, http://www.nbr.org/publications /element.aspx?id=836.

56. Minxin Pei, "Transition in China? More Likely Than You Think," *Journal of Democracy* 27, no. 4 (2016): 5–19.

57. For my take on China's real concerns regarding THAAD in South Korea, see Abraham M. Denmark, "China's Fear of US Missile Defense Is Disingenuous," *Foreign Policy*, March 20, 2017, https://foreignpolicy.com/2017/03/20/chinas -fear-of-u-s-missile-defense-is-disingenuous-north-korea-trump-united -states-tillerson-thaad/.

58. Richard C. Bush, "What Xi Jinping Said About Taiwan at the 19th Party Congress," Brookings Institution, October 19, 2017, https://www .brookings.edu/blog/order-from-chaos/2017/10/19/what-xi-jinping -said-about-taiwan-at-the-19th-party-congress/.

59. White House, *National Security Strategy of the United States of America, December 2017* (Washington: White House, 2017), https://www.whitehouse .gov/wp-content/uploads/2017/12/NSS-Final-12-18-2017-0905.pdf.

60. "Summary of the 2018 National Defense Strategy," https://www.defense .gov/Portals/1/Documents/pubs/2018-National-Defense-Strategy -Summary.pdf.

61. US Department of Defense, *Indo-Pacific Strategy Report: Preparedness, Partnerships, and Promoting a Networked Region*, June 1, 2019, https://media .defense.gov/2019/Jul/01/2002152311/-1/-1/1/department-of-defense -indo-pacific-strategy-report-2019.pdf.

62. Thomas J. T. Christensen, "Posing Problems Without Catching Up: China's Rise and Challenges for US Security Policy," *International Security* 25, no. 4 (2001): 5–40.

63. Shiping Tang, "China and the Future International Order(s)," *Ethics & International Affairs* 32, no. 1 (2018): 31–43, at 33–34, *https://doi.org/10.1017 /S0892679418000084.*

64. Tang, 40.

65. Tang, 38–39.

66. Alan Taylor, "Anti-Japan Protests in China," *The Atlantic*, September 17, 2012, https://www.theatlantic.com/photo/2012/09/anti-japan-protests -in-china/100370/.

67. "Profiles: Japan," Maritime Awareness Project, National Bureau of Asian Research, http://maritimeawarenessproject.org/profiles/japan/.

68. US Department of State, Bureau of Oceans and International Environmental and Scientific Affairs, *Limits in the Seas* no. 143, "China: Maritime Claims in the South China Sea," December 5, 2014, 19, https://www.state.gov /documents/organization/234936.pdf.

69. "The Indo-Pacific Maritime Security Strategy: Achieving US National Security Objectives in a Changing Environment," US Department of Defense, July 2015, https://www.defense.gov/Portals/1/Documents/pubs/NDAA percent20A-P_Maritime_SecuritY_Strategy-08142015-1300-finalformat .pdf.

70. Eliot Kim, "Water Wars: ASEAN No Longer 'Concerned' About China's Actions in the South China Sea," *Lawfare*, December 4, 2017, https:// lawfareblog.com/water-wars-asean-no-longer-concerned-about-chinas -actions-south-china-sea.

71. Kristine Lee and Alexander Sullivan, "People's Republic of the United Nations," Center for a New American Security, May 14, 2019, https://www .cnas.org/publications/reports/peoples-republic-of-the-united-nations.

72. Ralph Jennings, "China Demands Companies Stop Calling Taiwan a Country: Here's What They'll Do," *Forbes*, January 18, 2018, https://www.forbes.com /sites/ralphjennings/2018/01/17/corporations-will-quickly-comply-as -china-pressures-them-to-stop-calling-taiwan-a-country/#20887ba49bf4.

73. Brady, *Magic Weapons.*

74. Keith Bradsher, "Amid Tension, China Blocks Vital Exports to Japan," *New York Times*, September 23, 2010, https://www.nytimes.com/2010/09/23 /business/global/23rare.html.

75. Andrew Higgins, "In Philippines, Banana Growers Feel Effect of South China Sea Dispute," *Washington Post*, June 10, 2012, https://www.washingtonpost .com/world/asia_pacific/in-philippines-banana-growers-feel-effect-of -south-china-sea-dispute/2012/06/10/gJQA47WVTV_story.html?utm _term=.9d1e3d688698.

76. James Mayger and Jiyuen Lee, "China's Missile Sanctions Are Taking a Heavy Toll on Both Koreas," Bloomberg, August 29, 2017, https://www .bloomberg.com/news/articles/2017-08-29/china-s-missile-sanctions -are-taking-a-heavy-toll-on-both-koreas.

77. This is as described by Richard Fontaine, "Against Complacency: Risks and Opportunities for the Australia–US Alliance," United States Studies Centre, Sydney, October 2016, https://assets.ussc.edu.au/view/e6/b4/38

/ef/c9/ba/70/49/f6/da/78/36/02/48/c5/fa/original/959a3d25392702
0b0ed1a1bd671e65306f29b4f4/2016_Risks_Opportunities_Australia_US
_Alliance.pdf.

78. Bates Gill and Evan S. Medeiros, "Foreign and Domestic Influences on
     China's Arms Control and Nonproliferation Policies," *China Quarterly* 161
     (2000): 66–94.

79. Robert G. Sutter, *Chinese Foreign Relations: Power and Policy Since the Cold War*
     (Lanham, MD: Rowman & Littlefield, 2012), chap. 6.

80. Ministry of Foreign Affairs, People's Republic of China, "Chinese Foreign
     Minister Yang Jiechi Attends the Meeting of the Foreign Ministers of
     China, Russia, India and of Brazil," May 16, 2008, http://www.fmprc
     .gov.cn/mfa_eng/wjb_663304/zzjg_663340/ldmzs_664952/xwlb_664954
     /t455560.shtml.

81. "…是我国日益走近世界舞台中央、不断为人类作出更大贡献的时代";
     and "意味着中国特色社会主义道路、理论、制度、文化不断发展，拓
     展了发展中国家走向现代化的途径，给世界上那些既希望加快发展又
     希望保持自身独立性的国家和民族提供了全新选择，为解决人类问题
     贡献了中国智慧和中国方案." Xi Jinping, "Secure a Decisive Victory," 9.

82. Jane Perlez, "Tribunal Rejects Beijing's Claims in South China Sea," *New
     York Times*, July 12, 2016, https://www.nytimes.com/2016/07/13/world/asia
     /south-china-sea-hague-ruling-philippines.html.

83. Thayer, "Alarming Escalation."

84. Nadège Rolland, *China's Eurasian Century? Political and Strategic Implications of
     the Belt and Road Initiative* (Seattle: National Bureau of Asian Research, 2017).

85. Glen H. Snyder, "The Security Dilemma in Alliance Politics," *World Politics*
     36, no. 4 (1984): 461–95.

86. Bruce Vaughn, "US Strategic and Defense Relationships in the Asia-Pacific
     Region," Congressional Research Service, January 22, 2007, 15, https://fas
     .org/sgp/crs/row/RL33821.pdf.

87. Gordon Lubold, "US Spent $5.6 Trillion on Wars in Middle East and Asia:
     Study," *Wall Street Journal*, November 8, 2017, https://www.wsj.com/articles
     /study-estimates-war-costs-at-5-6-trillion-1510106400.

88. Andrew Marble, "China, the Financial Crisis, and Sino-American Relations:
     An Interview with Pieter Bottelier," *Asia Policy*, no. 9 (January 2010): 121–29.

89. World Bank, DataBank, World Development Indicators, http://databank
     .worldbank.org/data/reports.aspx?source=2&series=NY.GDP.MKTP
     .CD&country=USA,WLD.

90. This is in current dollars. SIPRI, Military Expenditure Database.

91. Andrew S. Erickson, Abraham M. Denmark, and Gabriel Collins, "Beijing's
     'Starter Carrier' and Future Steps: Alternatives and Implications," *Naval
     War College Review* 65, no. 1 (2012): 14–54.

92. See Michael Beckley, *Unrivaled: Why America Will Remain the World's Sole Superpower* (Ithaca, NY: Cornell University Press, 2018).

93. For a "present at the creation" account of the rebalance, see Kurt Campbell, *The Pivot: The Future of American Statecraft in Asia* (New York: Twelve, 2016).

94. Campbell, 32.

95. Campbell, 204.

96. Campbell, 267–68.

97. Full disclosure: the author was a senior official in the Obama administration from 2015 through 2017.

98. Barack Obama, "President Obama: The TPP Would Let America, Not China, Lead the Way on Global Trade," *Washington Post*, May 2, 2016, https://www.washingtonpost.com/opinions/president-obama-the-tpp-would-let-america-not-china-lead-the-way-on-global-trade/2016/05/02/680540e4-0fd0-11e6-93ae-50921721165d_story.html.

99. Adam Taylor, "A Timeline of Trump's Complicated Relationship with the TPP," *Washington Post*, April 13, 2018, https://www.washingtonpost.com/news/worldviews/wp/2018/04/13/a-timeline-of-trumps-complicated-relationship-with-the-tpp/.

100. "Transcript: Donald Trump Expounds on His Foreign Policy Views," *New York Times*, March 26, 2016, https://www.nytimes.com/2016/03/27/us/politics/donald-trump-transcript.html?hp&action=click&pgtype=Homepage&clickSource=story-heading&module=first-column-region&region=top-news&WT.nav=top-news&_r=0.

101. Alec Macfarlane and Taehoon Lee, "Trump: South Korea Should Pay for $1B Missile Defense System," *CNN Money*, April 28, 2017, http://money.cnn.com/2017/04/28/news/trump-south-korea-thaad-trade/index.html.

102. Richard Wike, Bruce Stokes, Jacob Poushter, and Janell Fetterolf, "Trump Unpopular Worldwide, American Image Suffers," Pew Research Center, Global Attitudes Project, June 26, 2017, http://www.pewglobal.org/2017/06/26/u-s-image-suffers-as-publics-around-world-question-trumps-leadership/.

103. ASEAN Studies Centre, "How Do Southeast Asians View the Trump Administration?," May 3, 2017, https://www.iseas.edu.sg/images/centres/asc/pdf/ASCSurvey40517.pdf.

104. Heather Long, "Analysis: Trump Has Officially Put More Tariffs on US Allies than on China," *Washington Post*, May 31, 2018, https://www.washingtonpost.com/news/wonk/wp/2018/05/31/trump-has-officially-put-more-tariffs-on-u-s-allies-than-on-china/?noredirect=on&utm_term=.6f4c4e186710.

105. Josh Rogin, "Opinion: Trump Still Holds Jimmy Carter's View on Withdrawing US Troops from South Korea," *Washington Post*, June 7, 2018, https://www.washingtonpost.com/news/josh-rogin/wp/2018/06/07

/trump-still-holds-jimmy-carters-view-on-withdrawing-u-s-troops
-from-south-korea/?utm_term=.fea7826655c9.

106. James Kirchick, "Why Donald Trump Keeps Dissing America's Allies in Europe
and Asia," *Daily Beast*, December 29, 2016, https://www.thedailybeast.com
/why-donald-trump-keeps-dissing-americas-allies-in-europe-and-asia.

107. Dina Smeltz, Ivo Daalder, Karl Friedhoff, and Craig Kafura, "What
Americans Think about America First," Chicago Council on Global Affairs,
2017, 10–16, https://www.thechicagocouncil.org/sites/default/files
/ccgasurvey2017_what_americans_think_about_america_first.pdf.

108. Van Jackson, "Power, Trust, and Network Complexity: Three Logics of
Hedging in Asian Security," *International Relations of the Asia-Pacific* 14, no. 3
(2014): 331–56, https://doi.org/10.1093/irap/lcu005.

109. For the purposes of clarity, this study includes as US allies and partners in
the Indo-Pacific the United States' five treaty allies (Australia, Japan, the
Philippines, South Korea, and Thailand) as well as its six regional partners
(India, Indonesia, New Zealand, Singapore, Taiwan, and Vietnam). All data
(in current US dollars) are from the World Bank, except for Taiwan's 1991
and 2016 GDP, which come from the Republic of China (Taiwan) Statistical
Bureau, https://eng.stat.gov.tw/ct.asp?xItem=37408&CtNode=5347&mp=5.

110. China data (in current US dollars) are from the World Bank, Data for East
Asia & Pacific, China, https://data.worldbank.org/?locations=Z4-CN.

111. World Bank; Republic of China (Taiwan) Statistical Bureau.

112. SIPRI, Military Expenditure Database, 2018.

113. Lowy Institute Asia Power Index, https://power.lowyinstitute.org/.

114. World Economic League Table 2018, Center for Economics and Business
Research, December 26, 2017, https://cebr.com/welt-2018/. Assuming
an average annual US growth rate of 2.5 percent and an average annual
Chinese growth rate of 6.0 percent would make China's GDP larger in
2032. Malcolm Scott and Cedric Sam, "Here's How Fast China's Economy Is
Catching Up to the US," Bloomberg, May 12, 2016, https://www.bloomberg
.com/graphics/2016-us-vs-china-economy/.

115. Homi Kharas, "The Unprecedented Expansion of the Global Middle Class:
An Update," Brookings Institution, 2017, https://www.brookings.edu/wp
-content/uploads/2017/02/global_20170228_global-middle-class.pdf.

116. Fang Tian, "China Rises to 16 Asian Countries' Biggest Trading Partners,"
People's Daily, January 12, 2018, http://en.people.cn/n3/2018/0112/c90000
-9314972.html.

117. Stefani Ribka and Linda Yulisman, "RCEP Talks Speed Up Amid TPP Failure,"
Jakarta Post, December 7, 2016, http://www.thejakartapost.com/news/2016
/12/07/rcep-talks-speed-up-amid-tpp-failure.html.

118. See Takashi Terada, "The Competing US and Chinese Models for East Asian Economic Order," *Asia Policy* 13, no. 2 (2018): 19–25.

119. I am grateful to Evan Medeiros for introducing me to this concept.

120. Bandwagoning is the strategic alignment of one state with another. Balancing is the alignment of one state against another, and can take at least two forms: internal (accumulation of military power) and external (alliances and military cooperation). For the most thorough discussion available of these ideal types of alignment, see Randall L. Schweller, "New Realist Research on Alliances: Refining, Not Refuting, Waltz's Balancing Proposition," *American Political Science Review* 91, no. 4 (2007): 927–30, as described and cited by Jackson, "Power," 333.

121. Tian, "China Rises."

122. Evan A. Feigenbaum, "Is Coercion the New Normal in China's Economic Statecraft?," Carnegie Endowment for International Peace, July 25, 2017, http://carnegieendowment.org/2017/07/25/is-coercion-new-normal-in-china-s-economic-statecraft-pub-72632.

123. Graham Bowley, "Cash Helped China Win Costa Rica's Recognition," *New York Times*, September 12, 2008, http://www.nytimes.com/2008/09/13/world/asia/13costa.html; J. R. Wu and Ben Blanchard, "Taiwan Loses Another Ally, Says Won't Help China Ties," Reuters, December 20, 2016, https://www.reuters.com/article/us-china-taiwan-saotome/taiwan-loses-another-ally-says-wont-help-china-ties-idUSKBN1492SO; Ben Blanchard, "After Ditching Taiwan, China Says Panama Will Get the Help It Needs," Reuters, November 17, 2017, https://www.reuters.com/article/us-china-panama/after-ditching-taiwan-china-says-panama-will-get-the-help-it-needs-idUSKBN1DH1FZ.

124. "Chinese Spending Lures Countries to Its Belt and Road Initiative," Bloomberg, September 5, 2017, https://www.bloomberg.com/graphics/2017-china-belt-and-road-initiative/.

125. Saibal Dasgupta and Anjana Pasricha, "Pakistan, Nepal, Myanmar Back Away from Chinese Projects," *Voice of America*, December 4, 2017, https://www.voanews.com/a/three-countries-withdraw-from-chinese-projects/4148094.html.

126. Bradsher, "Amid Tension, China Blocks Vital Exports."

127. Higgins, "In Philippines, Banana Growers Feel Effect."

128. Feigenbaum, "Is Coercion the New Normal?"

129. Ethan Meick and Nargiza Salidjanova, "China's Response to US–South Korean Missile Defense System Deployment and its Implications," US-China Economic and Security Review Commission, July 26, 2017, 7, https://www.uscc.gov/sites/default/files/Research/Report_China percent27s

percent20Response percent20to percent20THAAD percent20Deployment percent20and percent20its percent20Implications.pdf.

130. Thomas Lum, "Republic of the Philippines and US Interests," Congressional Research Service, April 5, 2012, https://fas.org/sgp/crs/row/RL33233.pdf.

131. Richard Javad Heydarian, "New Dawn for Philippine-China Relations?," *Al Jazeera*, June 5, 2016, http://www.aljazeera.com/indepth/opinion/2016/06/dawn-philippine-china-relations-duterte-160604101429033.html.

132. "Duterte Willing to Back Down on Sea Dispute with China," ABS-CBN News, October 7, 2016, http://news.abs-cbn.com/halalan2016/nation/04/11/16/duterte-willing-to-back-down-on-sea-dispute-with-china.

133. Richard Javad Heydarian, "Rodrigo Duterte Is Key to China's 'Post-American' Vision for Asia," *The National Interest*, May 24, 2017, http://nationalinterest.org/feature/rodrigo-duterte-key-chinas-post-american-vision-asia-20825?utm_content=buffer27c7d&utm_medium=social&utm_source=twitter.com&utm_campaign=buffer.

134. David Hutt, "China a Friend in Need to Malaysia," *Asia Times*, March 23, 2017, http://www.atimes.com/article/china-friend-need-malaysia/.

135. Roberta Rampton and David Brunnstrom, "Trump, Malaysia's Najib Skirt Round US Probe into 1MDB Scandal," Reuters, September 12, 2017, https://www.reuters.com/article/us-usa-malaysia/trump-malaysias-najib-skirt-round-u-s-probe-into-1mdb-scandal-idUSKCN1BN0DZ.

136. Kristen Bialik, "Views of Trump, US in Countries on His Asia Trip," Pew Research Center, November 3, 2017, http://www.pewresearch.org/fact-tank/2017/11/03/opinions-in-asian-countries-on-trump-trip/.

137. Motoko Rich, "TPP, the Trade Deal Trump Killed, Is Back in Talks Without US," *New York Times*, July 14, 2017, https://www.nytimes.com/2017/07/14/business/trans-pacific-partnership-trade-japan-china-globalization.html.

138. Bonnie S. Glaser, Scott Kennedy, Matthew P. Funaiole, and Derek Mitchell, "The New Southbound Policy," Center for Strategic and International Studies, January 19, 2018, https://www.csis.org/analysis/new-southbound-policy.

139. Kenneth Chung, "S'pore Must Work with Like-Minded Partners to Uphold Multilateralism, Says PM Lee," *Today*, July 14, 2018, https://www.todayonline.com/world/spore-must-work-minded-partners-uphold-multilateralism-says-pm-lee.

140. J. Weston Phippen, "South Korea Asks to Increase Its Firepower," *The Atlantic*, July 29 2017, https://www.theatlantic.com/news/archive/2017/07/south-korea-missile/535359/.

141. Mina Pollman, "What's in Japan's Record 2018 Defense Budget Request?," *The Diplomat*, August 28, 2017, https://thediplomat.com/2017/08/whats-in-japans-record-2018-defense-budget-request/.

142. "Korea's Defense Budget to Rise 7 Percent to W43.2tr," *Korea Herald*, December 6, 2017, http://www.koreaherald.com/view.php?ud=20171206000260&ACE _SEARCH=1.

143. Nc Bipindra, "India's Own Rules Are Tripping Up Its $250 Billion Military Upgrade," Bloomberg, September 4, 2017, https://www.bloomberg.com /news/articles/2017-09-04/modi-risks-trust-deficit-as-india-rips-up -weapons-contracts.

144. SIPRI, military expenditures by country, in millions of US dollars at current prices and exchange rates, 1949–2017. Figures are in millions of US dollars— in current prices for Indonesia, Malaysia, the Philippines, Singapore, and Vietnam—converted at the exchange rate for the given year.

145. Jess Macy Yu and Greg Torode, "Taiwan Plans to Invest in Advanced Arms as China Flexes Its Muscles," Reuters, January 12, 2018, https:// www.reuters.com/article/us-taiwan-defence-spending/taiwan-plans-to -invest-in-advanced-arms-as-china-flexes-its-muscles-idUSKBN1F00PC.

3. EMPOWERING US ALLIES AND PARTNERS IN THE INDO-PACIFIC

"To Conduct a Confirmation Hearing on the Expected Nomination of Mr. James N. Mattis to Be Secretary of Defense," January 12, 2017, https:// www.armed-services.senate.gov/imo/media/doc/17-03_01-12-17.pdf.

1. See Zbigniew Brzezinski, *Strategic Vision: America and the Crisis of Global Power* (New York: Basic Books, 2012), 21–26; Ian Bremmer, *Every Nation for Itself* (New York: Penguin, 2012); Dana Allin and Erik Jones, *Weary Policeman: American Power in an Age of Austerity* (London: International Institute for Strategic Studies, 2012); and Michael O'Hanlon, *The Wounded Giant: America's Armed Forces in an Age of Austerity* (New York: Penguin, 2011).

2. Keren Yarhi-Milo, Alexander Lanoszka, and Zack Cooper, "To Arm or to Ally? The Patron's Dilemma and the Strategic Logic of Arms Transfers and Alliances," *International Security* 41, no. 2 (2016): 90–139.

3. Jeffrey W. Taliaferro, *Balancing Risks: Great Power Intervention in the Periphery* (Ithaca, NY: Cornell University Press, 2004).

4. Rebecca Friedman Lissner and Mira Rapp Hooper, "American Strategy for a New International Order," *Washington Quaterly*, Spring 2018, 19–20.

5. Some of the points made in this section are derived from the author's testimony before the US Congress. Abraham M. Denmark, "The China Challenge: Military and Security Developments," Testimony before the Senate Foreign Relations Subcommittee on East Asia, the Pacific, and

International Security Policy, September 5, 2018, https://www.foreign.senate.gov/imo/media/doc/090518_Denmark_Testimony.pdf.

6. Ash Carter, "Remarks on 'Indo-Pacific's Principled Security Network' at 2016 IISS Shangri-La Dialogue," US Department of Defense, June 4, 2016, https://www.defense.gov/News/Speeches/Speech-View/Article/791213/remarks-on-Indo-Pacifics-principled-security-network-at-2016-iiss-shangri-la-di/.

7. Henry Kissinger, *World Order* (New York: Penguin Books, 2014), 1.

8. Joshua Kurlantzick, "Australia, New Zealand Face China's Influence," Council on Foreign Relations, December 13, 2017, https://www.cfr.org/expert-brief/australia-new-zealand-face-chinas-influence.

9. Natasha Bertrand, "Trump's Top Intelligence Officials Contradict Him on Russian Meddling," *The Atlantic*, February 13, 2018, https://www.theatlantic.com/politics/archive/2018/02/the-intelligence-community-warns-congress-russia-will-interfere-in-2018-elections/553256/.

10. Abha Bhattarai, "China Asked Marriott to Shut Down Its Website; The Company Complied," *Washington Post*, January 18, 2018, https://www.washingtonpost.com/news/business/wp/2018/01/18/china-demanded-marriott-change-its-website-the-company-complied/?utm_term=.03831fd1dd94.

11. David Shepardson, "US Condemns China for 'Orwellian Nonsense' over Airline Websites," Reuters, May 7, 2018, https://www.reuters.com/article/us-usa-airlines-china-exclusive/u-s-condemns-china-for-orwellian-nonsense-over-airline-websites-idUSKBN1I60NL.

12. Joshua Kurlantzick, "Southeast Asia's Democratic Decline in the America First Era," Council on Foreign Relations, October 27, 2017, https://www.cfr.org/expert-brief/southeast-asias-democratic-decline-america-first-era.

13. Parts of this subsection were previously published by the author in the Wilson Center's blog Asia Dispatches, or were recounted in his speech to the 2018 Seoul Defense Dialogue; see Abraham M. Denmark, "Competing with China in the Indo-Pacific," Asia Dispatches, February 27, 2018, https://www.wilsoncenter.org/blog-post/competing-china-the-indo-pacific; and Abraham M. Denmark, "US-China Competition and Implications for the Korean Peninsula," speech to Seoul Defense Dialogue, October 31, 2018, https://www.wilsoncenter.org/article/us-china-competition-and-implications-for-the-korean-peninsula.

14. Although Beijing has certainly outperformed Washington in its ability to link strategic objectives with investments and initiatives, there is also a structural element at play. Because of its authoritarian system, Beijing has the ability to aggregate its economic power and utilize it as a tool of the

state. This is markedly different from the United States' disaggregated, market-led approach. Though the latter is certainly more efficient and historically more successful, it is also a more complicated tool of power for American policymakers to wield.

15. Mike M. Mochizuki, "Japan's Shifting Strategy toward the Rise of China," *Journal of Strategic Studies* 30, nos. 4–5 (2007): 758–59; Mike M. Mochizuki, "Japan and China at a Crossroads," *East Asian Insights* 1, no. 2 (2006): 1–5, at 2–3, http://www.jcie.org/researchpdfs/EAI/1-2.pdf.

16. "Remarks by Prime Minister Shinzo Abe on the Occasion of Accepting Hudson Institute's 2013 Herman Kahn Award," Prime Minister of Japan and His Cabinet, September 25, 2013, http://japan.kantei.go.jp/96_abe /statement/201309/25hudson_e.html.

17. Balbina Hwang, "The US Pivot to Asia and South Korea's Rise," *Asian Perspective* 41 (2017): 83; Jae Ho Chung and Jiyoon Kim, "Is South Korea in China's Orbit? Assessing Seoul's Perceptions and Policies," *Asia Policy* 21 (2016): 126.

18. Chung and Kim, "Is South Korea in China's Orbit?," 135.

19. Evan A. Feigenbaum, "Is Coercion the New Normal in China's Economic Statecraft?," *MacroPolo*, July 25, 2017, https://macropolo.org/coercion -new-normal-chinas-economic-statecraft/.

20. "Summary of the 2018 National Defense Strategy," https://www.defense .gov/Portals/1/Documents/pubs/2018-National-Defense-Strategy -Summary.pdf.

21. International Monetary Fund, *World Economic Outlook Update* (Washington: International Monetary Fund, 2012), http://www.imf.org/external/pubs /ft/weo/2012/01/weodata/index.aspx.

22. International Monetary Fund, *World Economic Outlook Update*.

23. Richard Fontaine and Daniel M. Kliman, "At the G-20, Look to the Swing States," *World Politics Review*, November 2, 2011, http://www .worldpoliticsreview.com/articles/10532/at-the-g-20-look-to-the-swing -states.

24. See Nicholas Eberstadt, "Asia-Pacific Demographics in 2010–2040: Implications for Strategic Balance," in *Strategic Asia, 2010–11: Asia's Rising Power and America's Continued Purpose*, ed. Ashley J. Tellis, Andrew Marble, and Travis Tanner (Seattle: National Bureau of Asian Research, 2010), 237–78.

25. Stockholm International Peace Research Institute (SIPRI), Military Expenditures Database, http://milexdata.sipri.org/result.php4.

26. Chicago Council on Global Affairs and WorldPublicOpinion.org, *World Public Opinion 2007*, http://www.thechicagocouncil.org/userfiles/file/pos

_topline percent20reports/pos percent202007_global percent20issues /wpo_07 percent20full percent20report.pdf; Marvin C. Ott, *East Asia and the United States: Current Status and Five-Year Outlook* (Washington: Federation of American Scientists, 2000), http://www.fas.org/irp/nic /east_asia.html#link05; "US Eyes Return to Some Southeast Asia Military Bases," *Washington Post*, June 22, 2012, http://www.washingtonpost.com /world/national-security/us-seeks-return-to-se-asian-bases/2012/06/22 /gJQAKP83vV_story_1.html.

27. Lisa Daniel, "Flournoy: Asia Will Be Heart of US Security Policy," American Foreign Press Service, April 29, 2011, http://www.defense.gov/news /newsarticle.aspx?id=63755.

28. See David J. Berteau and Michael J. Green, "US Force Posture Strategy in the Asia Pacific Region: An Independent Assessment," Center for Strategic and International Studies, August 2012.

29. Joseph S. Nye Jr., "Recovering American Leadership," *Survival* 50, no. 1 (2008): 55–68.

30. Brian Weeden, "Testimony Before the US–China Economic and Security Review Commission, Hearing on China in Space: A Strategic Competition?," April 25, 2019, https://swfound.org/media/206425/weeden_uscc_testimony _april2019.pdf.

31. Weeden, "Testimony."

32. Specifically, this includes the Outer Space Treaty (1967), the Rescue Agreement (1968), the Liability Convention (1972), and the Registration Convention (1976).

33. Allison Peters, "Russia and China Are Trying to Set the UN's Rules on Cybercrime," *Foreign Policy*, September 16, 2019, https://foreignpolicy .com/2019/09/16/russia-and-china-are-trying-to-set-the-u-n-s-rules-on -cybercrime/.

34. Timothy Farnsworth, "China and Russia Submit Cyber Proposal," *Arms Control Today*, November 2011, https://www.armscontrol.org/act/2011-11 /china-russia-submit-cyber-proposal.

35. The Indo-Pacific region is the most natural disaster prone region of the world, according to a 2010 report by the UN Economic and Social Commission for Asia and the Pacific and the UN International Strategy for Disaster Reduction. See "Asia-Pacific Prone to Natural Disasters," UPI, October 27, 2010, http://www.upi.com/Business_News/Energy -Resources/2010/10/27/Asia-Pacific-prone-to-natural-disasters/UPI -40001288183258.

36. See Kurt M. Campbell et al., "The Age of Consequences: The Foreign Policy and National Security Implications of Global Climate Change," Center for a New American Security, November 2007.

37. In recent years, Indonesia and the Philippines have developed dedicated disaster response units as part of their military. Japan, Australia, Taiwan, and South Korea all highlight the intensifying threat of natural disasters to regional stability in their most recent defense white papers, and identify carrying out in humanitarian relief and disaster response missions as a core function of their respective militaries.

38. "South Korea to Temporarily Deploy Four Remaining THAAD Launchers: Ministry," Reuters, September 4, 2017, https://www.reuters.com/article/us-northkorea-missiles-thaad/south-korea-to-temporarily-deploy-four-remaining-thaad-launchers-ministry-idUSKCN1BF0PW.

39. Byun Duk-kun, "Moon, Trump Agree to Build Up Deterrence, Urge N. Korea to Give Up Nukes," Yonhap News Agency, November 7, 2017, http://english.yonhapnews.co.kr/national/2017/11/07/0301000000AEN20171107012553315.html?utm_source=Sailthru&utm_medium=email&utm_campaign=New percent20Campaign&utm_term=*Situation percent20Report.

40. Mari Yamaguchi, "Japan Approves Missile Defense System Amid NKorea Threat," Associated Press, December 19, 2017, https://apnews.com/39f053831e4f449c9be4186e7a0863a4/Japan-approves-missile-defense-system-amid-NKorea-threat.

41. Sheena Chestnut Greitens, "Analysis: Can Trump Count on Manila to Put Pressure on North Korea? 3 Points to Know," *Washington Post*, May 16, 2017, https://www.washingtonpost.com/news/monkey-cage/wp/2017/05/16/can-trump-count-on-manila-to-put-pressure-on-north-korea-3-points-to-know/?utm_term=.7a93b91d04bc.

42. Ellen Hallams, *The United States and NATO Since 9/11: The Transatlantic Alliance Renewed* (New York: Routledge, 2010), 58.

43. Edgar Buckley, "Invoking Article 5," *NATO Review*, June 1, 2006, https://www.nato.int/docu/review/2006/Invokation-Article-5/Invoking_Article_5/EN/index.htm.

44. President Nixon described his doctrine thusly: "Its central thesis is that the United States will participate in the defense and development of allies and friends, but that America cannot—and will not—conceive all the plans, design all the programs, execute all the decisions and undertake all the defense of the free nations of the world. We will help where it makes a real difference and is considered in our interest." Quoted from US Department of State, https://history.state.gov/historicaldocuments/frus1969-76v01/d60.

45. Leon Whyte, "Evolution of the US–ROK Alliance: Abandonment Fears," *The Diplomat*, June 22, 2015, https://thediplomat.com/2015/06/evolution-of-the-u-s-rok-alliance-abandonment-fears/.

46. Whyte, "Evolution."

47. Art Swift, "In US, Record-High 72 Percent See Foreign Trade as Opportunity," Gallup, February 16, 2017, http://news.gallup.com/poll/204044/record -high-foreign-trade-opportunity.aspx.

48. It should be noted that the author's spouse is currently a contractor for the US Agency for International Development.

49. "The FY 2018 Foreign Affairs Budget, Hearing Before the Committee on Foreign Affairs, House of Representatives," 115th Cong. 4-5 (2017), http:// docs.house.gov/meetings/FA/FA00/20170614/106115/HHRG-115-FA00 -Transcript-20170614.pdf.

50. "Fiscal Year 2018 USAID Development and Humanitarian Assistance Budget," USAID, May 24, 2017, https://www.usaid.gov/sites/default/files/documents /1869/USAIDFY2018BudgetFactsheet.pdf; "FY 2017 Development and Humanitarian Assistance Budget," USAID, https://www.usaid.gov/sites /default/files/documents/9276/FY2017_USAIDBudgetRequestFactSheet .pdf.

51. Rex Tillerson, "FY 2018 Congressional Budget Justification—Secretary's Letter," May 23, 2017, 1, https://www.state.gov/documents/organization /271282.pdf.

52. Tillerson, "FY 2018," 3.

53. "FY 2018 Foreign Affairs Budget."

54. Stockholm International Peace Research Institute (SIPRI), https://www .sipri.org/databases/milex.

55. John McCain, "Restoring American Power," January 16, 2017, https:// www.mccain.senate.gov/public/_cache/files/25bff0ec-481e-466a-843f -68ba5619e6d8/restoring-american-power-7.pdf; Yun Sun, "China and the Asia Pacific Stability Initiative," China-US Focus, May 23, 2017, https:// www.chinausfocus.com/finance-economy/2017/0523/15028.html.

56. John McCain, "Opening Statement by SASC Chairman John McCain at Hearing on US Policy & Strategy in the Indo-Pacific," April 25, 2017, https://www.mccain.senate.gov/public/index.cfm/floor-statements?ID =D03DC3B8-3901-44C5-8105-D435F0BDB718.

57. "Senators Urge Secretary Mattis to Create New Indo-Pacific Defense Fund," Senate website of Dan Sullivan, US senator for Alaska, March 1, 2017, https://www.sullivan.senate.gov/newsroom/press-releases/senators- urge-secretary-mattis-to-create-new-Indo-Pacific-defense-fund; letter from Madeleine Z. Bordallo, Joe Wilson, Colleen Hanabusa, Vicky Hartzler, and Stephanie Murphy to Secretary of Defense James Mattis, February 28, 2017, https://stephaniemurphy.house.gov/uploadedfiles/2.28.2017_house _letter_to_secdef_mattis_on_asia_pacific_stability_initiative_apsi.pdf.

58. Matthew Pennington, "Pentagon: Afghan War Costing $45 billion per Year," Military Times, February 6, 2018, https://www.militarytimes.com/news

/pentagon-congress/2018/02/07/pentagon-afghan-war-costing-us-45
-billion-per-year/.

59. Jen Judson, "Funding to Deter Russia Reaches $6.5B in FY19 Defense Budget
Request," *Defense News*, February 12, 2018, https://www.defensenews.com
/land/2018/02/12/funding-to-deter-russia-reaches-65b-in-fy19-defense
-budget-request/.

60. David H. Berger, "Commandant's Planning Guidance," July 2019, https://
www.hqmc.marines.mil/Portals/142/Docs/%2038th%20Commandant
%27s%20Planning%20Guidance_2019.pdf?ver=2019-07-16-200152-700.

61. Jennifer Hansler, "State Department Hiring Freeze Undermined Safety
and Gutted Morale, Report Finds," CNN, August 12, 2019, https://www.cnn
.com/2019/08/12/politics/state-oig-report-hiring-freeze/index.html.

62. "China Now Has More Diplomatic Posts Than Any Other Country," BBC
News, November 27, 2019, https://www.bbc.com/news/world-asia-china
-50569237.

63. See, e.g., Jane Wardell and Jonathan Barrett, "Analysis: Silk Roads and
Chilled Beef: How China Is Trying to Fill a Trump Vacuum in Australia,"
CNBC, March 29, 2017.

64. "Transcript: Donald Trump Expounds on His Foreign Policy Views," *New
York Times*, March 26, 2016, https://www.nytimes.com/2016/03/27/us
/politics/donald-trump-transcript.html?hp&action=click&pgtyp
e=Homepage&clickSource=story-heading&module=first-column
-region&region=top-news&WT.nav=top-news&_r=0.

65. Alec Macfarlane and Taehoon Lee, "Trump: South Korea Should Pay for
$1B Missile Defense, System," CNN Money, April 28, 2017, http://money
.cnn.com/2017/04/28/news/trump-south-korea-thaad-trade/index.html.

66. See, e.g., Euan McKirdy, "Trump Says He Would Consult with China's
Xi Before Speaking to Taiwan," CNN, April 28, 2017, http://www.cnn
.com/2017/04/28/asia/trump-taiwan-xi-comments/index.html.

67. Madeleine K. Albright, interview by Matt Lauer, *The Today Show*, NBC-TV,
February 19, 1998, https://1997-2001.state.gov/statements/1998/980219a.html.

68. This was one of the primary arguments in favor of the US–South Korea
free trade agreement, known as KORUS, negotiations for which were
begun in the George W. Bush administration and ratified in 2011.

69. Office of the Press Secretary, "Fact Sheet: Unprecedented US–ASEAN
Relations," White House, February 12, 2016, https://obamawhitehouse
.archives.gov/the-press-office/2016/02/12/fact-sheet-unprecedented
-us-asean-relations; Office of the State Department Historian, "Visits by
Foreign Leaders," https://history.state.gov/departmenthistory/visits.

70. Office of the State Department Historian, "Presidential and Secretaries
Travels Abroad—Barack Obama," https://history.state.gov/department

history/travels/president/obama-barack; Office of the State Department Historian, "Presidential and Secretaries Travels Abroad—George W. Bush," https://history.state.gov/departmenthistory/travels/president/bush -george-w.

71. Office of the State Department Historian, "Presidential and Secretaries Travel Abroad—Donald J. Trump," https://history.state.gov/department history/travels/president/trump-donald-j.

72. Prashanth Parameswaran, "China Blocked ASEAN Defense Meeting Pact Amid South China Sea Fears: US Official," *The Diplomat*, November 4, 2015, http://thediplomat.com/2015/11/china-blocked-asia-defense-meeting -pact-amid-south-china-sea-fears-us-official/.

73. See Office of the US Trade Representative, "Memorandum: National Security and Foreign Policy Authorities on President Obama's Trade Agenda," June 8, 2015, https://ustr.gov/memorandum-national-security -and-foreign-policy-authorities-president-obama percentE2 percent80 percent99s-trade-agenda; "The Trans-Pacific Partnership: Prospects for Greater US Trade, Before the Subcommittee on Asia and the Pacific of the Committee on Foreign Affairs, 114th Cong., March 4, 2015, https:// foreignaffairs.house.gov/hearing/subcommittee-hearing-the-trans -pacific-partnership-prospects-for-greater-u-s-trade.

74. See, e.g., Ana Swanson, " 'None of These Big Quagmire Deals': Trump Spells Out Historic Shift in Approach to Trade," *Washington Post*, February 24, 2017, https://www.washingtonpost.com/news/wonk/wp/2017/02/24/trump -spells-out-historic-shift-in-trade-that-could-weigh-on-companies -growth/?utm_term=.4db619e037d1; Donald J. Trump, "Presidential Memorandum Regarding Withdrawal of the United States from the Trans-Pacific Partnership Negotiations and Agreement," White House, January 23, 2017, https://www.whitehouse.gov/presidential-actions /presidential-memorandum-regarding-withdrawal-united-states-trans -pacific-partnership-negotiations-agreement/.

75. "Sec. Pompeo Remarks on 'America's Indo-Pacific Economic Vision,'" US Mission to ASEAN, July 30, 2018, https://asean.usmission.gov /sec-pompeo-remarks-on-americas-indo-pacific-economic-vision/.

76. US International Development Finance Corporation, https://www.opic .gov/build-act/faqs-build-act-implementation.

77. Alejandro Salas, "Slow, Imperfect Progress across Asia Pacific," Transparency International, February 21, 2018, https://www.transparency.org /news/feature/slow_imperfect_progress_across_asia_pacific.

78. E.g., see Damien Cave, "A New Battle for Guadalcanal, This Time with China," *New York Times*, July 21, 2018, https://www.nytimes.com/2018/07/21/world /asia/china-australia-guadalcanal-solomon-islands.html.

79. This argument was first made by the author in "Partnering to Protect Democracy," by Abraham M. Denmark, *Taipei Times,* June 25, 2018, http://www.taipeitimes.com/News/editorials/archives/2018/06/25/2003695487.

80. See Andrew T. H. Tan, *The Arms Race in Asia: Trends, Causes and Implications* (New York: Routledge, 2013).

81. Stockholm International Peace Research Institute (SIPRI), "Military Expenditure by Region in Constant US Dollars," https://www.sipri.org/sites/default/files/Milex-regional-totals.pdf; Military Expenditure Database, https://www.sipri.org/databases/milex. Percentage changes are calculated in constant (2015) US dollars.

82. SIPRI, "Military Expenditure." Percentage changes are calculated in constant (2016) US dollars.

83. National Archives and Records Administration, "Fact Sheet: US Building Maritime Capacity in Southeast Asia," November 17, 2017, https://obamawhitehouse.archives.gov/the-press-office/2015/11/17/fact-sheet-us-building-maritime-capacity-southeast-asia.

84. Prashanth Parameswaran, "America's New Maritime Security Initiative for Southeast Asia," *The Diplomat,* April 3, 2016, http://thediplomat.com/2016/04/americas-new-maritime-security-initiative-for-southeast-asia/.

85. Max Bearak and Lazaro Gamio, "The US Foreign Aid Budget, Visualized," *Washington Post,* October 18, 2016, https://www.washingtonpost.com/graphics/world/which-countries-get-the-most-foreign-aid/.

86. "Foreign Military Financing Account Summary," US Department of State, https://2009-2017.state.gov/t/pm/ppa/sat/c14560.htm.

87. Edward Linczer, "The Role of Security Assistance in Washington's Pivot to Southeast Asia," *China-US Focus,* August 26, 2016, https://www.chinausfocus.com/peace-security/the-role-of-security-assistance-in-washingtons-pivot-to-southeast-asia.

88. Aaron Mehta, "FY18 Budget Request Cuts $1B from State's Foreign Military Financing," Defense News, May 23, 2017, https://www.defensenews.com/congress/budget/2017/05/23/fy18-budget-request-cuts-1b-from-state-s-foreign-military-financing/.

89. US State Department, "Congressional Budget Justification: Department of State, Foreign Operations, and Related Programs, Fiscal Year 2018," 381–85, https://www.state.gov/documents/organization/271013.pdf; "America First: A Budget Blueprint to Make America Great Again," Office of Management and Budget, Executive Office of the President of the United States, 34, https://www.whitehouse.gov/wp-content/uploads/2017/11/2018_blueprint.pdf.

90. Aaron Mehta and Joe Gould, "Trump Budget to Cut Foreign Military Financing, with Loans Looming," *Defense News,* May 19, 2017, https://www

.defensenews.com/pentagon/2017/05/19/trump-budget-to-cut-foreign
-military-financing-with-loan-option-looming/; Rachel Stohl and Shannon
Dick, "Trump on Arms Sales," Forum on the Arms Trade, April 25, 2017,
https://www.forumarmstrade.org/looking-ahead-blog/trump-on-arms
-sales.

91. Jeremy Page and Paul Sonne, "Unable to Buy US Military Drones, Allies
Place Orders with China," *Wall Street Journal*, July 17, 2017, https://www
.wsj.com/amp/articles/unable-to-buy-u-s-military-drones-allies-place
-orders-with-china-1500301716?mg=prod/accounts-wsj.

92. Lauren Dickey, "Taiwan's Search for Security Partners: Looking Beyond
Washington," Jamestown Foundation, March 31, 2017, https://jamestown
.org/program/taiwans-search-security-partners-looking-beyond
-washington/.

93. "US Pledges Nearly $300 Million Security Funding for Indo-Pacific
Region," Reuters, August 5, 2018, https://www.reuters.com/article/us
-asean-singapore-usa-security/u-s-pledges-nearly-300-million-security
-funding-for-southeast-asia-idUSKBN1KP022.

94. Tommy Ross, "Congressional Oversight on Security Assistance," Center
for Strategic and International Studies, September 26, 2017, https://www
.csis.org/analysis/congressional-oversight-security-assistance.

95. Ross, "Congressional Oversight."

96. Ross, "Congressional Oversight."

97. "US Export Policy."

98. Elisa Catalano Ewers et al., "Drone Proliferation: Policy Choices for the
Trump Administration," Center for a New American Security, http://
drones.cnas.org/reports/drone-proliferation/; "US Export Policy for
Military Unmanned Aerial Systems," Office of the Spokesperson, US
Department of State, February 17, 2015, https://2009-2017.state.gov/r/pa
/prs/ps/2015/02/237541.htm.

99. Michael C. Horowitz and Joshua A. Schwartz, "A New US Policy Makes
It (Somewhat) Easier to Export Drones," *Washington Post*, April 20, 2018,
https://www.washingtonpost.com/news/monkey-cage/wp/2018/04/20
/a-new-u-s-policy-makes-it-somewhat-easier-to-export-drones/.

100. The RAND Corporation's 2010 study on foreign military assistance
analyzed this issue in depth. See "Security Cooperation Organizations in
the Country Team: Options for Success," by Terrence K. Kelly, Jefferson P.
Marquis, Cathryn Quantic Thurston, Jennifer D. P. Moroney, and Charlotte
Lynch, http://www.rand.org/content/dam/rand/pubs/technical_reports
/2010/RAND_TR734.sum.pdf.

101. Lyle J. Morris, "Blunt Defenders of Sovereignty: The Rise of Coast Guards of
East and Southeast Asia," *Naval War College Review* 70, no. 2 (2017): 75–112,

https://usnwc2.usnwc.edu/getattachment/eaa0678e-83a0-4c67-8aab
-0f829d7a2b27/Blunt-Defenders-of-Sovereignty—-The-Rise-of-Coast.aspx.

102. Ronald O'Rourke, "China Naval Modernization: Implications for US Navy
Capabilities—Background and Issues for Congress," Congressional Research
Service, December 13, 2017, https://fas.org/sgp/crs/row/RL33153.pdf.

103. Japanese Ministry of Defense, "Defense of Japan (Annual White Paper),"
http://www.mod.go.jp/e/publ/w_paper/.

104. See Lyle J. Morris, "The New 'Normal' in the East China Sea," *The
Diplomat*, March 2017, https://magazine.thediplomat.com/#/issues
/-KdYNdv6QWeKhsKfC5hO.

105. US Department of Defense, "The Indo-Pacific Maritime Security Strategy:
Achieving US National Security Objectives in a Changing Environment,"
July 2015, https://www.defense.gov/Portals/1/Documents/pubs/NDAA
percent20A-P_Maritime_SecuritY_Strategy-08142015-1300-FINAL
FORMAT.PDF.

106. "China Is Not Militarizing South China Sea, Premier Li Says," Reuters,
March 23, 2017, https://www.reuters.com/article/us-southchinasea-china
/china-is-not-militarizing-south-china-sea-premier-li-says
-idUSKBN16V04A.

107. E.g., see Natalie Sambhi, "Hokowi's Maritime Dreams Thwarted by Land-
Based Challenges," *The Diplomat*, October 17, 2019, https://thediplomat
.com/2019/10/jokowis-maritime-dreams-thwarted-by-land-based
-challenges/.

108. Morris, "Blunt Defenders."

109. See US House Subcommittee on Seapower and Projection Forces,
"Seapower and Projection Forces in the South China Sea," September 21,
2016, https://republicans-armedservices.house.gov/legislation/hearings
/seapower-and-projection-forces-south-china-sea.

110. "North Korea—Chemical," Nuclear Threat Initiative, December 2017, http://
www.nti.org/learn/countries/north-korea/chemical/.

111. Joby Warrick, "Microbes by the Ton: Officials See Weapons Threat as
North Korea Gains Biotech Expertise," *Washington Post*, December 10, 2017,
https://www.washingtonpost.com/world/national-security/microbes
-by-the-ton-officials-see-weapons-threat-as-north-korea-gains-biotech
-expertise/2017/12/10/9b9d5f9e-d5f0-11e7-95bf-df7c19270879_story
.html?utm_term=.54190a689fd1; Yoshihiro Makino, "North Korea Said to
Be Testing Anthrax-Tipped Ballistic Missiles," *Asahi Shimbun*, December 20,
2017, http://www.asahi.com/ajw/articles/AJ201712200036.html.

112. Wyatt Olson, "US, Japan, S. Korea Conducting First Joint Ballistic Missile
Defense Drill," *Stars and Stripes*, June 27, 2016, https://www.stripes.com/news/us
-japan-s-korea-conducting-first-joint-ballistic-missile-defense-drill-1.416554.

113. Franz-Stefan Gady, "Japan, US, South Korea Hold Missile Defense Drill," *The Diplomat*, January 24, 2017, https://thediplomat.com/2017/01/japan-us-south-korea-hold-missile-defense-drill/; Brad Lendon, "US, South Korea, Japan Start Drills Off North Korea," CNN, March 14, 2017, http://www.cnn.com/2017/03/14/asia/us-south-korea-japan-aegis-missile-defense-ship-exercises/index.html; Dagyum Ji, "US, South Korea, Japan Staging Missile Warning Exercises Near Korean Peninsula," *NK News*, October 24, 2017, https://www.nknews.org/2017/10/u-s-south-korea-japan-staging-missile-warning-exercises-near-korean-peninsula/; Ankit Panda, "US, Japan, South Korea to Hold Missile Tracking Exercises," *The Diplomat*, December 11, 2017, https://thediplomat.com/2017/12/us-japan-south-korea-to-hold-missile-tracking-exercises/.

114. Jon Grevatt, "South Korean Military Exports Climb 25 Percent," *Jane's 360*, January 15, 2018, http://www.janes.com/article/77044/south-korean-military-exports-climb-25.

115. Joyce Lee and Tony Munroe, "South Korea Wants to Turn Its Arms Industry into an Export Powerhouse," *Business Insider*, April 22, 2015, http://www.businessinsider.com/r-south-korea-seeks-bigger-role-in-global-arms-bazaar-2015-4.

116. Jonathan Soble, "With Ban on Exports Lifted, Japan Arms Makers Cautiously Market Wares Abroad," *New York Times*, July 12, 2015, https://www.nytimes.com/2015/07/13/business/international/with-ban-on-exports-lifted-japan-arms-makers-cautiously-market-wares-abroad.html.

117. Khanh Lynh, "Vietnam Hails Burgeoning Defense Ties with India," VnExpress International, August 18, 2017, https://e.vnexpress.net/news/news/vietnam-hails-burgeoning-defense-ties-with-india-3629191.html.

118. "Australia Aims to Become 'Top 10' Defence Exporter," BBC News, January 29, 2018, https://www.bbc.com/news/world-australia-42854839.

119. Bruce Stokes, "Japanese Divided on Democracy's Success at Home, but Value Voice of the People: Public Sees Threats Abroad amid Declining Views of US," Pew Research Center, October 17, 2017, 7, http://assets.pewresearch.org/wp-content/uploads/sites/2/2017/10/04141151/Pew-Research-Center_Japan-Report_2017.10.17.pdf.

120. Roy Kamphausen, John S. Park, Ryo Sahashi, and Alison Szalwinski, "The Case for US–ROK–Japan Trilateralism: Strengths and Limitations," National Bureau of Asian Research, February 2018, 17, http://www.nbr.org/publications/element.aspx?id=980.

121. Choe Sang-hun, "South Korea and China End Dispute Over Missile Defense System," *New York Times*, October 30, 2017, https://www.nytimes.com/2017/10/30/world/asia/north-korea-nuclear-test-radiation.html.

122. Kamphausen et al., "Case," 17.

123. Yuki Tatsumi, "The Japan–South Korea 'Comfort Women' Agreement Survives (Barely)," *The Diplomat*, January 11, 2018, https://thediplomat .com/2018/01/the-japan-south-korea-comfort-women-agreement -survives-barely/.

124. Tatsumi.

125. Kamphausen et al., "Case," 3.

126. See, e.g., Amitav Acharya, "Doomed by Dialogue? Will ASEAN Survive Great Power Rivalry in Asia?," *Asan Forum*, June 29, 2015; and Amitav Acharya, "Is ASEAN Losing Its Way?," YaleGlobal Online, September 24, 2015, https:// yaleglobal.yale.edu/content/asean-losing-its-way.

127. Organization for Economic Cooperation and Development, "OECD Sees Global Economy Strengthening, but Says Further Policy Action Needed to Catalyse the Private Sector for Stronger and More Inclusive Growth," November 28, 2017, https://www.oecd.org/newsroom/oecd-sees-global -economy-strengthening-but-says-further-policy-action-needed-to -catalyse-the-private-sector-for-stronger-and-more-inclusive-growth .htm.

128. International Monetary Fund, "Asia's Dynamic Economies Continue to Lead Global Growth," May 9, 2017, https://www.imf.org/en/News/Articles /2017/05/08/NA050917-Asia-Dynamic-Economies-Continue-to-Lead -Global-Growth.

129. Rolland Nadège, *China's Eurasian Century? Political and Strategic Implications of the Belt and Road Initiative* (Seattle: National Bureau of Asian Research, 2017).

130. "ASEAN Needs to Re-Think Approach to US$2.8 Trillion Infrastructure Gap," *Business Times* (Singapore), April 3, 2019, https://www.sc.com/en /feature/asean-needs-to-re-think-approach-to-us2-8-trillion -infrastructure-gap/.

131. Siegfrid Alegado, "Japan Still Beating China in Southeast Asia Infrastructure Race," Bloomberg, February 8, 2018, https://www.bloomberg .com/news/articles/2018-02-08/japan-still-beating-china-in-southeast -asia-infrastructure-race.

132. Shannon Tiezzi, "In Japan, Trump and Abe Offer Alternative to China's 'Belt and Road,'" *The Diplomat*, November 8, 2017, https://thediplomat .com/2017/11/in-japan-trump-and-abe-offer-alternative-to-chinas-belt -and-road/.

133. Saki Hayashi, "Japan, US and India Team to Fund Indo-Pacific Infrastructure," *Nikkei Asian Review*, April 10, 2018, https://asia.nikkei.com /Politics/International-Relations/Japan-US-and-India-team-to-fund -Indo-Pacific-infrastructure.

134. "Asia Africa Growth Corridor: Partnership for Sustainable and Innovative Development—A Vision Document," Research and Information System for Developing Countries, Economic Research Institute for ASEAN and East Asia, and Institute of Developing Economies, May 2017, http://www.eria .org/Asia-Africa-Growth-Corridor-Document.pdf.

135. Nirav Patel, "US Should Offer a Digital Highway Initiative for Asia," *Straits Times*, February 7, 2018, http://www.straitstimes.com/opinion/us-should -offer-a-digital-highway-initiative-for-asia.

136. "Sec. Pompeo Remarks on 'America's Indo-Pacific Economic Vision,'" US Mission to ASEAN, July 30, 2018, https://asean.usmission.gov/sec -pompeo-remarks-on-americas-indo-pacific-economic-vision/.

137. Jane Perlez, "Tribunal Rejects Beijing's Claims in South China Sea," *New York Times*, July 12, 2016, https://www.nytimes.com/2016/07/13/world /asia/south-china-sea-hague-ruling-philippines.html?mtrref=www .google.com&gwh=18D0ECABC520A6579443152609880200&gwt=pay.

138. Other international agreements that focus on specific aspects of the use of space have entered into force generally, but have not sought to generally govern the use of space. They include the "Outer Space Treaty," "Rescue Agreement," "Liability Convention," "Registration Convention," and the "Moon Agreement"; see http://www.unoosa.org/oosa/en/ourwork/spacelaw /treaties.html.

139. "Beyond the Stalemate in the Space Commons," in *Contested Commons: The Future of American Power in a Multipolar World*, ed. Abraham M. Denmark and James Mulvenon (Washington: Center for a New American Security, 2010), 105–37.

140. Sandra Erwin, "In Space and Cyber, China Is Closing in on the United States," *Space News*, January 10, 2018, http://spacenews.com/in-space -and-cyber-china-is-closing-in-on-the-united-states/.

141. Secretary of Defense Ash Carter, "Remarks on 'Asia-Pacific's Principled Security Network' at 2016 IISS Shangri-La Dialogue," Singapore, June 4, 2016, https://www.defense.gov/News/Speeches/Speech-View/Article /791213/remarks-on-asia-pacifics-principled-security-network-at-2016 -iiss-shangri-la-di/.

142. Kiran Sharma, "India and Vietnam to Strengthen Defense Ties Against Assertive China," *Nikkei Asian Review*, March 1, 2018, https://asia.nikkei .com/Politics-Economy/International-Relations/India-and-Vietnam-to -strengthen-defense-ties-against-assertive-China.

143. Shinzo Abe, "Asia's Democratic Security Diamond by Shinzo Abe," Project Syndicate, December 27, 2012, https://www.project-syndicate.org/onpoint/a -strategic-alliance-for-japan-and-india-by-shinzo-abe?barrier=accesspaylog.

4. COUNTRY STUDIES

John F. Kennedy, "Inaugural Address," January 20, 1961, https://www
.jfklibrary.org/learn/about-jfk/historic-speeches/inaugural-address.

1. See *Strategic Asia, 2015–2016: Foundations of National Power in the Asia-Pacific*, ed. Michael Wills, Ashley J. Tellis, and Alison Szalwinski (Seattle: National Bureau of Asian Research, 2015); *Strategic Asia 2016–2017: Understanding Strategic Cultures in the Asia-Pacific*, ed. Michael Wills, Ashley J. Tellis, and Alison Szalwinski (Seattle: National Bureau of Asian Research, 2016); *and Strategic Asia, 2017–2018: Power, Ideas, and Military Strategy in the Asia-Pacific*, ed. Ashley J. Tellis, Alison Szalwinski, and Michael Wills (Seattle: National Bureau of Asian Research, 2017).

2. Vinayak HV, Fraser Thompson, and Oliver Tonby, "Understanding ASEAN: Seven Things You Need to Know," McKinsey & Company, New York, May 2014, https://www.mckinsey.com/industries/public-sector/our-insights /understanding-asean-seven-things-you-need-to-know.

3. "Asia Matters for America," http://www.asiamattersforamerica.org /asean/, as cited in "ASEAN's Bright Future: Growth Opportunities for Corporates in the ASEAN Region," J. P. Morgan, n.d., https://www.jpmorgan .com/country/US/EN/cib/investment-banking/trade-asean-future.

4. "Investing in ASEAN 2013–2014," http://www.usasean.org/system/files /downloads/Investing-in-ASEAN-2013-14.pdf, as cited in "ASEAN's Bright Future."

5. International Monetary Fund, World Economic Outlook Database, April 2019, April 2019, https://www.imf.org/external/pubs/ft/weo/2019/01 /weodata/index.aspx.

6. East-West Center in Washington, "ASEAN Matters for America / America Matters for ASEAN," https://www.eastwestcenter.org/system/tdf/private /aseanmatters2017.pdf?file=1&type=node&id=36244.

7. Prashanth Parameswaran, "Assessing ASEAN's New Indo-Pacific Outlook," *The Diplomat*, June 24, 2019, https://thediplomat.com/2019/06/assessing -aseans-new-indo-pacific-outlook/.

8. "ASEAN Outlook on the Indo-Pacific," June 2019, https://asean.org /storage/2019/06/ASEAN-Outlook-on-the-Indo-Pacific_FINAL_22062019 .pdf.

9. *ASEAN Outlook on the Indo-Pacific*, June 2019.

10. Prashanth Parameswaran, "Will a China–ASEAN South China Sea Code of Conduct Really Matter?," *The Diplomat*, August 5, 2017, https:// thediplomat.com/2017/08/will-a-china-asean-south-china-sea-code-of -conduct-really-matter/.

11. Yeganeh Torbati and Trinna Leong, "ASEAN Defense Chiefs Fail to Agree on South China Sea Statement," Reuters, November 4, 2015, https://www.reuters.com/article/us-asean-malaysia-statement /asean-defense-chiefs-fail-to-agree-on-south-china-sea-statement -idUSKCN0ST07G20151104.

12. Victoria Zaretskaya, "Australia Is on Track to Become World's Largest LNG Exporter," *Today in Energy*, August 12, 2019, https://www.eia.gov /todayinenergy/detail.php?id=40853.

13. Hugh White, "America or China? Australia Is Fooling Itself That It Doesn't Have to Choose," *The Guardian*, November 26, 2017, https://www .theguardian.com/australia-news/2017/nov/27/america-or-china-were -fooling-ourselves-that-we-dont-have-to-choose.

14. "Without America," *Quarterly Essay*, November 2017, https://www.quarterly essay.com.au/essay/2017/11/without-america.

15. Paul Dibb, "Why I Disagree with Hugh White on China's Rise," *The Australian*, August 13, 2012, http://www.theaustralian.com.au/opinion/why -i-disagree-with-hugh-white-on-chinas-rise/news-story/5a69eb06fefd28 a68b5b597313f66cf0?sv=ddf1076fb959bb965d36f114a8203bd9.

16. IISS Shangri-La Dialogue, keynote address by Malcolm Turnbull, prime minister of Australia, June 2, 2017, https://srilanka.embassy.gov.au/files /clmb/Keynote%20Address%20-%20Malcolm%20Turnbull-%202017.pdf.

17. Australian Government, "2017 Foreign Policy White Paper," November 21, 2017, https://www.fpwhitepaper.gov.au/foreign-policy-white-paper.

18. John Pomfret, "Opinion: China's Meddling in Australia—and What the US Should Learn from It," *Washington Post*, June 14, 2017, https://www.washington post.com/news/global-opinions/wp/2017/06/14/how-should-the-u-s-deal -with-chinas-rise-look-to-australia/?utm_term=.b23f878ab241.

19. Quoted by Pomfret.

20. Harry Krejsa, "Under Pressure: The Growing Reach of Chinese Influence Campaigns in Democratic Societies," CNAS, April 2018.

21. Primrose Riordan, "ASIO Battling Spy Threat from China and Russia," *The Australian*, October 19, 2017, https://www.theaustralian.com.au /national-affairs/national-security/asio-battling-spy-threat-from-china -and-russia/news-story/78ae4df93a6e9e3e664b28bdd1e88b96.

22. John Power, "Australia Sounds the Alarm over Chinese 'Interference,'" *Nikkei Asian Review*, April 11, 2018, https://asia.nikkei.com/Politics/International -Relations/Australia-sounds-the-alarm-over-Chinese-interference.

23. David Wroe, "China Eyes Vanuatu Military Base in Plan with Global Ramifications," *Sydney Morning Herald*, April 9, 2018, https://www.smh .com.au/politics/federal/china-eyes-vanuatu-military-base-in-plan -with-global-ramifications-20180409-p4z8j9.html.

24. Australian Department of Defence, "Defence at a Glance: 2016–17 Report," June 30, 2017, https://www.defence.gov.au/AnnualReports/16-17/Defence Glance.asp.

25. "Remarks by President Obama and Prime Minister Gillard of Australia in Joint Press Conference," National Archives and Records Administration, November 16, 2011, https://obamawhitehouse.archives.gov/the-press -office/2011/11/16/remarks-president-obama-and-prime-minister -gillard-australia-joint-press.

26. Krishnadev Calamur, "China vs. America in a Financial Game of 'Risk,'" *The Atlantic*, October 18, 2017, https://www.theatlantic.com/international /archive/2017/10/china-investments/543321/.

27. Australian Government, "The Sydney Declaration," March 18, 2018, https://aseanaustralia.pmc.gov.au/Declaration.html.

28. Chris Duckett, "Australia Using Foreign Aid to Lock Huawei Out of PNG-Solomon Islands Subsea Cable," ZDNet, June 13, 2018, https://www.zdnet .com/article/australia-using-foreign-aid-to-lock-huawei-out-of-png -solomon-islands-subsea-cable/.

29. Geideon Rachman, "The EU Needs to Be a Power Project," *Financial Times*, October 7, 2019, https://www.ft.com/content/ff92106c-e8e0-11e9-85f4 -d00e5018f061.

30. Jonathan E. Hillman and Maesea McCalpin, "Will China's '16+1' Format Divide Europe?," Center for Strategic and International Studies, April 11, 2019, https://www.csis.org/analysis/will-chinas-161-format-divide-europe.

31. European Commission, "EU-China: A Strategic Outlook," March 12, 2019, https://ec.europa.eu/commission/sites/beta-political/files/communication -eu-china-a-strategic-outlook.pdf.

32. Ana Neves, William Becker, and Marcos Dominguez-Torreiro, "Explained, the Economic Ties between Europe and Asia," World Economic Forum, May 14, 2019, https://www.weforum.org/agenda/2019/05/ways-asia-and -europe-together-connected/.

33. Florence Parly, "Asia's Evolving Security Order and Its Challenges," remarks to IISS Shangri-La Dialogue, June 1, 2019, https://in.ambafrance.org/French -Defence-Minister-Florence-Parly-s-speech-at-the-Shangri-La-Dialogue.

34. UK House of Commons Foreign Affairs Committee, "China and the Rules-Based International System," March 26, 2019, https://publications .parliament.uk/pa/cm201719/cmselect/cmfaff/612/612.pdf.

35. UK House of Commons Foreign Affairs Committee, "China," citing Foreign and Commonwealth Office, *Annual Report and Accounts: 2017–2018* (London: Her Majesty's Stationery Office, 2017), 42, https://assets.publishing .service.gov.uk/government/uploads/system/uploads/attachment_data /file/722730/FCO1119_FCO_Annual_Report_2018_-_ONLINE.PDF.

36. Arne Delfs, "Merkel Wants Government and Industry to Take on Asia Together," Bloomberg, February 27, 2019, https://www.bloomberg.com /news/articles/2019-02-26/merkel-wants-government-and-industry-to -take-on-asia-together.

37. "Germany's Merkel Faces Balancing Act in Beijing," *Straits Times*, September 6, 2019, https://www.straitstimes.com/asia/east-asia/germanys -merkel-faces-balancing-act-in-beijing.

38. John Mair and Colin Packham, "NATO Needs to Address China's Rise, Says Stoltenberg," Reuters, August 7, 2019, https://uk.reuters.com/article /uk-australia-nato/nato-needs-to-address-chinas-rise-says-stoltenberg -idUKKCN1UX0YV.

39. Andrew Small, "Why Europe Is Getting Tough on China," *Foreign Affairs*, April 3, 2019.

40. Brad Lendon, "A British Military Base on the South China Sea Is Not a Far-Fetched Idea," CNN, January 3, 2019, https://www.cnn.com/2019/01/03 /asia/britain-mliitary-bases-asia-intl/index.html.

41. NATO, "Relations with Japan," September 12, 2018, https://www.nato.int /cps/en/natohq/topics_50336.htm.

42. International Monetary Fund, "Report for Selected Country Groups and Subjects (PPP Valuation of Country GDP)," 2017.

43. Zackary Keck, "Are America and India Building an 'Aircraft Carrier' Alliance?," *The National Interest*, November 11, 2017, http://nationalinterest.org/blog /the-buzz/are-america-india-building-aircraft-carrier-alliance-23147.

44. Sandeep Unnithan, "A Peek into India's Top Secret and Costliest Defence Project, Nuclear Submarines," *India Today*, December 10, 2017, https://www .indiatoday.in/magazine/the-big-story/story/20171218-india-ballistic -missile-submarine-k-6-submarine-launched-drdo-1102085-2017-12-10.

45. Prashanth Parameswaran, "Modi Unveils India's 'Act East Policy' to ASEAN in Myanmar," *The Diplomat*, November 17, 2014, https://thediplomat.com /2014/11/modi-unveils-indias-act-east-policy-to-asean-in-myanmar/.

46. Manpreet Singh Anand, "3 Areas of Opportunity for the US–India Relationship," *The Diplomat*, March 2, 2017, https://thediplomat.com/2017 /03/3-areas-of-opportunity-for-the-us-india-relationship/.

47. US Department of Defense and US Department of State, "Enhancing Defense and Security Cooperation with India," July 2017, https://www .defense.gov/Portals/1/Documents/pubs/NDAA-India-Joint-Report-FY -July-2017.pdf.

48. US Department of Defense "Report to the Congress on US–India Security Cooperation," November 3, 2011, https://www.defense.gov/Portals/1 /Documents/pubs/20111101_NDAA_Report_on_US_India_Security _Cooperation.pdf.

49. US Department of State, "US Relations with India," June 21, 2019, https://www.state.gov/r/pa/ei/bgn/3454.htm.

50. Rajesh Rajagopalan, "India's Unrealized Power," in *Strategic Asia, 2015–16: Foundations of National Power in the Asia-Pacific*, ed. Michael Wills, Ashley J. Tellis, and Alison Szalwinski (Seattle: National Bureau of Asian Research, 2015), 160–89.

51. Quoted by Tellis, Szalwinski, and Wills, *Power*, 142.

52. Ian Hall, Ashley J. Tellis, Alison Szalwinski, and Michael Wills, "The Persistence of Nehruvianism in India's Strategic Culture," *Strategic Asia* 17 (2016): 141–67.

53. Nayanima Basu, "US Looking at Free Trade Agreement with India," *The Hindu BusinessLine*, January 11, 2018, https://www.thehindubusinessline.com/economy/policy/us-looking-at-free-trade-agreement-with-india/article10026929.ece.

54. Prabhash Ranjan, "Bit of a Bumpy Ride, *The Hindu*, September 16, 2016, http://www.thehindu.com/opinion/op-ed/Bit-of-a-bumpy-ride/article14378406.ece.

55. "US–India Joint Strategic Vision for the Asia-Pacific and Indian Ocean Region," National Archives and Records Administration, January 25, 2015, https://obamawhitehouse.archives.gov/the-press-office/2015/01/25/us-india-joint-strategic-vision-asia-pacific-and-indian-ocean-region.

56. US Embassy in New Delhi, "US–India Defense Relations Fact Sheet," December 9, 2016, https://in.usembassy.gov/u-s-india-defense-relations-fact-sheet-december-8-2016/.

57. US Embassy in New Delhi.

58. "India and the United States Sign the Logistics Exchange Memorandum of Agreement (LEMOA)," Press Information Bureau, Government of India, August 30, 2016, http://pib.nic.in/newsite/mbErel.aspx?relid=149322.

59. For an exceptional review of these documents and debates about them, see Mark Rosen and Douglas Jackson, "The US–India Defense Relationship: Putting the Foundational Agreements in Perspective," CNA, February 2017, https://www.cna.org/cna_files/pdf/DRM-2016-U-013926-Final2.pdf.

60. This ambitious objective was first proposed by the Center for American Progress in its laudable report "The United States and India: Forging an Indispensable Democratic Partnership," January 14, 2018, https://www.americanprogress.org/issues/security/reports/2018/01/14/444786/united-states-india-forging-indispensable-democratic-partnership/.

61. International Monetary Fund, World Economic Outlook Database, October 2017.

62. Office of US Trade Representative, "Japan," n.d., https://ustr.gov/countries-regions/japan-korea-apec/japan.

63. Mie Oba, "What Now for Economic Integration in the Asia-Pacific?," *The Diplomat*, February 9, 2018, https://thediplomat.com/2018/02/what-now-for-economic-integration-in-the-asia-pacific/.

64. Ian Rinehart, "New US–Japan Defense Guidelines Deepen Alliance Cooperation," Congressional Research Service, April 28, 2015, 1, https://fas.org/sgp/crs/row/IN10265.pdf.

65. Rinehart, 2; Japanese Ministry of Defense, "The Guidelines for US–Japan Defense Cooperation," April 27, 2015, http://www.mod.go.jp/e/d_act/anpo/pdf/shishin_20150427e.pdf.

66. Rinehart, "New US–Japan Defense Guidelines," 2.

67. White House, "Remarks by President Trump at APEC CEO Summit in Da Nang, Vietnam," November 10, 2017, https://www.whitehouse.gov/briefings-statements/remarks-president-trump-apec-ceo-summit-da-nang-vietnam/.

68. "Asia Africa Growth Corridor: Partnership for Sustainable and Innovative Development—A Vision Document," Research and Information System for Developing Countries, Economic Research Institute for ASEAN and East Asia, and Institute of Developing Economies, May 2017, http://www.eria.org/Asia-Africa-Growth-Corridor-Document.pdf.

69. "Address by Prime Minister Shinzo Abe at the Seventy-Second Session of the United Nations General Assembly," Ministry of Foreign Affairs of Japan, September 20, 2017, http://www.mofa.go.jp/fp/unp_a/page4e_000674.html.

70. "Address by Prime Minister Shinzo Abe to a Joint Meeting of the US Congress: 'Toward an Alliance of Hope,'" Ministry of Foreign Affairs of Japan, April 29, 2015, http://www.mofa.go.jp/na/na1/us/page4e_000241.html.

71. Japanese Ministry of Defense, "Guidelines."

72. Japanese Ministry of Foreign Affairs, "Trends in Chinese Government and Other Vessels in the Waters Surrounding the Senkaku Islands, and Japan's Response: Records of Intrusions of Chinese Government and Other Vessels into Japan's Territorial Sea," April 5, 2018, http://www.mofa.go.jp/region/page23e_000021.html.

73. Japanese Ministry of Foreign Affairs, "Trends."

74. Lyle J. Morris, "The New 'Normal' in the East China Sea," RAND Corporation, February 27, 2017, https://www.rand.org/blog/2017/02/the-new-normal-in-the-east-china-sea.html.

75. Benoit Hardy-Chartrand and J. Berkshire Miller, "Japan's Delicate Balancing Act in the South China Sea," *The National Interest*, June 27, 2017, http://nationalinterest.org/feature/japans-delicate-balancing-act-the-south-china-sea-21343.

76. Nirav Patel, "US Should Offer a Digital Highway Initiative for Asia," *Straits Times*, February 7, 2018, http://www.straitstimes.com/opinion/us-should -offer-a-digital-highway-initiative-for-asia.

77. For more on the Scarborough Standoff, see Michael Green, Kathleen Hicks, Zack Cooper, John Schaus, and Jake Douglas, "Counter-Coercion Series: Scarborough Shoal Standoff," Asia Maritime Transparency Initiative, May 22, 2017, https://amti.csis.org/counter-co-scarborough-standoff/.

78. Beijing denies that any such agreement was made.

79. Keith Bradsher, "Philippine Leader Sounds Alarm on China," *New York Times*, February 4, 2014, https://www.nytimes.com/2014/02/05/world /asia/philippine-leader-urges-international-help-in-resisting-chinas -sea-claims.html?_r=0.

80. "Arbitration between the Republic of the Philippines and the People's Republic of China," Permanent Court of Arbitration, The Hague, October 29, 2015, https://www.pcacases.com/web/sendAttach/1503.

81. Michael Sullivan, "Demanding Greater Respect from US, Philippines Looks to China," NPR, October 24, 2016, https://www.npr.org/sections /parallels/2016/10/24/499147427/demanding-greater-respect-from-u-s -philippines-looks-to-china.

82. Pia Ranada, "Duterte Wants to Scrap EDCA," *Rappler*, October 25, 2016, https://www.rappler.com/nation/150262-duterte-edca-no-foreign -troops.

83. "1987 Constitution of the Republic of the Philippines," http://www.wipo .int/edocs/lexdocs/laws/en/ph/ph020en.pdf.

84. "Mutual Defense Treaty between the United States and the Republic of the Philippines, August 30, 1951," Avalon Project, Yale Law School, August 30, 1951, http://avalon.law.yale.edu/20th_century/phil001.asp.

85. Japanese Ministry of Foreign Affairs, "Treaty of Mutual Cooperation and Security between Japan and the United States of America," January 19, 1960, https://www.mofa.go.jp/region/n-america/us/q&a/ref/1.html.

86. "Rep. Alejano: US–PHL Defense Pact Review Chance to Clarify 'Ambiguous' Provisions," GMA News Online, December 29, 2018, https://www.gmanet work.com/news/news/nation/679791/us-phl-defense-pact-review-chance -to-clarify-ambiguous-provisions/story/.

87. "Philippines Official: US Defense Treaty Could Start War with China," KXLY-TV Spokane, March 6, 2019, https://www.kxly.com/news/national -news/philippines-official-us-defense-treaty-could-start-war-with -china/1051335533.

88. Jim Gomez, "Philippines Frets about War at Sea for US," *Navy Times*, March 5, 2019, https://www.navytimes.com/news/your-navy/2019 /03/05/philippines-frets-about-war-at-sea-for-us/.

89. Jeff Himmelman, "A Game of Shark and Minnow," *New York Times*, October 24, 2013, http://www.nytimes.com/newsgraphics/2013/10/27/south-china-sea/index.html.

90. Simon Denyer, "North Korean Leader Says He Has 'Nuclear Button' but Won't Use It Unless Threatened," *Washington Post*, January 1, 2018, https://www.washingtonpost.com/world/north-korea-leader-says-he-hasnuclear-button-but-wont-use-unless-threatened/2017/12/31/af3dc188-ee96-11e7-90ed-77167c6861f2_story.html?utm_term=.b4c9d478ded5.

91. In his role as deputy assistant secretary of defense for East Asia, the author played a significant role in negotiating and finalizing this agreement.

92. Franz-Stefan Gady "US, ROK Agree to Scrap Warhead Weight Limit for Ballistic Missiles," *The Diplomat*, September 8, 2017, https://thediplomat.com/2017/09/us-rok-agree-to-scrap-warhead-weight-limit-for-ballistic-missiles/.

93. Kyle Mizokami, "This Is How South Korea Plans to Stop a Nuclear Attack from North Korea," *The National Interest*, July 10, 2017, http://nationalinterest.org/blog/the-buzz/how-south-korea-plans-stop-nuclear-attack-north-korea-21472.

94. Julian Ryall, "North Korea Carries Out 'Unprecedented' Test of Submarine Missile System," *The Telegraph*, August 1, 2017, http://www.telegraph.co.uk/news/2017/08/01/north-koreas-submarine-missile-tests-critical-advance-highly/.

95. Donghui Park, "Cybersecurity Strategy Advice for the Trump Administration: US–South Korea Relations," Henry M. Jackson School of International Studies, University of Washington, February 7, 2017, https://jsis.washington.edu/news/cybersecurity-strategy-advice-trump-administration-us-south-korea-relations/.

96. Park, "Cybersecurity."

97. Organization for Economic Cooperation and Development, "DAC Member Profile: Korea," n.d., http://www.oecd.org/dac/korea.htm.

98. Scott A. Snyder and Seukhoon Paul Choi, "From Aid to Development Partnership: Strengthening US–Republic of Korea Cooperation in International Development," Council on Foreign Relations, February 2012, 3, https://www.cfr.org/sites/default/files/pdf/2012/02/CFR_Working Paper10_Snyder_Choi.pdf.

99. Snyder and Seukhoon Paul Choi, "From Aid to Development," 5.

100. Audrey Young, "Rice Hints at Thaw in US–NZ Relations," *New Zealand Herald*, July 26, 2008, https://www.nzherald.co.nz/politics/news/article.cfm?c_id=280&objectid=10523634.

101. Charlotte Graham-Mclay, "New Zealand Fears Fraying Ties with China, Its Biggest Customer," *New York Times*, February 14, 2019, https://www.nytimes.com/2019/02/14/world/asia/new-zealand-china-huawei-tensions.html.

102. "New Zealand Agonises about Chinese Meddling," *The Economist*, November 8, 2018, https://www.economist.com/asia/2018/11/08/new-zealand-agonises-about-chinese-meddling.

103. Rob Schmitz, "Australia and New Zealand Are Ground Zero for Chinese Influence," NPR, October 2, 2018, https://www.npr.org/2018/10/02/627249909/australia-and-new-zealand-are-ground-zero-for-chinese-influence.

104. Stats NZ, "Goods and Services Trade by Country: Year Ended March 2019," June 5, 2019, https://www.stats.govt.nz/information-releases/goods-and-services-trade-by-country-year-ended-march-2019.

105. Stats NZ, "Foreign Direct Investment in New Zealand Continues to Increase," September 26, 2019, https://www.stats.govt.nz/news/foreign-direct-investment-in-new-zealand-continues-to-increase.

106. New Zealand Ministry of Foreign Affairs and Trade, "Our Aid Partnerships in the Pacific," n.d., https://www.mfat.govt.nz/en/aid-and-development/our-work-in-the-pacific/.

107. Charlotte Greenfield, "New Zealand Hikes Foreign Aid Budget with Eye on Contested South Pacific," Reuters, May 8, 2018, https://www.reuters.com/article/us-newzealand-pacific/new-zealand-hikes-foreign-aid-budget-with-eye-on-contested-south-pacific-idUSKBN1I90X8.

108. Jamie Smyth, "New Zealand Boosts Aid to Counter China's Influence in South Pacific," *Financial Times*, May 17, 2018, https://www.ft.com/content/0fca1c20-5988-11e8-bdb7-f6677d2e1ce8.

109. New Zealand Navy, "RIMPAC 2018," http://www.navy.mil.nz/oae/ex/rimpac/rimpac18.htm.

110. Seth Robson, "Destroyer Will Be 1st US Navy Ship to Visit New Zealand in 3 Decades," *Stars and Stripes*, October 18, 2016, https://www.stripes.com/news/pacific/destroyer-will-be-1st-us-navy-ship-to-visit-new-zealand-in-3-decades-1.434597.

111. "Full Text of President Tsai's Inaugural Address," May 20, 2016, Focus Taiwan, http://focustaiwan.tw/news/aipl/201605200008.aspx.

112. "您所查詢的網址無法顯示," n.d., 行政院全球資訊網, https://www.ey.gov.tw/state/News_Content3.aspx?n=1DA8EDDD65ECB8D4&sms=474D9346A19A4989&s=8A1DCA5A3BFAD09C.

113. Peter C. Y. Chou, "US–Taiwan Relations: Prospects for Security and Economic Ties," Woodrow Wilson International Center for Scholars,

April 2017, 21, https://www.wilsoncenter.org/publication/us-taiwan -relations-prospects-for-security-and-economic-ties.

114. For US arms sales with Taiwan between 2004 and 2011, see Shirley Kan, "Taiwan: Major US Arms Sales since 1990," Congressional Research Service, August 29, 2014, https://fas.org/sgp/crs/weapons/RL30957.pdf. For the two arms sales agreements since 2011, see David Brunnstrom and Arshad Mohammed, "US Plans to Sell Taiwan about $1.42 Billion in Arms," Reuters, June 29, 2017, https://www.reuters.com/article/us-usa-taiwan-arms/u-s -plans-to-sell-taiwan-about-1-42-billion-in-arms-idUSKBN19K2XO.

115. "H.R.2479—96th Congress (1979–1980): Taiwan Relations Act," US House Foreign Affairs Committee, April 10, 1979, https://www.congress.gov /bill/96th-congress/house-bill/2479.

116. "歷年貿易國家(地區)名次值表," Bureau of Foreign Trade, https://cus93 .trade.gov.tw/FSC3050F/FSC3050F?menuURL=FSC3050F.

117. "GDP, Current Prices," International Monetary Fund, http://www.imf.org /external/datamapper/NGDPD@WEO/CHN/TWN.

118. "Real GDP Growth," International Monetary Fund, http://www.imf.org /external/datamapper/NGDP_RPCH@WEO/CHN/TWN.

119. "105 年國人赴海外工作人數統計結果," January 1, 2018, Chinese Directorate General of Budget, Accounting, and Statistics, https://www .dgbas.gov.tw/public/Attachment/813018211L3E53FL6.pdf.

120. Austin Ramzy, "As Taiwan's Workers Flock to China, Concerns About Economy Grow," *New York Times*, January 13, 2016, https://www.nytimes .com/2016/01/14/world/asia/taiwan-elections-china.html.

121. *Global Taiwan Brief*, May 24, 2017, http://globaltaiwan.org/2017/05/24 -gtb-2-21/.

122. M. Balasubramaniam, "Tsai Ing-wen's Administration and Taiwan's Shrinking International Space," *Asia Dialogue*, July 6, 2017, https://theasiadialogue .com/2017/07/06/tsai-ing-wens-administration-and-taiwans-shrinking -international-space/.

123. For Taiwan's sustainability in air defense, see Michael Lostumbo, David R. Frelinger, James Williams, and Barry Wilson, *Air Defense Options for Taiwan: An Assessment of Relative Costs and Operational Benefits* (Santa Monica, CA: RAND Corporation, 2016).

124. Brad Lendon, "Chinese Stealth Fighters Are Combat-Ready, Beijing Says," CNN, February 11, 2018, https://www.cnn.com/2018/02/11/asia/china-j -20-stealth-fighter-combat-ready-intl/index.html.

125. Office of the Secretary of Defense, "Military and Security Developments Involving the People's Republic of China 2017," May 15, 2017, https://www .defense.gov/Portals/1/Documents/pubs/2017_China_Military_Power

_Report.pdf; "Russia Starts Shipping S-400 Air Defense Missile System to China: TASS Cites Source," Reuters, January 18, 2018, https://www.reuters .com/article/us-russia-china-missiles/russia-starts-shipping-s-400-air -defense-missile-system-to-china-tass-cites-source-idUSKBN1F70MH.

126. Mike Yeo, "China Launches Its Most Advanced Homegrown Class of Guided-Missile Destroyers," *Defense News*, June 28, 2017, https://www .defensenews.com/naval/2017/06/28/china-launches-its-most -advanced-homegrown-class-of-guided-missile-destroyers/.

127. Stockholm International Peace Research Institute, "Data for All Countries from 1988–2016 as a Share of GDP," https://www.sipri.org/sites/default /files/Milex-share-of-GDP.pdf.

128. 黃煌雄, 台灣國防變革: *1982–2016* (Taipei: China Time Publishing, 2017).

129. 程嘉文, "全募兵尚未落實 國軍人數已跌破「最低防衛需求," *United Daily News*, September 14, 2017, https://udn.com/news/story/10930/2702401.

130. Dee Wu, "Taiwan's All-Volunteer Force and Military Transformation," Project 2049 Institute, December 2017, https://project2049.net/wp -content/uploads/2017/12/P2049_Wu_Taiwan_AVF_Strategy_122017.pdf.

131. "India Signs 12 Agreements with Vietnam, Extends $500m for Defence Cooperation," *Firstpost*, January 6, 2017, https://www.firstpost.com/world /india-signs-12-agreements-with-vietnam-extends-500m-for-defence -cooperation-2989334.html.

132. "Obama Lifts US Embargo on Lethal Arms Sales to Vietnam," BBC News, May 23, 2016, https://www.bbc.com/news/world-asia-36356695.

133. US Census Bureau, Foreign Trade Data Dissemination Branch, "Foreign Trade: Data—US Trade with Vietnam," n.d., http://www.census.gov /foreign-trade/balance/c5520.html.

134. Tran Viet Thai, "The Evolving Regional Order in East Asia: A View from Vietnam," *Asia Policy* 13, no. 2 (2018): 64–68.

135. Nyshka Chandran, "China Reportedly Threatens Vietnam into Ending Energy Exploration in South China Sea," CNBC, July 24, 2017, https://www .cnbc.com/2017/07/23/china-threatens-vietnam-over-south-china-sea -drilling.html.

136. Derek Grossman, "US Striking Just the Right Balance with Vietnam in South China Sea," *The Diplomat*, November 22, 2017, https://thediplomat .com/2017/11/us-striking-just-the-right-balance-with-vietnam-in -south-china-sea/.

137. Ngo Di Lam, "Vietnam's Foreign Policy after the 12th National Party Congress: Expanding Continuity," CogitASIA CSIS Asia Policy Blog, February 9, 2016, https://www.cogitasia.com/vietnams-foreign-policy -after-the-12th-national-party-congress-expanding-continuity/.

CONCLUSION: TOWARD AN ALLIED STRATEGY IN THE INDO-PACIFIC

Barack Obama, "Remarks by the President at the United States Military Academy Commencement Ceremony," May 28, 2014, https://obamawhitehouse.archives.gov/the-press-office/2014/05/28/remarks-president-united-states-military-academy-commencement-ceremony.

1. E.g., see Michael J. Green, *By More Than Providence: Grand Strategy and American Power in the Asia Pacific Since 1783* (New York: Columbia University Press, 2017).

SELECTED BIBLIOGRAPHY

Abe, Shinzo. "Asia's Democratic Security Diamond by Shinzo Abe." Project Syndicate, December 27, 2012. https://www.project-syndicate.org/onpoint /a-strategic-alliance-for-japan-and-india-by-shinzo-abe?barrier =accesspaylog.

Acharya, Amitav. "Doomed by Dialogue? Will ASEAN Survive Great Power Rivalry in Asia?" *Asan Forum*, June 29, 2015.

——. "Is ASEAN Losing Its Way?" YaleGlobal Online, September 24, 2015. https:// yaleglobal.yale.edu/content/asean-losing-its-way.

Albright, Madeleine K. Interview by Matt Lauer. *The Today Show*, NBC-TV, February 19, 1998. https://1997-2001.state.gov/statements/1998/980219a .html.

Alegado, Siegfrid. "Japan Still Beating China in Southeast Asia Infrastruc- ture Race." Bloomberg, February 8, 2018. https://www.bloomberg.com/news /articles/2018-02-08/japan-still-beating-china-in-southeast-asia-infrastructure -race.

Allin, Dana, and Erik Jones. *Weary Policeman: American Power in an Age of Austerity.* London: International Institute for Strategic Studies, 2012.

Allison, Graham. *Destined for War: Can America and China Escape Thucydides's Trap?* Boston: Houghton Mifflin Harcourt, 2017.

Anand, Manpreet Singh. "3 Areas of Opportunity for the US-India Relationship." *The Diplomat*, March 2, 2017. https://thediplomat.com/2017/03/3-areas-of -opportunity-for-the-us-india-relationship/.

Balasubramaniam, M. "Tsai Ing-wen's Administration and Taiwan's Shrinking International Space." 2017. https://cpianalysis.org/2017/07/06/tsai-ing -wens-administration-and-taiwans-shrinkinginternational-space/#.

BBC News. "China Now Has More Diplomatic Posts Than Any Other Country." November 27, 2019. https://www.bbc.com/news/world-asia-china-50569237.

Bearak, Max, and Lazaro Gamio. "The US Foreign Aid Budget, Visualized." *Washington Post*, October 18, 2016. https://www.washingtonpost.com/graphics /world/which-countries-get-the-most-foreign-aid/.

Beckley, Michael. *Unrivaled: Why America Will Remain the World's Sole Superpower.* Ithaca, NY: Cornell University Press, 2018.

Berger, David H. "Commandant's Planning Guidance." July 2019. https://www .hqmc.marines.mil/Portals/142/Docs/%2038th%20Commandant%27s %20Planning%20Guidance_2019.pdf?ver=2019-07-16-200152-700.

Berteau, David J., and Michael J. Green. "US Force Posture Strategy in the Asia Pacific Region: An Independent Assessment." Center for Strategic and International Studies, August 2012.

Bertrand, Natasha. "Trump's Top Intelligence Officials Contradict Him on Russian Meddling." *The Atlantic*, February 13, 2018. https://www.theatlantic .com/politics/archive/2018/02/the-intelligence-community-warns -congress-russia-will-interfere-in-2018-elections/553256/.

Bhattarai, Abha. "China Asked Marriott to Shut Down Its Website; The Company Complied." *Washington Post*, January 18, 2018. https://www.washingtonpost .com/news/business/wp/2018/01/18/china-demanded-marriott-change -its-website-the-company-complied/?utm_term=.03831fd1dd94.

Bialik, Kristen. "Views of Trump, US in Countries on His Asia Trip." Pew Research Center, November 3, 2017. http://www.pewresearch.org/fact -tank/2017/11/03/opinions-in-asian-countries-on-trump-trip/.

Bipindra, Nc. "India's Own Rules Are Tripping Up Its $250 Billion Military Upgrade." Bloomberg, September 4, 2017. https://www.bloomberg.com /news/articles/2017-09-04/modi-risks-trust-deficit-as-india-rips-up-weapons -contracts.

Blanchard, Ben. "After Ditching Taiwan, China Says Panama Will Get the Help It Needs." Reuters, November 17, 2017. https://www.reuters.com/article /us-china-panama/after-ditching-taiwan-china-says-panama-will-get-the -help-it-needs-idUSKBN1DH1FZ.

Bowley, Graham. "Cash Helped China Win Costa Rica's Recognition." *New York Times*, September 12, 2008. http://www.nytimes.com/2008/09/13/world /asia/13costa.html.

Bradsher, Keith. "Amid Tension, China Blocks Vital Exports to Japan." *New York Times*, September 22, 2010. http://www.nytimes.com/2010/09/23/business /global/23rare.html.

——. "Philippine Leader Sounds Alarm on China." *New York Times*, February 4, 2014. https://www.nytimes.com/2014/02/05/world/asia/philippine-leader -urges-international-help-in-resisting-chinas-sea-claims.html?_r=0.

Brady, Anne-Marie. *Magic Weapons: China's Political Influence Activities Under Xi Jinping*. Washington: Woodrow Wilson International Center for Scholars, 2017. https://www.wilsoncenter.org/sites/default/files/for_website_magic weaponsanne-mariesbradyseptember2017.pdf.

Bremmer, Ian. *Every Nation For Itself*. New York: Penguin, 2012.

Brzezinski, Zbigniew. *Strategic Vision: America and the Crisis of Global Power*. New York: Basic Books, 2012.

——. Twitter post, May 4, 2017. https://twitter.com/zbig/status/860177803194 630144?lang=en.

Buckley, Edgar. "Invoking Article 5." *NATO Review*, June 1, 2006. https://www .nato.int/docu/review/2006/Invokation-Article-5/Invoking_Article_5/EN /index.htm.

Bull, Hedley. *The Anarchical Society: A Study of Order in World Politics*. London: Macmillan, 1977. https://doi.org/10.1007/978-1-349-24028-9.

Bush, Richard C. 2017. "What Xi Jinping Said About Taiwan at the 19th Party Congress." Brookings Institution, October 19, 2017. https://www.brookings .edu/blog/order-from-chaos/2017/10/19/what-xi-jinping-said-about -taiwan-at-the-19th-party-congress/.

Calamur, Krishnadev. "China vs. America in a Financial Game of 'Risk.'" *The Atlantic*, October 18, 2017. https://www.theatlantic.com/international/archive /2017/10/china-investments/543321/.

Campbell, Kurt M. *The Pivot: The Future of American Statecraft in Asia*. New York: Twelve Books, 2016.

Campbell, Kurt M., et al. "The Age of Consequences: The Foreign Policy and National Security Implications of Global Climate Change." Center for a New American Security, November 2007.

Campbell, Kurt M., and Ely Ratner. "The China Reckoning." *Foreign Affairs*, March–April 2018. https://www.foreignaffairs.com/articles/china/2018-02-13 /china-reckoning.

Carter, Ash. "Remarks on 'Indo-Pacific's Principled Security Network' at 2016 IISS Shangri-La Dialogue." US Department of Defense, June 4, 2016. https:// www.defense.gov/News/Speeches/Speech-View/Article/791213/remarks -on-Indo-Pacifics-principled-security-network-at-2016-iiss-shangri-la-di/.

Cave, Damien. "A New Battle for Guadalcanal, This Time with China." *New York Times*, July 21, 2018. https://www.nytimes.com/2018/07/21/world/asia /china-australia-guadalcanal-solomon-islands.html.

Cha, Victor D. *Powerplay: The Origins of the American Alliance System in Asia*. Princeton, NJ: Princeton University Press, 2018.

Chandran, Nyshka. "China Reportedly Threatens Vietnam into Ending Energy Exploration in South China Sea." CNBC, July 24, 2017. https://www.cnbc.com/2017/07/23/china-threatens-vietnam-over-south-china-sea-drilling.html.

Chou, Peter C. Y. "US–Taiwan Relations: Prospects for Security and Economic Ties." Woodrow Wilson International Center for Scholars, April 2017. https://www.wilsoncenter.org/publication/us-taiwan-relations-prospects-for-security-and-economic-ties.

Christensen, Thomas J. T. "Posing Problems Without Catching Up: China's Rise and Challenges for US Security Policy." International Security 25, no. 4 (2001): 5–40.

Chung, Jae Ho, and Jiyoon Kim, "Is South Korea in China's Orbit? Assessing Seoul's Perceptions and Policies." National Bureau of Asian Research, January 1, 2016. https://www.nbr.org/publication/is-south-korea-in-chinas-orbit-assessing-seouls-perceptions-and-policies/.

Chung, Kenneth. "S'pore Must Work with Like-minded Partners to Uphold Multilateralism, Says PM Lee." Today, July 14, 2018. https://www.todayonline.com/world/spore-must-work-minded-partners-uphold-multilateralism-says-pm-lee.

Daniel, Lisa. "Flournoy: Asia Will Be Heart of US Security Policy." American Foreign Press Service, April 29, 2011. http://www.defense.gov/news/news article.aspx?id=63755.

Dasgupta, Saibal, and Anjana Pasricha. "Pakistan, Nepal, Myanmar Back Away from Chinese Projects." Voice of America, December 4, 2017. https://www.voanews.com/a/three-countries-withdraw-from-chinese-projects/4148094.html.

Delfs, Arne. "Merkel Wants Government and Industry to Take on Asia Together." Bloomberg, February 27, 2019. https://www.bloomberg.com/news/articles/2019-02-26/merkel-wants-government-and-industry-to-take-on-asia-together.

Denmark, Abraham M. "Partnering to Protect Democracy." Taipei Times, June 25, 2018. http://www.taipeitimes.com/News/editorials/archives/2018/06/25/2003695487.

Denmark, Abraham M., and Nirav Patel. "China's Arrival: A Strategic Framework for a Global Relationship." Center for a New American Security, September 22, 2009. https://www.cnas.org/publications/reports/chinas-arrival-a-strategic-framework-for-a-global-relationship.

Denyer, Simon. "North Korean Leader Says He Has 'Nuclear Button' But Won't Use It Unless Threatened." Washington Post, January 1, 2018. https://www.washingtonpost.com/world/north-korea-leader-says-he-hasnuclear-button-but-wont-use-unless-threatened/2017/12/31/af3dc188-ee96-11e7-90ed-77167c6861f2_story.html?utm_term=.b4c9d478ded5.

Diamond, Larry, and Orville Schell. "China's Influence and American Interests: Promoting Constructive Vigilance." Hoover Institution, November 29, 2018. https://www.hoover.org/research/chinas-influence-american-interests -promoting-constructive-vigilance.

Dibb, Paul. "Why I Disagree with Hugh White on China's Rise." *The Australian*, August 13, 2012. http://www.theaustralian.com.au/opinion/why-i-disagree -with-hugh-white-on-chinas-rise/news-story/5a69eb06fefd28a68b5b59731 3f66cf0?sv=ddf1076fb959bb965d36f114a8203bd9.

Dickey, Lauren. "Taiwan's Search for Security Partners: Looking Beyond Washington." Jamestown Foundation, March 31, 2017. https://jamestown .org/program/taiwans-search-security-partners-looking-beyond -washington/.

Duckett, Chris. "Australia Using Foreign Aid to Lock Huawei Out of PNG -Solomon Islands Subsea Cable." ZDNet, June 13, 2018. https://www.zdnet .com/article/australia-using-foreign-aid-to-lock-huawei-out-of-png -solomon-islands-subsea-cable/.

Duk-kun, Byun. "Moon, Trump Agree to Build Up Deterrence, Urge N. Korea to Give Up Nukes." Yonhap News Agency, November 7, 2017.

Eberstadt, Nicholas. "Asia-Pacific Demographics in 2010–2040: Implications for Strategic Balance." In *Strategic Asia, 2010–11: Asia's Rising Power and America's Continued Purpose*, ed. Ashley J. Tellis, Andrew Marble, and Travis Tanner. Seattle: National Bureau of Asian Research, 2010.

Erickson, Andrew S., Abraham M. Denmark, and Gabriel Collins. "Beijing's 'Starter Carrier' and Future Steps: Alternatives and Implications." *Naval War College Review* 65, no. 1 (2012): 14–54.

Erwin, Sandra. "In Space and Cyber, China Is Closing In on the United States." SpaceNews.com, January 10, 2018. http://spacenews.com/in-space-and-cyber -china-is-closing-in-on-the-united-states/.

European Commission. "EU-China: A Strategic Outlook." March 12, 2019. https://ec.europa.eu/commission/sites/beta-political/files/communication -eu-china-a-strategic-outlook.pdf.

Ewers, Elisa Catalano, et al. "Drone Proliferation: Policy Choices for the Trump Administration." Center for a New American Security, http://drones.cnas .org/reports/drone-proliferation/.

Fairbank, John King. *The Chinese World Order: Traditional China's Foreign Relations*. Cambridge, MA: Harvard University Press, 1974.

Farnsworth, Timothy. "China and Russia Submit Cyber Proposal." *Arms Control Today*, November, 2011. https://www.armscontrol.org/act/2011-11/china -russia-submit-cyber-proposal.

Fazal, Tanisha M. "Dead Wrong?" *International Security* 39, no. 1 (Summer 2014): 95–125. doi:10.1162/ISEC_a_00166.

Feigenbaum, Evan A. "Is Coercion the New Normal in China's Economic Statecraft?" Carnegie Endowment for International Peace, July 25, 2017. http://carnegieendowment.org/2017/07/25/is-coercion-new-normal -in-china-s-economic-statecraft-pub-72632.

Florence Parly. "Asia's Evolving Security Order and Its Challenges." Remarks to Shangri-La Dialogue, June 1, 2019. https://in.ambafrance.org/French -Defence-Minister-Florence-Parly-s-speech-at-the-Shangri-La-Dialogue.

Fontaine, Richard. "Against Complacency: Risks and Opportunities for the Australia–US Alliance." United States Studies Centre, Sydney, October 2016. https://assets.ussc.edu.au/view/e6/b4/38/ef/c9/ba/70/49/f6/da/78/36 /02/48/c5/fa/original/959a3d253927020b0ed1a1bd671e65306f29b4f4/2016 _Risks_Opportunities_Australia_US_Alliance.pdf.

Fontaine, Richard, and Daniel M. Kliman. "At the G-20, Look to the Swing States." World Politics Review, November 2, 2011. http://www.worldpoliticsreview .com/articles/10532/at-the-g-20-look-to-the-swing-states.

Fravel, M. Taylor., J. Stapleton Roy, Michael D. Swaine, Susan A. Thornton, and Ezra Vogel. "China Is Not an Enemy." Washington Post, July 3, 2019. https://www.washingtonpost.com/opinions/making-china-a-us-enemy-is -counterproductive/2019/07/02/647d49d0-9bfa-11e9-b27f-ed2942f73d70 _story.html?noredirect=on.

Freeman, C. W., Jr. "The United States and China: Game of Superpowers." Remarks to National War College, February 8, 2018. https://chasfreeman .net/the-united-states-and-china-game-of-superpowers/.

French, Howard W. Everything Under the Heavens: How the Past Helps Shape China's Push for Global Power. New York: Vintage Books, 2017.

French, Howard W., Ian Johnson, Jeremiah Jenne, Pamela Kyle Crossley, Robert A. Kapp, and Tobie Meyer-Fong. "How China's History Shapes, and Warps, Its Policies Today." Foreign Policy, March 22, 2017. https://foreign policy.com/2017/03/22/how-chinas-history-shapes-its-foreign-policy -empire-humiliation/.

Friedberg, Aaron. "Will Europe's Past Be Asia's Future?" Survival 42, no. 3 (2010): 147–60. https://doi.org/10.1093/survival/42.3.147.

Gady, Franz-Stefan. "Japan, US, South Korea Hold Missile Defense Drill." The Diplomat, January 24, 2017. https://thediplomat.com/2017/01/japan -us-south-korea-hold-missile-defense-drill/.

——. "US, ROK Agree to Scrap Warhead Weight Limit for Ballistic Missiles." The Diplomat, September 8, 2017. https://thediplomat.com/2017/09/us-rok -agree-to-scrap-warhead-weight-limit-for-ballistic-missiles/.

Gardner, John. "Legal Positivism: 51/2 Myths." American Journal of Jurisprudence 46, no 1 (2001): 199–227. https://doi.org/10.1093/ajj/46.1.199.

Gill, Bates, and Evan S. Medeiros. "Foreign and Domestic Influences on China's Arms Control and Nonproliferation Policies." *China Quarterly* 161 (2000): 66–94.

Glaser, Bonnie S., Scott Kennedy, Matthew P. Funaiole, and Derek Mitchell. "The New Southbound Policy." Center for Strategic and International Studies, January 19, 2018. https://www.csis.org/analysis/new-southbound-policy.

Gomez, Jim. "Philippines Frets about War at Sea for US." *Navy Times*, March 5, 2019. https://www.navytimes.com/news/your-navy/2019/03/05/philippines -frets-about-war-at-sea-for-us/.

Graham-Mclay, Charlotte. "New Zealand Fears Fraying Ties with China, Its Biggest Customer." *New York Times*, February 14, 2019. https://www.nytimes .com/2019/02/14/world/asia/new-zealand-china-huawei-tensions.html.

Green, Michael J. *By More Than Providence: Grand Strategy and American Power in the Asia Pacific Since 1783.* New York: Columbia University Press, 2017.

Green, Michael, Kathleen Hicks, Zack Cooper, John Schaus, and Jake Douglas. "Counter-Coercion Series: Scarborough Shoal Standoff." Asia Maritime Transparency Initiative, May 22, 2017. https://amti.csis.org/counter-co -scarborough-standoff/.

Greenfield, Charlotte. "New Zealand Hikes Foreign Aid Budget with Eye on Contested South Pacific." Reuters, May 8, 2018. https://www.reuters.com /article/us-newzealand-pacific/new-zealand-hikes-foreign-aid-budget -with-eye-on-contested-south-pacific-idUSKBN1I90X8.

Greer, Tanner. "Xi Jinping in Translation: China's Guiding Ideology." *Palladium Magazine*, May 31, 2019. https://palladiummag.com/2019/05/31/xi-jinping -in-translation-chinas-guiding-ideology/.

Greitens, Sheena Chestnut. "Analysis: Can Trump Count on Manila to Put Pressure on North Korea? 3 Points to Know." *Washington Post*, May 16, 2017. https://www.washingtonpost.com/news/monkey-cage/wp/2017/05/16 /can-trump-count-on-manila-to-put-pressure-on-north-korea-3-points-to -know/?utm_term=.7a93b91d04bc.

Grevatt, Jon. "South Korean Military Exports Climb 25%." *Jane's 360*, January 15, 2018. http://www.janes.com/article/77044/south-korean-military-exports -climb-25.

Grossman, Derek. "US Striking Just the Right Balance with Vietnam in South China Sea." *The Diplomat*, November 22, 2017. https://thediplomat.com/2017 /11/us-striking-just-the-right-balance-with-vietnam-in-south-china-sea/.

Hall, Ian, Ashley J. Tellis, Alison Szalwinski, and Michael Wills. "The Persistence of Nehruvianism in India's Strategic Culture." *Strategic Asia* 17 (2016): 141–67.

Hallams, Ellen. *The United States and NATO Since 9/11: The Transatlantic Alliance Renewed.* New York: Routledge, 2010.

Hardy-Chartrand, Benoit, and J. Berkshire Miller. "Japan's Delicate Balancing Act in the South China Sea." *The National Interest*, June 27, 2017. http://nationalinterest.org/feature/japans-delicate-balancing-act-the-south-china-sea-21343.

Hass, Ryan. "Democracy, the China Challenge, and the 2020 Elections in Taiwan." *Taipei Times*, March 18, 2019. http://www.taipeitimes.com/News/editorials/archives/2019/03/18/2003711694.

Havard, Hegre. "Predicting Armed Conflict, 2010–2050." University of Oslo, November 21, 2011. http://folk.uio.no/hahegre/Papers/PredictionISQ_Final.pdf.

Hayashi, Saki. "Japan, US and India Team to Fund Indo-Pacific Infrastructure." *Nikkei Asian Review*, April 10, 2018. https://asia.nikkei.com/Politics/International-Relations/Japan-US-and-India-team-to-fund-Indo-Pacific-infrastructure.

Hayton, Bill: Twitter post, April 12, 2018. https://twitter.com/bill_hayton/status/984416871184257024.

Heydarian, Richard Javad. "New Dawn for Philippine-China Relations?" *Al Jazeera*, June 5, 2016. http://www.aljazeera.com/indepth/opinion/2016/06/dawn-philippine-china-relations-duterte-160604101429033.html.

——. "Rodrigo Duterte Is Key to China's 'Post-American' Vision for Asia." *The National Interest*, May 24, 2017. http://nationalinterest.org/feature/rodrigo-duterte-key-chinas-post-american-vision-asia-20825?utm_content=buffer27c7d&utm_medium=social&utm_source=twitter.com&utm_campaign=buffer.

Higgins, Andrew. "In Philippines, Banana Growers Feel Effect of South China Sea Dispute." *Washington Post*, June 10, 2012. https://www.washingtonpost.com/world/asia_pacific/in-philippines-banana-growers-feel-effect-of-south-china-sea-dispute/2012/06/10/gJQA47WVTV_story.html?utm_term=.c32d4d965742.

Hillman, Jonathan E., and Maesea McCalpin. "Will China's '16+1' Format Divide Europe?" Center for Strategic and International Studies, April 11, 2019. https://www.csis.org/analysis/will-chinas-161-format-divide-europe.

Himmelman, Jeff. "A Game of Shark and Minnow." *New York Times*, October 24, 2013. http://www.nytimes.com/newsgraphics/2013/10/27/south-china-sea/index.html.

Horowitz, Michael C., and Joshua A. Schwartz. "A New US Policy Makes It (Somewhat) Easier to Export Drones." *Washington Post*, April 20, 2018. https://www.washingtonpost.com/news/monkey-cage/wp/2018/04/20/a-new-u-s-policy-makes-it-somewhat-easier-to-export-drones/.

Hutt, David. "China a Friend in Need to Malaysia." *Asia Times*, March 23, 2017. http://www.atimes.com/article/china-friend-need-malaysia/.

HV, Vinayak, Fraser Thompson, and Oliver Tonby. "Understanding ASEAN: Seven Things You Need to Know." McKinsey & Company, New York, May 2014.

https://www.mckinsey.com/industries/public-sector/our-insights
/understanding-asean-seven-things-you-need-to-know.

Hwang, Balbina. "The US Pivot to Asia and South Korea's Rise." *Asian Perspective* 41 (2017): 83.

Ikenberry, G. John. *Liberal Leviathan: The Origins, Crisis, and Transformation of the American World Order.* Princeton, NJ: Princeton University Press, 2011.

Ip, Greg. "Has America's China Backlash Gone Too Far?" *Wall Street Journal*, August 28, 2019. https://www.wsj.com/articles/has-americas-china-backlash -gone-too-far-11566990232.

Jackson, Van. "Power, Trust, and Network Complexity: Three Logics of Hedging in Asian Security." *International Relations of the Asia-Pacific* 14, no. 3 (2014): 331–56. https://doi.org/10.1093/irap/lcu005.

Jennings, Ralph. "China Demands Companies Stop Calling Taiwan a Country: Here's What They'll Do." *Forbes*, January 18, 2018. https://www.forbes.com /sites/ralphjennings/2018/01/17/corporations-will-quickly-comply-as -china-pressures-them-to-stop-calling-taiwan-a-country/#20887ba49bf4.

Ji, Dagyum. "US, South Korea, Japan Staging Missile Warning Exercises Near Korean Peninsula." *NK News*, October 24, 2017. https://www.nknews.org /2017/10/u-s-south-korea-japan-staging-missile-warning-exercises-near -korean-peninsula/.

Jinping, Xi. "Secure a Decisive Victory in Building a Moderately Prosperous Society in All Respects and Strive for the Great Success of Socialism with Chinese Characteristics for a New Era." Xinhua.net, October 18, 2017. http:// www.xinhuanet.com/english/download/Xi_Jinping's_report_at_19th_CPC _National_Congress.pdf.

Judson, Jen. "Funding to Deter Russia Reaches $6.5B in FY19 Defense Budget Request." *Defense News*, February 12, 2018. https://www.defensenews.com/land/2018/02 /12/funding-to-deter-russia-reaches-65b-in-fy19-defense-budget-request/.

Kamphausen, Roy, John S. Park, Ryo Sahashi, and Alison Szalwinski. "The Case for US–ROK–Japan Trilateralism: Strengths and Limitations." National Bureau of Asian Research, February 2018. http://www.nbr.org/publications /element.aspx?id=980.

Kang, David C. *East Asia Before the West: Five Centuries of Trade and Tribute.* New York: Columbia University Press, 2012.

Keck, Zachary. "Are America and India Building an 'Aircraft Carrier' Alliance?" *The National Interest*, November 11, 2017. http://nationalinterest.org/blog /the-buzz/are-america-india-building-aircraft-carrier-alliance-23147.

——. "China's J-20 Stealth Fighter Is Now Training for War." *The National Interest*, January 20, 2018. https://nationalinterest.org/blog/the-buzz/chinas -j-20-stealth-fighter-now-training-war-24147.

Kennedy, John F. "Inaugural Address." January 20, 1961. https://www.jfklibrary .org/learn/about-jfk/historic-speeches/inaugural-address.

Keohane, Robert O. *After Hegemony: Cooperation and Discord in the World Political Economy.* Princeton, NJ: Princeton University Press, 2005.

Khanna, Parag. "Opinion: Asia Is Building Its Own World Order." CNN, August 8, 2017. https://www.cnn.com/2017/08/08/opinions/china-and-the-asian-world-order-parag-khanna-opinion/index.html.

Kharas, Homi. "The Unprecedented Expansion of the Global Middle Class: An Update." Brookings Institution, 2017. https://www.brookings.edu/wp-content/uploads/2017/02/global_20170228_global-middle-class.pdf.

Kim, Eliot. "Water Wars: ASEAN No Longer 'Concerned' About China's Actions in the South China Sea." *Lawfare*, December 4, 2017. https://lawfareblog.com/water-wars-asean-no-longer-concerned-about-chinas-actions-south-china-sea.

Kirchick, James. "Why Donald Trump Keeps Dissing America's Allies in Europe and Asia." *The Daily Beast*, December 29, 2016. https://www.thedailybeast.com/why-donald-trump-keeps-dissing-americas-allies-in-europe-and-asia.

Kissinger, Henry. "Kissinger on the Controversy Over the Shah." *Washington Post*, November 29, 1979. https://www.washingtonpost.com/archive/politics/1979/11/29/kissinger-on-the-controversy-over-the-shah/a3153d91-02be-40d5-958b-8784c4991941/?utm_term=.aa6cdcbc088a.

——. *World Order.* New York: Penguin Books, 2015.

Krejsa, Harry. 2018. "Under Pressure: The Growing Reach of Chinese Influence Campaigns in Democratic Societies." CNAS, April 2018.

Kurlantzick, Joshua. "Australia, New Zealand Face China's Influence." Council on Foreign Relations, December 13, 2017. https://www.cfr.org/expert-brief/australia-new-zealand-face-chinas-influence.

——. "Southeast Asia's Democratic Decline in the America First Era." Council on Foreign Relations, October 27, 2017. https://www.cfr.org/expert-brief/southeast-asias-democratic-decline-america-first-era.

Lam, Ngo Di. 2016. "Vietnam's Foreign Policy after the 12th National Party Congress: Expanding Continuity." CogitASIA CSIS Asia Policy Blog, February 9, 2016. https://www.cogitasia.com/vietnams-foreign-policy-after-the-12th-national-party-congress-expanding-continuity/.

Lardy, Nicholas R. "Zhu Rongji's Promise." Brookings Institution, October 28, 2002. https://www.brookings.edu/opinions/zhu-rongjis-promise.

Lee, Joyce, and Tony Munroe. "South Korea Wants to Turn Its Arms Industry into an Export Powerhouse." *Business Insider*, April 22, 2015. http://www.businessinsider.com/r-south-korea-seeks-bigger-role-in-global-arms-bazaar-2015-4.

Lee, Kristine, and Alexander Sullivan. "People's Republic of the United Nations." Center for a New American Security, May 14, 2019. https://www.cnas.org/publications/reports/peoples-republic-of-the-united-nations.

Lendon, Brad. "A British Military Base on the South China Sea Is Not a Far-Fetched Idea." CNN, January 3, 2019. https://www.cnn.com/2019/01/03/asia/britain-mliitary-bases-asia-intl/index.html.

——. "Chinese Stealth Fighters Are Combat-Ready, Beijing Says." CNN, February 11, 2018. https://www.cnn.com/2018/02/11/asia/china-j-20-stealth-fighter-combat-ready-intl/index.html.

——. "US, South Korea, Japan Start Drills Off North Korea." CNN, March 14, 2017. http://www.cnn.com/2017/03/14/asia/us-south-korea-japan-aegis-missile-defense-ship-exercises/index.html.

Lincoln, Abraham. "Annual Message to Congress—Concluding Remarks." December 1, 1862.

Linczer, Edward. "The Role of Security Assistance in Washington's Pivot to Southeast Asia." *China-US Focus*, August 26, 2016. https://www.chinausfocus.com/peace-security/the-role-of-security-assistance-in-washingtons-pivot-to-southeast-asia.

Lissner, Rebecca Friedman, and Mira Rapp Hooper. "American Strategy for a New International Order." *Washington Quarterly*, Spring 2018, 19–20.

Long, Heather. "Analysis: Trump Has Officially Put More Tariffs on US Allies Than on China." *Washington Post*, May 31, 2018. https://www.washingtonpost.com/news/wonk/wp/2018/05/31/trump-has-officially-put-more-tariffs-on-u-s-allies-than-on-china/?noredirect=on&utm_term=.6f4c4e186710.

Lubold, Gordon. "US Spent $5.6 Trillion on Wars in Middle East and Asia: Study." *Wall Street Journal*, November 8, 2017. https://www.wsj.com/articles/study-estimates-war-costs-at-5-6-trillion-1510106400.

Lum, Thomas. "Republic of the Philippines and US Interests." Congressional Research Service, April 5, 2012. https://fas.org/sgp/crs/row/RL33233.pdf.

Lynh, Khanh. "Vietnam Hails Burgeoning Defense Ties with India." VnExpress International, August 18, 2017. https://e.vnexpress.net/news/news/vietnam-hails-burgeoning-defense-ties-with-india-3629191.html.

Macfarlane, Alec, and Taehoon Lee. "Trump: South Korea Should Pay for $1B Missile Defense System." CNN Money, April 28, 2017.

Mair, John, and Colin Packham. "NATO Needs to Address China's Rise, Says Stoltenberg." Reuters, August 7, 2019. https://uk.reuters.com/article/uk-australia-nato/nato-needs-to-address-chinas-rise-says-stoltenberg-idUKKCN1UX0YV.

Makino, Yoshihiro. "North Korea Said to Be Testing Anthrax-Tipped Ballistic Missiles." *Asahi Shimbun*, December 20, 2017. http://www.asahi.com/ajw/articles/AJ201712200036.html.

Mann, James. "America's Dangerous 'China Fantasy.'" *New York Times*, October 27, 2016. https://www.nytimes.com/2016/10/28/opinion/americas-dangerous-china-fantasy.html.

Marble, Andrew. "China, the Financial Crisis, and Sino-American Relations: An Interview with Pieter Bottelier." *Asia Policy* 9 (2010): 121–29.

Mardell, Jacob. "The 'Community of Common Destiny' in Xi Jinping's New Era." *The Diplomat*, October 25, 2017. https://thediplomat.com/2017/10/the -community-of-common-destiny-in-xi-jinpings-new-era/.

Mastro, Oriana Skylar. "Ideas, Perceptions, and Power: An Examination of China's Military Strategy." In *Strategic Asia, 2017–2018: Power, Ideas, and Military Strategy in the Asia-Pacific*, ed. Ashley J. Tellis, Alison Szalwinski, and Michael Wills. Seattle: National Bureau of Asian Research, 2017.

Mattis, Peter. "China's Digital Authoritarianism: Surveillance, Influence, and Political Control." Testimony Before the House Permanent Select Committee on Intelligence, May 16, 2019. https://docs.house.gov/meetings/IG/IG00 /20190516/109462/HHRG-116-IG00-Wstate-MattisP-20190516.pdf.

Mayger, James, and Jiyuen Lee. "China's Missile Sanctions Are Taking a Heavy Toll on Both Koreas." Bloomberg, August 29, 2017. https://www.bloomberg .com/news/articles/2017-08-29/china-s-missile-sanctions-are-taking-a -heavy-toll-on-both-koreas.

Mazarr, Michael J., Miranda Priebe, Andrew Radin, and Astrid Stuth Cevallos. *Understanding the Current International Order*. Santa Monica, CA: RAND Corporation, 2016.

McCain, John. "Restoring American Power." January 16, 2017. https://www .mccain.senate.gov/public/_cache/files/25bff0ec-481e-466a-843f -68ba5619e6d8/restoring-american-power-7.pdf.

McKirdy, Euan. "Trump Says He Would Consult with China's Xi Before Speaking to Taiwan." CNN, April 28, 2017. http://www.cnn.com/2017/04/28/asia /trump-taiwan-xi-comments/index.html.

Mead, Walter Russell. "In the Footsteps of the Kaiser: China Boosts US Power in Asia." *The American Interest*, September 26, 2010.

Mearsheimer, John J. "Bound to Fail: The Rise and Fall of the Liberal International Order." *International Security* 43, no. 4 (Spring 2019): 7–50. https://doi .org/10.1162/ISEC_a_00342.

——. *The Tragedy of Great Power Politics*. New York: Norton, 2002.

Mehta, Aaron. "FY18 Budget Request Cuts $1B from State's Foreign Military Financing." *Defense News*, May 23, 2017. https://www.defensenews.com /congress/budget/2017/05/23/fy18-budget-request-cuts-1b-from-state-s -foreign-military-financing/.

Mehta, Aaron, and Joe Gould. "Trump Budget to Cut Foreign Military Financing, with Loans Looming." *Defense News*, May 19, 2017. https://www.defensenews .com/pentagon/2017/05/19/trump-budget-to-cut-foreign-military-financing -with-loan-option-looming/.

Meick, Ethan, and Nargiza Salidjanova. "China's Response to US–South Korean Missile Defense System Deployment and Its Implications." US-China Economic and Security Review Commission, July 26, 2017. https://www.uscc .gov/sites/default/files/Research/Report_China%27s%20Response %20to%20THAAD%20Deployment%20and%20its%20Implications.pdf.

Mizokami, Kyle. "This Is How South Korea Plans to Stop a Nuclear Attack from North Korea." *The National Interest*, July 10, 2017. http://nationalinterest.org/blog /the-buzz/how-south-korea-plans-stop-nuclear-attack-north-korea-21472.

Mochizuki, Mike M. "Japan and China at a Crossroads." *East Asian Insights* 1, no. 2 (2006): 1–5. http://www.jcie.org/researchpdfs/EAI/1-2.pdf.

Morgenthau, Hans J. *Politics Among Nations: The Struggle for Power and Peace.* New York: Alfred A. Knopf, 1973.

Morris, Lyle J. "Blunt Defenders of Sovereignty: The Rise of Coast Guards of East and Southeast Asia." *Naval War College Review* 70, no. 2 (2017): 75–112. https://usnwc2.usnwc.edu/getattachment/eaa0678e-83a0-4c67-8aab -0f829d7a2b27/Blunt-Defenders-of-Sovereignty—-The-Rise-of-Coast.aspx.

——. "The New 'Normal' in the East China Sea." RAND Corporation, February 27, 2017. https://www.rand.org/blog/2017/02/the-new-normal-in-the-east -china-sea.html.

Neves, Ana, William Becker, and Marcos Dominguez-Torreiro. "Explained, the Economic Ties between Europe and Asia." World Economic Forum, May 14, 2019. https://www.weforum.org/agenda/2019/05/ways-asia-and-europe -together-connected/.

Nixon, Richard M. "Asia After Viet Nam." *Foreign Affairs* 46, no. 1 (1967): 111. https://doi.org/10.2307/20039285.

Nye, Joseph S., Jr. "Recovering American Leadership." *Survival* 50, no. 1 (2008): 55–68.

Oba, Mie. "What Now for Economic Integration in the Asia-Pacific?" *The Diplomat*, February 9, 2018. https://thediplomat.com/2018/02/what-now -for-economic-integration-in-the-asia-pacific/.

Obama, Barack. "President Obama: The TPP Would Let America, Not China, Lead the Way on Global Trade." *Washington Post*, May 2, 2016. https://www .washingtonpost.com/opinions/president-obama-the-tpp-would-let-america -not-china-lead-the-way-on-global-trade/2016/05/02/680540e4-0fd0-11e6 -93ae-50921721165d_story.html.

O'Hanlon, Michael. *The Wounded Giant: America's Armed Forces in an Age of Austerity.* New York: Penguin, 2011.

Olson, Wyatt. "US, Japan, S. Korea Conducting First Joint Ballistic Missile Defense Drill." *Stars and Stripes*, June 27, 2016. https://www.stripes.com/news/us-japan -s-korea-conducting-first-joint-ballistic-missile-defense-drill-1.416554.

O'Rourke, Ronald. "China Naval Modernization: Implications for US Navy Capabilities: Background and Issues for Congress." Congressional Research Service, December 13, 2017. https://fas.org/sgp/crs/row/RL33153.pdf.

Ott, Marvin C. *East Asia and the United States: Current Status and Five-Year Outlook.* Federation of American Scientists, September 2000. http://www.fas.org /irp/nic/east_asia.html#link05.

Page, Jeremy, and Paul Sonne. "Unable to Buy US Military Drones, Allies Place Orders with China." *Wall Street Journal*, July 17, 2017. https://www.wsj.com /amp/articles/unable-to-buy-u-s-military-drones-allies-place-orders -with-china-1500301716?mg=prod/accounts-wsj.

Panda, Ankit. "US, Japan, South Korea to Hold Missile Tracking Exercises." *The Diplomat*, December 11, 2017. https://thediplomat.com/2017/12/us-japan -south-korea-to-hold-missile-tracking-exercises/.

Parameswaran, Prashanth. "America's New Maritime Security Initiative for Southeast Asia." *The Diplomat*, April 3, 2016. http://thediplomat.com/2016/04 /americas-new-maritime-security-initiative-for-southeast-asia/.

——. "Assessing ASEAN's New Indo-Pacific Outlook." *The Diplomat*, June 24, 2019. https://thediplomat.com/2019/06/assessing-aseans-new-indo-pacific -outlook/.

——. "China Blocked ASEAN Defense Meeting Pact Amid South China Sea Fears: US Official." *The Diplomat*, November 4, 2015. http://thediplomat .com/2015/11/china-blocked-asia-defense-meeting-pact-amid-south -china-sea-fears-us-official/.

——. "Modi Unveils India's 'Act East Policy' to ASEAN in Myanmar." *The Diplomat*, November 17, 2014. https://thediplomat.com/2014/11/modi-unveils-indias -act-east-policy-to-asean-in-myanmar/.

——. "Will a China–ASEAN South China Sea Code of Conduct Really Matter?" *The Diplomat*, August 5, 2017. https://thediplomat.com/2017/08/will-a-china -asean-south-china-sea-code-of-conduct-really-matter/.

Park, Donghui. "Cybersecurity Strategy Advice for the Trump Administration: US–South Korea Relations." Henry M. Jackson School of International Studies, University of Washington, February 7, 2017. https://jsis.washington .edu/news/cybersecurity-strategy-advice-trump-administration-us-south -korea-relations/.

Patel, Nirav. "US Should Offer a Digital Highway Initiative for Asia." *Straits Times*, February 7, 2018. http://www.straitstimes.com/opinion/us-should -offer-a-digital-highway-initiative-for-asia.

Pei, Minxin. "Transition in China? More Likely Than You Think." *Journal of Democracy* 27, no. 4 (2016): 5–19.

Pennington, Matthew. "Pentagon: Afghan War Costing $45 Billion Per Year." *Military Times*, February 6, 2018. https://www.militarytimes.com/news /pentagon-congress/2018/02/07/pentagon-afghan-war-costing-us-45-billion -per-year/.

Perlez, Jane. "Tribunal Rejects Beijing's Claims in South China Sea." *New York Times*, July 12, 2016. https://www.nytimes.com/2016/07/13/world/asia /south-china-sea-hague-ruling-philippines.html?mtrref=www.google .com&gwh=18D0ECABC520A6579443152609880200&gwt=pay.

Peters, Allison. "Russia and China Are Trying to Set the UN's Rules on Cybercrime." *Foreign Policy*, September 16, 2019. https://foreignpolicy.com/2019/09/16 /russia-and-china-are-trying-to-set-the-u-n-s-rules-on-cybercrime/.

Phippen, J. Weston. "South Korea Asks to Increase Its Firepower." *The Atlantic*, July 29 2017. https://www.theatlantic.com/news/archive/2017/07/south-korea -missile/535359/.

Pinker, Steven. *The Better Angels of Our Nature: Why Violence Has Declined*. New York: Penguin Books, 2011.

Pollman, Mina. "What's in Japan's Record 2018 Defense Budget Request?" *The Diplomat*, August 28, 2017. https://thediplomat.com/2017/08/whats-in -japans-record-2018-defense-budget-request/.

Pomfret, John. "Opinion: China's Meddling in Australia—and What the US Should Learn From It." *Washington Post*, June 14, 2017. https://www .washingtonpost.com/news/global-opinions/wp/2017/06/14/how-should -the-u-s-deal-with-chinas-rise-look-to-australia/?utm_term=.b23f878ab241.

Porter, Patrick. "Sorry, Folks, There Is No Rules-Based World Order." *The National Interest*, August 29, 2016. https://nationalinterest.org/blog/the-skeptics /sorry-folks-there-no-rules-based-world-order-17497.

Power, John. "Australia Sounds the Alarm Over Chinese 'Interference.' " *Nikkei Asian Review*, April 11, 2018. https://asia.nikkei.com/Politics/International -Relations/Australia-sounds-the-alarm-over-Chinese-interference.

Rachman, Geideon. "The EU Needs to Be a Power Project." *Financial Times*, October 7, 2019. https://www.ft.com/content/ff92106c-e8e0-11e9-85f4 -d00e5018f061.

Rajagopalan, Rajesh. "India's Unrealized Power." In *Strategic Asia, 2015–16: Founda- tions of National Power in the Asia-Pacific*, ed. Michael Wills, Ashley J. Tellis, and Alison Szalwinski. Seattle: National Bureau of Asian Research, 2015.

Rampton, Roberta, and David Brunnstrom. "Trump, Malyaysia's Najib Skirt Round US Probe into 1MDB Scandal." Reuters, September 12, 2017. https:// www.reuters.com/article/us-usa-malaysia/trump-malaysias-najib-skirt -round-u-s-probe-into-1mdb-scandal-idUSKCN1BN0DZ.

Ramzy, Austin. "As Taiwan's Workers Flock to China, Concerns About Economy Grow." *New York Times*, January 13, 2016. https://www.nytimes.com/2016/01/14/world/asia/taiwan-elections-china.html.

Ranada, Pia. "Duterte Wants to Scrap EDCA." *Rappler*, October 25, 2016. https://www.rappler.com/nation/150262-duterte-edca-no-foreign-troops.

Ranjan, Prabhash. "Bit of a Bumpy Ride." *The Hindu*, September 16, 2016. http://www.thehindu.com/opinion/op-ed/Bit-of-a-bumpy-ride/article14378406.ece.

Rapoza, Kenneth. "China's Mostly Closed, Communist Party–Run Economy Touts Free Markets." *Forbes*, July 18, 2017. https://www.forbes.com/sites/kenrapoza/2017/07/18/chinas-mostly-closed-communist-party-run-economy-touts-free-markets/#5c1b0fae731c.

Ribka, Stefani, and Linda Yulisman. "RCEP Talks Speed Up Amid TPP Failure." *Jakarta Post*, December 7, 2016. http://www.thejakartapost.com/news/2016/12/07/rcep-talks-speed-up-amid-tpp-failure.html.

Rich, Motoko. "TPP, the Trade Deal Trump Killed, Is Back in Talks Without US." *New York Times*, July 14, 2017. https://www.nytimes.com/2017/07/14/business/trans-pacific-partnership-trade-japan-china-globalization.html.

Rinehart, Ian. "New US–Japan Defense Guidelines Deepen Alliance Cooperation." Congressional Research Service, April 28, 2015. https://fas.org/sgp/crs/row/IN10265.pdf, 1.

Riordan, Primrose. "ASIO Battling Spy Threat from China and Russia." *The Australian*, October 19, 2017. https://www.theaustralian.com.au/national-affairs/national-security/asio-battling-spy-threat-from-china-and-russia/news-story/78ae4df93a6e9e3e664b28bdd1e88b96.

Robson, Seth. "Destroyer Will Be 1st US Navy Ship to Visit New Zealand in 3 Decades." *Stars and Stripes*, October 18, 2016. https://www.stripes.com/news/pacific/destroyer-will-be-1st-us-navy-ship-to-visit-new-zealand-in-3-decades-1.434597.

Rogin, Josh. "Opinion: Trump Still Holds Jimmy Carter's View on Withdrawing US Troops from South Korea." *Washington Post*, June 7, 2018.

Rolland, Nadège. *China's Eurasian Century? Political and Strategic Implications of the Belt and Road Initiative.* Seattle: National Bureau of Asian Research, 2017.

——. "China's National Power: A Colossus with Iron or Clay Feet." *Strategic Asia* 16 (2015): 23–54. http://www.nbr.org/publications/element.aspx?id=836.

Ross, Tommy. "Congressional Oversight on Security Assistance." Center for Strategic and International Studies, September 26, 2017. https://www.csis.org/analysis/congressional-oversight-security-assistance.

Ryall, Julian. "North Korea Carries Out 'Unprecedented' Test of Submarine Missile System." *The Telegraph*, August 1, 2017. http://www.telegraph.co.uk/news/2017/08/01/north-koreas-submarine-missile-tests-critical-advance-highly/.

Salas, Alejandro. "Slow, Imperfect Progress Across Asia Pacific." Transparency International, February 21, 2018. https://www.transparency.org/news /feature/slow_imperfect_progress_across_asia_pacific.

Sang-hun, Choe. "South Korea and China End Dispute Over Missile Defense System." *New York Times*, October 30, 2017. https://www.nytimes.com/2017 /10/30/world/asia/north-korea-nuclear-test-radiation.html.

Schell, Orville, and John Delury. *Wealth and Power: China's Long March to the Twenty-First Century*. London: Abacus, 2016.

Schmitz, Rob. "Australia and New Zealand Are Ground Zero for Chinese Influence." NPR, October 2, 2018. https://www.npr.org/2018/10/02/627249909 /australia-and-new-zealand-are-ground-zero-for-chinese-influence.

Schram, Stuart R. "Mao Tse-Tung and the Theory of the Permanent Revolution, 1958–69." *China Quarterly* 46 (1971): 221–44. https://doi.org/10.1017 /s0305741000010675.

Schweller, Randall L., and Xiaoyu Pu. "After Unipolarity: China's Visions of International Order in an Era of US Decline." *International Security* 36, no. 1 (2011): 41–72.

Shambaugh, David. *China's Future*. Cambridge: Polity Press, 2016.

——. "The Coming Chinese Crack Up." *Wall Street Journal*, March 6, 2015. https://www.wsj.com/articles/the-coming-chinese-crack-up-1425659198.

——. "Writing China: David Shambaugh, *China's Future*; Interview by Andrew Browne." *Wall Street Journal*, March 14, 2016. https://blogs.wsj.com/chinareal time/2016/03/14/writing-china-david-shambaugh-chinas-future.

Sharma, Kiran. "India and Vietnam to Strengthen Defense Ties against Assertive China." *Nikkei Asian Review*, March 1, 2018. https://asia.nikkei .com/Politics-Economy/International-Relations/India-and-Vietnam-to -strengthen-defense-ties-against-assertive-China.

Shepardson, David. "US Condemns China for 'Orwellian Nonsense' over Airline Websites." Reuters, May 7, 2018. https://www.reuters.com/article/us-usa -airlines-china-exclusive/u-s-condemns-china-for-orwellian-nonsense -over-airline-websites-idUSKBN1I60NL.

Small, Andrew. "Why Europe Is Getting Tough on China." *Foreign Affairs*, April 3, 2019.

Smeltz, Dina, Ivo Daalder, Karl Friedhoff, and Craig Kafura. "What Americans Think about America First." Chicago Council on Global Affairs, 2017. https:// www.thechicagocouncil.org/sites/default/files/ccgasurvey2017_what _americans_think_about_america_first.pdf.

Smyth, Jamie. "New Zealand Boosts Aid to Counter China's Influence in South Pacific." *Financial Times*, May 17, 2018. https://www.ft.com/content/0fca1c20 -5988-11e8-bdb7-f6677d2e1ce8.

Snyder, Glen H. "The Security Dilemma in Alliance Politics." *World Politics* 36, no. 4 (1984): 461–95.

Snyder, Scott A., and Seukhoon Paul Choi. "From Aid to Development Partnership: Strengthening US–Republic of Korea Cooperation in International Development." Council on Foreign Relations, February 2012. https://www.cfr.org/sites/default/files/pdf/2012/02/CFR_WorkingPaper10_Snyder_Choi.pdf.

Soble, Jonathan. "With Ban on Exports Lifted, Japan Arms Makers Cautiously Market Wares Abroad." *New York Times*, July 12, 2015. https://www.nytimes.com/2015/07/13/business/international/with-ban-on-exports-lifted-japan-arms-makers-cautiously-market-wares-abroad.html.

Spetalnick, Matt, and Mike Stone. "Exclusive: Game of Drones—US Poised to Boost Unmanned Aircraft Exports." Reuters, October 11, 2017. https://www.reuters.com/article/us-trump-effect-drones-exclusive/exclusive-game-of-drones-u-s-poised-to-boost-unmanned-aircraft-exports-idUSKBN1CG0F4.

Steinberg, James B. 2017. "Keynote Address at the Center for a New American Security." Keynote Address at Center for a New American Security, September 24. https://2009-2017.state.gov/s/d/former/steinberg/remarks/2009/169332.htm.

Stohl, Rachel, and Shannon Dick. "Trump on Arms Sales." Paper presented at forum on the arms trade, April 25, 2017. https://www.forumarmstrade.org/looking-ahead-blog/trump-on-arms-sales.

Stokes, Bruce. "Japanese Divided on Democracy's Success at Home, but Value Voice of the People: Public Sees Threats Abroad Amid Declining Views of US." Pew Research Center, October 17, 2017. http://assets.pewresearch.org/wp-content/uploads/sites/2/2017/10/04141151/Pew-Research-Center_Japan-Report_2017.10.17.pdf.

Sullivan, Michael. 2016. "Demanding Greater Respect from US, Philippines Looks to China." NPR, October 24, 2016. https://www.npr.org/sections/parallels/2016/10/24/499147427/demanding-greater-respect-from-u-s-philippines-looks-to-china.

Sun, Yun. "China and the Asia Pacific Stability Initiative." *China-US Focus*, May 23, 2017. https://www.chinausfocus.com/finance-economy/2017/0523/15028.html.

Sutter, Robert G. *Chinese Foreign Relations: Power and Policy Since the Cold War.* Lanham, MD: Rowman & Littlefield, 2012.

Swanson, Ana. " 'None of These Big Quagmire Deals': Trump Spells Out Historic Shift in Approach to Trade." *Washington Post*, February 24, 2017. https://www.washingtonpost.com/news/wonk/wp/2017/02/24/trump-spells-out-historic-shift-in-trade-that-could-weigh-on-companies-growth/?utm_term=.4db619e037d1.

Swift, Art. "In US, Record-High 72% See Foreign Trade as Opportunity." Gallup, February 16, 2017. http://news.gallup.com/poll/204044/record-high-foreign -trade-opportunity.aspx.

Taliaferro, Jeffrey W. *Balancing Risks: Great Power Intervention in the Periphery*. Ithaca, NY: Cornell University Press, 2004.

Tan, Andrew T. H. *The Arms Race in Asia: Trends, Causes and Implications*. New York: Routledge, 2013.

Tanaka, Hitoshi. "Japan's Shifting Strategy toward the Rise of China." *Journal of Strategic Studies* 30, nos. 4–5 (2007): 758–59.

Tang, Shiping. "China and the Future International Order(s)." *Ethics & International Affairs* 32, no. 1 (2018): 33–34. https://doi.org/10.1017/S0892679418000084.

Tatsumi, Yuki. "The Japan–South Korea 'Comfort Women' Agreement Survives (Barely)." *The Diplomat*, January 11, 2018. https://thediplomat.com/2018/01 /the-japan-south-korea-comfort-women-agreement-survives-barely/.

Taylor, Adam. "A Timeline of Trump's Complicated Relationship with the TPP." *Washington Post*, April 13, 2018. https://www.washingtonpost.com/news /worldviews/wp/2018/04/13/a-timeline-of-trumps-complicated-relationship -with-the-tpp/.

Taylor, Alan. "Anti-Japan Protests in China." *The Atlantic*, September 17, 2012. https://www.theatlantic.com/photo/2012/09/anti-japan-protests-in -china/100370/.

Tellis, Ashley J. *US Alliances and Partnerships at the Center of Global Power*. Seattle: National Bureau of Asian Research, 2014.

Tellis, Ashley J., Alison Szalwinski, and Michael Wills, eds. *Power, Ideas, and Military Strategy in the Asia-Pacific*. Seattle: National Bureau of Asian Research, 2017.

Terada, Takashi. "The Competing US and Chinese Models for East Asian Economic Order." *Asia Policy* 13, no. 2 (2018): 19–25.

Thai, Tran Viet. "The Evolving Regional Order in East Asia: A View from Vietnam." *Asia Policy* 13, no. 2 (2018): 64–68.

Thayer, Carl. "Alarming Escalation in the South China Sea: China Threatens Force If Vietnam Continues Oil Exploration in Spratlys." *The Diplomat*, July 25, 2017. https://thediplomat.com/2017/07/alarming-escalation-in-the-south -china-sea-china-threatens-force-if-vietnam-continues-oil-exploration-in -spratlys/.

Thies, Cameron G., and Mark David Nieman. *Rising Powers and Foreign Policy Revisionism: Understanding BRICS Identity and Behavior through Time*. Ann Arbor: University of Michigan Press, 2017.

Tian, Fang. "China Rises to 16 Asian Countries' Biggest Trading Partners." *People's Daily*, January 12, 2018. http://en.people.cn/n3/2018/0112/c90000 -9314972.html.

Tiezzi, Shannon. "In Japan, Trump and Abe Offer Alternative to China's 'Belt and Road.'" *The Diplomat*, November 8, 2017. https://thediplomat.com/2017/11/in-japan-trump-and-abe-offer-alternative-to-chinas-belt-and-road/.

Tillerson, Rex. "FY 2018 Congressional Budget Justification: Secretary's Letter." US Department of State, May 23, 2017. https://www.state.gov/documents/organization/271282.pdf.

Tobin, Liza. "Xi's Vision for Transforming Global Governance: A Strategic Challenge for Washington and Its Allies." *Texas National Security Review* 2, no. 1 (2018). http://dx.doi.org/10.26153/tsw/863.

Torbati, Yeganeh, and Trinna Leong. "ASEAN Defense Chiefs Fail to Agree on South China Sea Statement." Reuters, November 4, 2015. https://www.reuters.com/article/us-asean-malaysia-statement/asean-defense-chiefs-fail-to-agree-on-south-china-sea-statement-idUSKCN0ST07G20151104.

Trump, Donald J. "Presidential Memorandum Regarding Withdrawal of the United States from the Trans-Pacific Partnership Negotiations and Agreement." White House, January 23, 2017. https://www.whitehouse.gov/presidential-actions/presidential-memorandum-regarding-withdrawal-united-states-trans-pacific-partnership-negotiations-agreement/.

——. "Press Conference by President Trump." White House, June 12, 2018. https://www.whitehouse.gov/briefings-statements/press-conference-president-trump/.

Unnithan, Sandeep. "A Peek into India's Top Secret and Costliest Defence Project, Nuclear Submarines." *India Today*, December 10, 2017. https://www.indiatoday.in/magazine/the-big-story/story/20171218-india-ballistic-missile-submarine-k-6-submarine-launched-drdo-1102085-2017-12-10.

US International Development Finance Corporation. "Who We Are." No date. https://www.opic.gov/build-act/faqs-build-act-implementation.

Vaughn, Bruce. "US Strategic and Defense Relationships in the Asia-Pacific Region." Congressional Research Service, January 22, 2007. https://fas.org/sgp/crs/row/RL33821.pdf, 15..

Waltz, Kenneth Neal. *Theory of International Politics*. Long Grove, IL: Waveland Press, 2010.

Wardell, Jane, and Jonathan Barrett. "Analysis: Silk Roads and Chilled Beef: How China Is Trying to Fill a Trump Vacuum in Australia." CNBC, March 29, 2017.

Warrick, Joby. "Microbes by the Ton: Officials See Weapons Threat as North Korea Gains Biotech Expertise." *Washington Post*, December 10, 2017. https://www.washingtonpost.com/world/national-security/microbes-by-the-ton-officials-see-weapons-threat-as-north-korea-gains-biotech-expertise/2017/12/10/9b9d5f9e-d5f0-11e7-95bf-df7c19270879_story.html?utm_term=.54190a689fd1.

Washington, George. "Washington's Farewell Address." 1796. Avalon Project. http://avalon.law.yale.edu/18th_century/washing.asp.

Weeden, Brian. "Testimony Before the US–China Economic and Security Review Commission, Hearing on China in Space: A Strategic Competition?" April 25, 2019. https://swfound.org/media/206425/weeden_uscc_testimony _april2019.pdf.

Whyte, Leon. "Evolution of the US–ROK Alliance: Abandonment Fears." *The Diplomat*, June 22, 2015. https://thediplomat.com/2015/06/evolution-of-the -u-s-rok-alliance-abandonment-fears/.

Wike, Richard, Bruce Stokes, Jacob Poushter, and Janell Fetterolf. "Trump Unpopular Worldwide, American Image Suffers." Pew Research Center, Global Attitudes Project. June 26, 2017. http://www.pewglobal.org/2017/06/26/u -s-image-suffers-as-publics-around-world-question-trumps-leadership/.

Wroe, David. "China Eyes Vanuatu Military Base in Plan with Global Ramifications." *Sydney Morning Herald*, April 9, 2018. https://www.smh.com.au /politics/federal/china-eyes-vanuatu-military-base-in-plan-with-global -ramifications-20180409-p4z8j9.html.

Wu, Dee. "Taiwan's All-Volunteer Force and Military Transformation." Project 2049 Institute, 2017. https://project2049.net/wp-content/uploads/2017/12 /P2049_Wu_Taiwan_AVF_Strategy_122017.pdf.

Wu, J. R., and Ben Blanchard. "Taiwan Loses Another Ally, Says Won't Help China Ties." Reuters, December 20, 2016. https://www.reuters.com/article/us-china -taiwan-saotome/taiwan-loses-another-ally-says-wont-help-china-ties -idUSKBN1492SO.

Yamaguchi, Mari. "Japan Approves Missile Defense System Amid NKorea Threat." Associated Press, December 19, 2017. https://apnews.com/39f053831e4f449c9be 4186e7a0863a4/Japan-approves-missile-defense-system-amid-NKorea-threat.

Yarhi-Milo, Keren, Alexander Lanoszka, and Zack Cooper. "To Arm or to Ally? The Patron's Dilemma and the Strategic Logic of Arms Transfers and Alliances." *International Security* 41, no. 2 (2016): 90–139.

Yeo, Mike. "China Launches Its Most Advanced Homegrown Class of Guided-Missile Destroyers." *Defense News*, June 28, 2017. https://www.defensenews .com/naval/2017/06/28/china-launches-its-most-advanced-homegrown -class-of-guided-missile-destroyers/.

Young, Audrey. "Rice Hints at Thaw in US–NZ Relations." *New Zealand Herald*, July 26, 2008. https://www.nzherald.co.nz/politics/news/article.cfm?c_id =280&objectid=10523634.

Yu, Jess Macy, and Greg Torode. "Taiwan Plans to Invest in Advanced Arms as China Flexes Its Muscles." Reuters, January 12, 2018. https://www.reuters .com/article/us-taiwan-defence-spending/taiwan-plans-to-invest-in -advanced-arms-as-china-flexes-its-muscles-idUSKBN1F00PC.

Zaretskaya, Victoria. "Australia Is on Track to Become World's Largest LNG Exporter." *Today in Energy*, August 12, 2019. https://www.eia.gov/today inenergy/detail.php?id=40853.

Zemin, Jiang. "Build a Well-Off Society in an All-Round Way and Create a New Situation in Building Socialism with Chinese Characteristics." Report at 16th National Congress of the Communist Party of China, November 8, 2002. As quoted by Evan Medeiros, *China's International Behavior: Activism, Opportunism, and Diversification* (Santa Monica, CA: RAND Corporation, 2009).

Zoellick, Robert B. "Whither China: From Membership to Responsibility?" *NBR Analysis* 16, no. 4 (2005): 5.

INDEX